Case Studies in
Japanese
Management

Case Studies in
Japanese
Management

Parissa Haghirian
Sophia University, Japan

Philippe Gagnon
Economist Intelligence Unit, Canada

World Scientific

NEW JERSEY • LONDON • SINGAPORE • BEIJING • SHANGHAI • HONG KONG • TAIPEI • CHENNAI

Published by

World Scientific Publishing Co. Pte. Ltd.

5 Toh Tuck Link, Singapore 596224

USA office: 27 Warren Street, Suite 401-402, Hackensack, NJ 07601

UK office: 57 Shelton Street, Covent Garden, London WC2H 9HE

British Library Cataloguing-in-Publication Data
A catalogue record for this book is available from the British Library.

ISBN-13 978-981-4340-87-8
ISBN-10 981-4340-87-1

Typeset by Stallion Press
Email: enquiries@stallionpress.com

Printed in Singapore.

Contents

About the Authors

Ali AL Dhamen received his BS in Business Administration from Northeastern University and is currently pursuing his Masters in International Business and Development at Sophia University's Graduate Program of Global Studies. His research interests include cross-cultural product design and the effects of organizational structure on business.

Vincent Agulhon graduated in 2010 from the ESCEM School of Business and Management, France. He owns a Master's degree in Management and did a one-year graduate exchange program at Sophia University in Tokyo. He is currently working as a Brand Ambassador for a French luxury company in Japan.

Chenming Bi was born in Shanghai, moved to Tokyo at age 13 and is an undergraduate student at Sophia University majoring in International Business and Economics. In 2011, he studies in France, specializing in International Finance. After his graduation, he plans to return to Japan and start a career in banking.

Nathan Michael Echols holds a Master of Arts in International Business and Development Studies from Sophia University. His research primarily focused on variations in managerial methods of famous Japanese corporations.

Philippe Gagnon is a graduating student in finance who studied at Sophia University in 2009–2010. His work experience at the Economist Intelligence Unit's Tokyo office made him discover an interest for researching and understanding Japan's strengths and potential in tomorrow's global economy.

Paul Gaspari is an Adjunct Professor of International Management at the Faculty of Economics at Sophia University, Japan. His research interests include the modern keiretsu and international entrepreneurship in Japan.

Parissa Haghirian is an Associate Professor of International Management at Sophia University in Japan. Her research focuses on Asian management styles, Japanese management and cross-cultural management challenges.

Ekaterina Ignatova holds a Bachelor's degree in Business Administration from Roanoke College, VA, USA and is currently a master student at Sophia University, majoring in International Business and Development.

Pascal Kalbermatten graduated in 2008 from the University of St. Gallen, Switzerland. He owns a Bachelor's degree in Business Administration, a Master's degree in Information and Technology Management (IMT) and spent study visits at Stanford University in California as well as Sophia University in Tokyo.

Kaoru Kusuma was a graduate student at Sophia University, Faculty of Liberal Arts (Global Studies) and researches on Japanese Marketing and Management. She is currently working as Document Control executive in a Japan-based company in Singapore.

Roy Martinez is currently a senior at Arizona State University and is a member of The Barrett Honors College. Being an avid technology enthusiast since the age of six has led to him pursue a Bachelor of Science degree in Computer Science, with a concentration in Information Assurance. Roy's accomplishments include a semester at Sophia University in Tokyo, a 2010 Google Scholarship Award, a 2010

Motorola Scholarship from the Ira Fulton School of Engineering at ASU, and an internship with Microsoft in summer of 2010.

Julie Lafage is a Marketing professional and currently a Product Manager at Renault. She received her Master degree in International Business and Marketing from the ESCEM-Ecole Superieure de Commerce Tours-Poitiers in France in 2009.

Elena Neufeld is a student of Baltic Management Studies at the University of Applied Science in Stralsund, Germany. She spent a study visit at the Institute of Technology in Carlow, Ireland and worked as a research and teaching assistant with Professor. Haghirian at Sophia University in Tokyo. She will graduate in 2011 with a Bachelor of Business Administration in Baltic Management Studies.

Greg Taylor has ten years of experience in the video game industry. He now works at Sucker Punch Productions on the infamous 2 team. Greg received his Masters of International Business from Sophia University in Spring 2009.

Aaron Toussaint is currently Research Manager at *Five by Fifty*, a Tokyo-based trend forecasting and ethnographic marketing research agency. Aaron's current research interests include the effect of consumer ethnocentrism on product evaluation, as well as trends in Japan's FMCG markets, especially alcoholic beverages.

Christina Wright graduated from Sophia University, Faculty of Comparative Culture, where she earned her degree in International Business and Economics. She is currently working in the fashion industry in Tokyo.

What Can We Learn from Japanese Management?

Parissa Haghirian

Japan and Japanese management have produced a lot of international interest over the past decades. After an unprecedented economic miracle, catapulting Japan from being one of the poorest countries after World War II to become the second most important global economic player, Japanese management practices were seen not only as exotic but also superior to Western management practices until the end of the 1980s.

However, a decade of economic stagnation followed, in which the very same management practices which were responsible for Japan's success were suddenly named as the influence factors for slow recovery. Japanese companies were forced to restructure and internationalize. Their traditional strength — manufacturing — was not able to compete with cheaper Asian competitors. Successful strategies of the past such as lifetime employment and seniority system were suddenly becoming burdens which hindered flexibility and slowed the way out of the recession. At the same time, Japan's neighbors, China and India, became the new economic superstars and are expected to challenge Japan's economic power and supremacy in Asia.

Japanese companies took the challenge and did change. Many changes were not prominently covered in Western media or by Western researchers; they happened in a Japanese "kaizen" oriented way, step-by-step. Even after restructuring, Japanese companies still face many challenges to keep up with the challenges of globalization and international business. They have been famous for adapting extremely quickly to all their customers' wishes and yet find it difficult to abandon their traditional management styles. They still show a too rigid process orientation, but still manage to develop successful and innovative products which excite consumers all over the world. They are caught between traditional management practices, which have been successful for many decades and the wish to change and keep their dominant role in an increasingly globalized business world. Their decision-making processes need to become faster and many of them lack assertive leaders. At the same time, Japan is still the world's second largest consumer market and a highly profitable place for international investment.

The catastrophe of March 2011 has shown how different Japanese people manage crisis and uncertainty, how dedicated and loyal they are to their peers and how different their view on the world is from ours. For all these reasons, Japan is still a very interesting and inspiring place to study and research management. Despite the interesting economic history and changes in the Japanese economy, there is still little coverage about Japan's business world today. Particularly teaching material on the topic is often old and outdated; the number of contemporary case studies on the topic is scant.

This book presents case studies on Western and Japanese companies operating in today's Japanese market. All cases present a typical situation in which the company faces challenges dealing with Japanese clients, developing a strategy to succeed in the sophisticated Japanese market and also discuss critical situations in which some Japanese companies have recently found themselves. We cover a wide array of topics starting from market entry into the Japanese market to strategic issues. Marketing aspects are also covered as well as the question of how Western and Japanese players deal with crisis. We further present three mini-cases which discuss cross-cultural challenges when dealing with Japanese firms. In doing so, we hope that we can provide a vivid picture on how diverse the Japanese business environment is today. The number of foreign investors has increased over the past years despite difficulties they may face when entering the market. Japanese consumers and the enormous size of the market still provide business opportunities and the possibility to discover new marketing and product trends. At the same time, we can learn from the struggles Japanese companies face when dealing with an increasingly globalized world.

"Case Studies in Japanese Management" starts with a topic which challenges most Western companies in Japan: entering the Japanese market. In the first case, Aaron Toussaint discusses the entry of Wal-Mart in Japan. The company, whose business model is based on the distribution of cheap products, found very idiosyncratic and not always easy to deal with customers in Japan. Although Wal-mart entered the market with an established partner, Seiyu, their business procedures were influenced mainly by cross-cultural misunderstandings and false judgments. The case presents the history of the company in Japan and provides an insight into the Japanese consumer market and how it differs from consumers in other industrialized markets.

The second case deals with another American giant and the challenges of the Japanese market. Julie Lafage shows how eBay found Japan out of the markets in which it could not get a strong foothold. The reasons for this are not only found in particularities of Japanese consumer behavior, but also in the strong Japanese competition. Ebay retired after an unsuccessful first attempt and abandoned the market, but decided to give the Japanese market another chance. The case discusses Ebay's history in Japan, how the first attempts failed and which market situation the company found when trying to re-enter.

The second part of this book discusses strategic management challenges when managing in Japan. The first case in this section was written by Greg Taylor and investigates the return of Nintendo, a leading software firm, which was synonymous with video games in the 1990s. Yet, by 2000, it was Sony's "Playstation" that held that honor. This case covers the strategic changes made at Nintendo to reclaim its former market-leader position. By innovating the game experience and developing products to expand the market (by reaching out to "non-traditional" gamers), Nintendo was able to disprove its skeptics and rebuild its gaming empire. The case shows how the company developed over the past two decades and how its strategy catapulted it back to the top in its industry.

Kaoru Kusuma presents another Japanese giant in her case "NTT DoCoMo — Beyond i-mode and FOMA". NTT DoCoMo is Japan's leading mobile phone carrier. Over the years, NTT DoCoMo has emerged as the market leader in Japan after its successful launch of the mobile internet i-mode. i-mode, the first mobile internet in the world, made internet available on the phone without the need to dial-up. Following i-mode's success, NTT DoCoMo began establishing a foothold in overseas mobile phone markets by investing in foreign mobile phone carriers such as Hutchison Telecom, AT&T Wireless, KPN and KTF. However, the company's global expansion drive showed minimal success. At the same time, technical problems with NTT DoCoMo's 3G networks and the 3G service were not as well-received as was expected to be. As the competition among the mobile phone operators intensified, it remained to be seen how NTT DoCoMo reacts to sustain its market leader position.

The case study "Xbox in the land of the rising sun" describes the struggles that Microsoft had to face when selling its product in Japan. Ali AL Dhamen describes how Microsoft launched its Xbox video game system very successfully save for one market: Japan. Here Microsoft faced a particular harsh competition and was even trumped by competitors who could not succeed outside Japan. The case discusses how Microsoft struggled with the Japanese market over the past decade and which factors were responsible for these problems. It raises the question of whether the software can turn around its business in the land of the rising sun.

Paul Gaspari in his case study "Big Gulps and Big Business: Seven Eleven Japan and the New Keiretsu" presents another main player in the Japanese market as well as in many other markets, including Seven Eleven Japan. Starting as an idea imported from the United States by the company, Ito-Yokado, convenience stores in Japan became an instant success and a standard sight in every Japanese city.

The company grew so successful that it did not only take over Seven Eleven in the United States, but also built a keiretsu of its own style in Japan. The case discusses the rise of Seven Eleven in Japan and the internationalization of the convenience store concept as well as the new keiretsu, which was formed out of importing an American idea successfully to Japan.

The last case in the strategic section deals with another software company, Sony, and its product, Playstation 3. In this case, Vincent Agulhon shows how the company, after being very successful with earlier versions of the famous Playstation, is dealing with the massive change and severe sales shrinkages in the Japanese video game market and the fact that their hit product, Playstation 3, did not live up to expectations. The case further discusses the *otaku* phenomenon, which is a major influence on the software and gaming industry in Japan.

The third part of the book investigates marketing issues in Japan. Marketing in Japan is a topic which was fairly neglected in Western management research. In her case, "The Rise and Fall of the Japanese Luxury Market", Ekaterina Ignatova describes the latest developments in the Japanese luxury brand retail market. The Japanese market has long been considered the only luxury mass market with millions of consumers spending enormous amounts of money on branded fashion products especially from Europe. Since the year 2008, however, this development has stopped and Japanese consumers have started to become more careful on how they spend and which items they spend on. Buying cheaper fashion items became more socially acceptable within Japanese society and leaves Western luxury retailers with the question of whether the Japanese luxury market is only showing signs of fatigue or whether this is going to be a worldwide trend.

Another luxury product, which is not perceived as a luxury product in its home country, is the center of attention in Nathan Echols' case "Toyota Lexus: Number One Overseas but Struggling at Home". Since many Japanese consumers perceive Western products as more luxurious than Japanese, the Lexus-even if well, perceived in other markets, struggles to sell luxury cars in Japan. The case describes how the brand was developed and how it is perceived in Japan.

The fourth part of the book deals with companies which gained a lot of media attention recently. Both companies were "dealing with crisis" and had to endure often very negative media coverage in both Japan and the West. The first case deals with Swiss manufacturer, Schindler Elevators, and its biggest crisis in Japan. Schindler, being world market leader in the elevator and escalator business in numerous markets all over the world, has struggled to enter the Japanese market which is dominated by powerful Japanese for a while. The company faced a major crisis when a lethal accident involved one of their elevators in a Tokyo building. Reacting in a very European way, the company did not only upset the Japanese public, but also made serious mistakes in dealing with a Public Relation crisis. The case describes the accident and how the company reacted. Both Japanese and European point of view are presented and support the discussion of cross-cultural differences when dealing with crisis.

Elena Neufeld in her case, "Lost in Translation? Toyota and the Recall Scandal", portrays the biggest scandal a Japanese company faced in the past years. She describes the case history of Toyota and its biggest scandal that was covered in most media and how differently it was perceived from Japanese and American perspective.

In the fifth section of the book, we discuss cross-cultural challenges when working or studying in Japan or with the Japanese. Christina Wright describes how a Japanese fashion editor is shocked by "too" relaxed American work processes when working for the first time in the United States. Chenming Bi shows that being polite can take very complex forms in Japan and Roy Martinez describes his experience as an American in a Japanese university archery club.

The final section of the book deals with future technologies and how they are being promoted by Japanese firms. Here Nathan Michael Echols provides an overview on how the three major Japanese car makers, Toyota, Nissan and Honda, have very different strategies and assumption on which technology will dominate the future of the automotive industry. The book closes with a note on the contributors.

This book is supposed to help students of international management as well as managers working in Japan understand the Japanese market and the current changes in Japanese management. Each case comes with a teaching PPT presentation which are available for educators in the World Scientific Publishing Homepage.

With this book we hope to increase the understanding of Japanese management practices and the current Japanese economy and help students all over the world to get a better idea about how business should be done in one of the biggest and most powerful economies of the world.

Part 1

ENTERING THE JAPANESE MARKET

You Can't Please All of the People All of the Time: Wal-Mart's Adventures in Japan

Aaron Toussaint

INTRODUCTION

There are a few firms so successful in their respective fields that their names have become synonymous with the industry. When thinking of computer software, everyone immediately pictures Microsoft. What about cars? Today, the embodiment of the auto industry is Toyota. But what about retail? To any North American, the answer is simple: Wal-Mart. Wal-Mart is the largest retailer in the world and perhaps the world's most successful company. In tackling competition, it has swiftly come, seen and conquered. This does not mean that Wal-Mart is some sort of corporate monster, but that the firm is an uncommonly tough competitor. The company has expanded across North America, then the world, succeeding in almost every market that it has chosen to enter. Therefore, it is no surprise that when Wal-Mart moves to a new market, existing competitors get nervous.[1]

Wal-Mart is in many ways the quintessential American retailer, though this has not stopped the company from expanding aggressively to overseas markets in recent years. Not content with being

---

[1] The secrets of Wal-Mart's success (14 June 1999). *BBC News*.

number one in the United States, Mexico and Canada, Wal-Mart has entered South America, and is doing very well. Wal-Mart also operates successful ventures in numerous nations in Central America. Wal-Mart bought ASDA Group in Great Britain, making it one of the largest retailers in that country as well. Wal-Mart has stores in Hong Kong and a hugely successful joint venture in mainland China. However, Wal-Mart has hit a snag in Japan.

In 2002, Wal-Mart acquired a stake in the struggling retail corporation, Seiyu, as a way to enter the notoriously difficult and potentially lucrative Japanese market. Wal-Mart soon began to implement changes, but the hope for turnaround at Seiyu has been slow to materialize. Since it started investing in Japan, Wal-Mart has pulled out of Germany and South Korea after finding that it could not please customers in those demanding markets. In contrast, Wal-Mart doubled-down on Seiyu, making it a wholly-owned subsidiary in 2006.[2] Wal-Mart has sunk deeper and deeper into Japan, and has still not seen a return on its investment. Sales at Seiyu continue to decline, recently forcing Wal-Mart to abandon attempts to keep Seiyu's sales network in place and to proceed with major store closings in a drastic cost-cutting measure.[3] Seven years is a long time to not make money, yet heading into 2009, this is exactly the prospect that Wal-Mart faces. After several *faux-pas* and hastily rethought strategies, the retailing powerhouse that is Wal-Mart seems utterly out of its element in the land of the Rising Sun.

THE BIRTH OF WAL-MART

As already mentioned, Wal-Mart is perhaps the fiercest of competitors in the retail business. The company may be the dominant retailer on the planet today, but it was not always that way. Sam Walton, the man who founded the company that bears his name, started with a single

---

[2] Tak Kumakura. Wal-Mart seeks full ownership of Seiyu; Business Asia by Bloomberg (27 October 2007). *International Herald Tribune*.

[3] "Analysis: Wal-Mart puts profit ahead of sales volume in Seiyu revamp" (30 September 2008). *Nikkei Tuesday Morning Edition*.

store. Mr. Walton had a simple motto, which he tried to infuse into his new venture, "give your customers what they want". You can still find Sam Walton's thoughts on the company's website:

> "If you think about it from the point of view of the customer, you want everything: a wide assortment of quality merchandise; the lowest possible prices; guaranteed satisfaction; friendly, knowledgeable service; convenient hours; and a pleasant shopping experience. You love it when a store exceeds your expectations, and you hate it when a store inconveniences you, gives you a hard time, or pretends you're invisible".[4]

Though Wal-Mart started as a single discount store in Arkansas, the company steadily expanded throughout five states in the American south. However, Wal-Mart was unable to compete in the face of the rapid growth of such competitors as K-mart, another discount chain. In order to raise capital, Walton began to sell shares, listing on the New York Stock Exchange in 1972. With this infusion of capital, the real fun began. By the end of the decade, Wal-Mart had 276 stores in 11 states, 21,000 associates, and 1.248 billion dollars in sales.[5] Wal-Mart expanded steadily, even spectacularly during the 1980s, and in 1990, the company became the number one retailer in the United States.[6] The next year, Wal-Mart started operating internationally with a store in Mexico City. 1991 also marked the year that Wal-Mart introduced the store private brand, "Sam's American Choice", which has since become a best seller in the U.S.

Wal-Mart had become so famous in the U.S. and so important to the American economy that President George H.W. Bush awarded the Medal of Freedom, the highest honor that the U.S. bestows on non-military personal, to Sam Walton in 1992.[7] Sadly, Mr. Walton died later that year. The company he founded however, showed no

---

[4] Wal-Mart Corporate Website. History Timeline. http://walmartstores.com/AboutUs/297.aspx.
[5] *Ibid.*
[6] *Ibid.*
[7] Wal-Mart Corporate Website. History Timeline. http://walmartstores.com/AboutUs/297.aspx.

sign of a slowdown. The next year saw Wal-Mart expand into Canada as well as Hong Kong. International sales were becoming increasingly important to the company. Today, Wal-Mart operates in all 50 U.S. states, as well as 14 countries outside the U.S.

WAL-MART'S CORE COMPETENCIES

Wal-Mart's spectacular growth is due to a number of factors. Though many people may have an idea of retail firms as tradition-bound and not bent on innovation, Wal-Mart has changed the way retail firms operate. The company has introduced many innovations throughout its businesses. However, the firm's basic motto, "everyday low prices", is still the driving force behind the success of Wal-Mart. The motto neatly sums up Wal-Mart's goal of cheap products all the time. Their new motto, "Save money. Live better", is the same fare in slightly fancier packaging. The innovations touched on above, which will be discussed in more detail later on, all help achieve the ultimate end of passing cheaper prices onto consumers. Wal-Mart has gotten huge by giving customers a chance to get all their shopping — from motor oil to cold cuts, from circular saws to blue jeans — done under one roof, and letting them get all of these items for less money than they would have to pay anywhere else.

Economy of Scale

Margins in the retail business are not normally high, especially in the discount retail business; hence, Wal-Mart relies heavily on economy of scale to make money. Tens of millions of Americans shop at Wal-Mart each week.[8] Even with low prices and small margins, the company is able to move enough goods to make a profit. Perhaps more important than the sheer volume of Wal-Mart's sales is the sheer volume of Wal-Mart's purchases. As mentioned above, Wal-Mart is committed to passing savings along to consumers and as the largest retailer in the

---

[8] In 2003, this was estimated at more than 100 million customers a week. Jim Hopkins. Wal-Mart's influence grows. *USA Today*.

world, they are in a unique position to use this bulk to win concessions from suppliers. Consider these facts: Wal-Mart is the biggest customer for such household names as Kraft Foods, Gillette and Procter and Gamble (maker of Tide detergent and Palmolive dish soap).[9] In 2003, Wal-Mart accounted for 26% of annual revenue at Rayovac, a household name in batteries, 17% at Procter and Gamble, and 10% at both Kraft Foods and Heinz (famous purveyors of pickles and ketchup).[10] With such magnitude, Wal-Mart has special leverage over its suppliers, both giving them helpful advice on how to cut costs (and passing these savings on to consumers) and negotiating for lower prices with suppliers (generating price savings which are again passed down to the consumer). Suppliers play ball because they benefit from dealing closely with Wal-Mart. In the mid-1990s, Rubbermaid, a household name in home storage products, was forced into a merger because they tried to raise the prices they charged Wal-Mart. Wal-Mart responded by giving them less shelf space, resulting in drastically reduced sales, and financial ruin for Rubbermaid.[11]

The company also has the financial bulk to sit out losses that would bankrupt smaller firms. To quote a BBC article about Wal-Mart's debut in the UK, "losses that would wipe out some competitors are a mere pinprick for the company with headquarters in Bentonville, Arkansas". When entering new markets, this kind of firepower can be used to build a strategic position. Economy of scale has been a huge advantage for Wal-Mart and the company still seems to have room to grow.[12]

Distribution

Wal-Mart has also been innovative in finding other ways to save money. As America has moved into the suburbs, Wal-Mart has followed,

---

[9] *Ibid.*

[10] *Ibid.*

[11] Jim Hopkins. Wal-Mart's influence grows. *USA Today.*

[12] The secrets of Wal-Mart's success (14 June 1999). *BBC News.* http://news.bbc.co.uk/2/hi/business/325922.stm.

building huge stores on cheap land away from city centers, bringing stores to new population centers and keeping development costs low. Wal-Mart has also got the movement of goods down to a science. Wal-Mart tries to buy all of a particular type of good from one supplier and has distribution centers set up in numerous locations, also located on cheap land, to provide these goods to its stores. Wal-Mart stores across the country carry the same items, so specialization is not a problem. There is minimal variation between stores in different regions and between seasons.[13] Many of these goods are also Wal-Mart exclusives, like Sam's American Choice products, which also help to cement store loyalty.[14] These store brands sell for much cheaper than comparable name brands, and are of comparable quality.[15] Many consumers will make the special trip to Wal-Mart to save half the cost of a case of cola by buying Sam's American Choice brand instead of Coca Cola.

Technology

Wal-Mart may seem to be a standard retail business for the very reason that Wal-Mart set the standard. Assembly lines were a radical concept when Henry Ford first began building automobiles. Today, every manufacturer makes extensive use of them so that they no longer seem special. Similarly, the information systems that Wal-Mart uses have become so standard that they no longer seem revolutionary. Wal-Mart was the first of the big three U.S. discount retailers to introduce point-of-sale scanning of UPC barcodes.[16] Wal-Mart has developed unique

---

[13] This is not to say that there are no variations. Christmas merchandize, Halloween candy, Back to School supplies in August. Compared to a Japanese retail store, however, there are much fewer variations in seasons and regional items.

[14] Several brands, such as Sam's Choice and Ol' Roy Dog food, are national best sellers in the U.S.

[15] U.S. shoppers believe that they can buy the same products at Wal-Mart for 15–20% less. Ian Rowley. Japan isn't buying the Wal-Mart idea (28 February 2005). *Business Week*, Asian Business.

[16] Use of retail technology focuses on service (14 December 1995). *Discount Store News*.

information systems like SMART and Retail Link that can track what exactly is being sold in stores in real time, allowing stores to quickly replenish stock. It also keeps data on what is selling where, and orders new goods as soon as stocks are depleted, allowing a measure of tailoring. For example, if a store sells less Lego blocks for whatever reason, that store can simply receive less of them. The Retail Link system also allows Wal-Mart to search for products among multiple potential supplies, find the best price, and buy that item in bulk, which carries an appreciable discount.[17] Wal-Mart has risen to new heights of information management for a retailer. In fact, the company's communications and IT capabilities are so advanced that Wal-Mart now has the largest private satellite communications network in the U.S.[18]

Low prices, economy of scale and efficiency are the pillars of the Wal-Mart empire. Throw in store brands to build loyalty, greeters saying hello at the door and stores that sell everything under the sun, allowing customers to do all their shopping at once, you have one of the most competitive firms on the planet. These principles have been put into practice with some variations all over the world. More importantly, they have proven to be successful in a wide variety of markets.

WAL-MART TAKES THE PLUNGE

Wal-Mart entered the Japanese market with a measure of trepidation. The U.S. retail giant bought just over 6% of Seiyu in the initial deal, but had options to raise its investment incrementally to a majority, later acquiring the right to further raise their stake. Judging by their tepid entry, Wal-Mart had some idea of the high stakes of the Japanese retail market. Wal-Mart seemed bullish on the prospects of Seiyu, and quickly moved to increase its share, becoming the majority shareholder in December of 2002.[19] In fact, Wal-Mart's decision to

---

[17] Jim Hopkins. Wal-Mart's influence grows *USA Today*.

[18] Wal-Mart corporate. History Timeline. Website http://walmartstores.com/AboutUs/7603.aspx.

[19] Charles Smith. Wal-Mart stocks up on Seiyu. (13 December 2002). *Daily Deal*, M&A section.

become a majority stakeholder came on the news that Seiyu was initiating a major change, selling off Tokyo Finance, a money-losing consumer finance subsidiary, to focus on the core business of supermarkets.[20]

While becoming the largest shareholder at Seiyu, Wal-Mart moved quickly to make changes in the way Seiyu did business. While keeping in place the Japanese management structure, including Chairman Masao Kiuchi, the influence of Bentonville made itself known.[21] Wal-Mart began phasing its advanced computer systems into Seiyu, attempting to make the business more efficient. While keeping basic management structure in place, Wal-Mart also brought in advisors from the home office in Bentonville Arkansas to try and push Japanese management to make further changes. One of the first was to push for major restructuring, or the dreaded *risutora* in Japanese.[22]

TAKING A LOOK AT SEIYU

Seiyu (The Seiyu Co., LTD) is even older than its partner. Founded after World War II as part of the Seiyu Railway group, it was eventually split off as a main component of the Saison retail group. After the war, railway companies and retailers were a common pairing. In fact, some of Tokyo's most posh department stores, such as Odakyu and Seibu, were set up by transport companies after the war. The Saison Group was fairly broad based, branching out into many industries. This was another typical feature of Japanese companies, both before and after the war. Though it is now changing, Japanese industry used to be set up around large corporate conglomerates, usually based around a bank. The bank would be a major shareholder in each of the other businesses, lending at preferable rates. Meanwhile, the other

---

[20] *Ibid.*

[21] William J Holstein. Why Wal-Mart can't find happiness in Japan (27 July 2007). *Fortune.*

[22] William J Holstein. Why Wal-Mart can't find happiness in Japan (27 July 2007). *Fortune.*

companies would also do much of their business among themselves. For example, Mitsubishi steel would sell metal to Mitsubishi automobiles, who would outfit their factory with machines bought from Mitsubishi heavy industry. These conglomerates were called *zaibatsu* before the war and *keiretsu* afterwards. While not an internationally known conglomerate like Mitsubishi or Nissan, Seiyu was in a group of linked firms with Sumitomo bank as the primary shareholder. This ended only when Wal-Mart bought out Sumitomo's shares.

Seiyu expanded heavily in the 1980s but when the bubble economy burst in the mid 90's and land values dropped correspondingly, Seiyu started to have serious financial problems. Even before Wal-Mart bought a stake in Seiyu, the retailer had been struggling, though its core grocery business was profitable.[23] In an attempt to reach new markets Seiyu was expanding into newly built residential areas and experimenting with new types of stores, for example "The Mall, Mizuho 16", a large complex with a Seiyu-managed store as the anchor and numerous other retailers renting space, and Livin, a department store with groceries on the first floor, a common practice in higher-end Japanese retailing. Seiyu was also re-building and re-modeling several stores a year, though it simply did not have the capital to move as fast as it needed to. Seiyu was a firm that expanded too much in the heady days of Japan's bubble economy, had lost sight of its core business and was no longer nimble enough to fight off rivals. Interestingly, one of Seiyu's sister firms from that era is Mujirushi, the hip home furnishing store where everything comes in only three colors. Though Muji has gone from strength to strength in recent years, time has not been so kind to Seiyu.

While Seiyu was struggling, competitors were moving in. In 1990, Seiyu was the third largest retailer in Japan.[24] The top two spots were occupied by Daiei and Ito Yokado, respectively, both in

---

[23] Charles Smith. Wal-Mart stocks up on Seiyu (13 December 2002). *Daily Deal*, M&A section.

[24] Yuko Aoyama. Why foreign retailers fail in Japan, Carrefour vs. Wal-Mart (paper presented at *Globalizing Retail* Surrey, United Kingdom, July 17–18, 2006). www.sorn.surry.ac.uk/research/groups/globalizingretailseminar/Aoyama.pdf.

general merchandise stores like Seiyu. By 2003, Seiyu had been knocked out of the top five, while Daiei, Jusco and Ito Yokado remained. The first and fifth spots respectively, were held by convenience store chains Lawson and Seven Eleven.[25,26] Seiyu was suffering declining sales and declining profits. One reason may be due to Seiyu's image. Many consumers seem confused as to what exactly Seiyu is offering them. It is just one more name in a crowded retail field, a name that many consumers do not feel particularly drawn too. In a recent poll, only 5% of those asked responded that the reason they shop at Seiyu was quality, versus around 12% for Jusco and nearly 20% for Ito Yokado (see Table 1).[27] In all three categories polled, quality, display, and variety/inventory, Seiyu ranked near the bottom, besting only Daei.[28-30]

Table 1.   Attitude towards Japanese retailers.

Retailer	Quality (percent of respondents)	Display (percent of respondents)	Inventory (percent of respondents)
Ito Yokado	, 16.9	12.6	36.1
JUSCO	12.1	9.2	29.5
AEON	7.9	3.9	34.5
Seiyu	5.4	3.3	17.0
Daiei	3.6	3.0	14.3

[25] Yuko Aoyama. Why foreign retailers fail in Japan, Carrefour vs. Wal-Mart (paper presented at *Globalizing Retail* Surrey, United Kingdom, July 17–18, 2006). www.sorn.surry.ac.uk/research/groups/globalizingretailseminar/Aoyama.pdf.

[26] Seven and I holding owns both Seven Eleven convenience stores and Ito Yokado.

[27] Yuko Aoyama. Why foreign retailers fail in Japan, Carrefour vs. Wal-Mart (paper presented at *Globalizing Retail* Surrey, United Kingdom, July 17–18, 2006). www.sorn.surry.ac.uk/research/groups/globalizingretailseminar/Aoyama.pdf.

[28] *Ibid.*

[29] It is perhaps worth mentioning here that Wal-Mart also attempted to acquire Daiei after their purchase of Seiyu.

[30] Chart Data: Yuko Aoyama. Why foreign retailers fail in Japan, Carrefour vs. Wal-Mart (paper presented at *Globalizing Retail* Surrey, United Kingdom, July17–18, 2006). www.sorn.surry.ac.uk/research/groups/globalizingretailseminar/Aoyama.pdf.

In 2002, Seiyu was thrown a lifeline in the form of capital investment from Wal-Mart. After some years of financial trouble, a tie-up with the biggest retailer in the world must have seemed a windfall. Indeed, looking at media reports from the time, there are many voices urging caution, but predicting that with the right moves, Wal-Mart and Seiyu could make money in Japan.[31] Wal-Mart was seeking to expand its operations overseas at this time, having acquired stores in Germany, South Korea, and Great Britain in the late 1990s.[32] Seiyu presented an opportunity to enter the Japanese market, which has historically been reluctant to allow foreign companies to operate. Seiyu's financial troubles also gave Wal-Mart more of a free hand to make drastic yet necessary changes.[33]

The two companies also seemed to be a good fit. Both were general merchandise stores. Both had built extensively in the suburbs, and Seiyu and Wal-Mart both tried to undercut the competition on price. Wal-Mart had what many were seeing as a golden chance to enter Japan with a well-established partner. They could thus forego the risks that firms like Ikea and Carrefour incurred by deciding to venture alone.

Public Perception of Wal-Mart

To understand the impact of Wal-Mart's restructuring in Japan, a brief note on Japan's corporate-based culture in the decades after the Second World War is necessary. The chief engines of the Japanese economic miracle after the Second World War were favored corporations, aforementioned *keiretsu*. Though white-collar company employees, or salarymen as they are known in Japan, never became the norm of the working population, the salaryman and his

---

[31] "...an inexpensive, low-risk way to enter a market with tremendous long-term potential..." Mike Troy. Wal-Mart invests in Japan, buys 6% share of Seiyu — brief article (25 March 2002). *DSN Retailing Today.*

[32] The secrets of Wal-Mart's success (14 June 1999). *BBC News.* http://news.bbc.co.uk/2/hi/business/325922.stm.

[33] Tak Kumakura. Wal-Mart seeks full ownership of Seiyu; Business Asia by Bloomberg (27 October 2007). *International Herald Tribune.* Finance section.

accompanying company culture came to dominate Japanese society. Comic books like *Tsuribaka* (Fool for Fishing) and the *Shima Kousaku* Series, about a man who climbs the corporate ladder from humble office worker to company president, became best sellers. Salaryman influence was so pervasive that a line from the eleventh century novel, *Tale of Genji*, was adopted to fit the times, "If you aren't a salaryman, then you aren't a man" (*sarariman ni arazunba, ningen ni arazu*).[34] These companies supported society by providing good jobs with lifetime guarantees of employment. These large corporations succeeded in creating a kind of private welfare state where the needs of employees were looked after from the moment they entered the company until the end of their lives. Though Japanese companies were still geared to make money, this shepherding instinct was very important to Japanese capitalism. While in the U.S., the objective of companies came to be seen as generating profits for shareholders, Japanese companies tended to be viewed as job-creating machines. Of course profit was necessary, but it was not as central a concept as in U.S. capitalism.

Japanese companies are changing with the times, but the Japanese public, including the government, has been slow to change its view of corporate responsibility. Japanese labor laws are still very protective of the worker and it remains difficult to get rid of surplus employees.[35] Generous severance must be provided, even for a firm in trouble, and the court of public opinion is especially severe. Full-time employees, called *seishain* have been decreasing in recent years to be replaced with less expensive temporary and part-time workers. This has prompted national soul-searching. Even the government has gotten involved, with lawmakers, especially opposition lawmakers, regularly calling for new measures to protect workers from layoffs and calling for an increase of full-time workers.

---

[34] The original quote is 「平家にあらずんば人にあらず」 Heike ni arazunba, hito ni arazu, if you are not a Heike (one of the two warring factions in the *Tale*) you are not a person.

[35] Jonathan Soble. Manager@work: If you must get sacked, then Japan's the place (27 October 2008). *The Edge Malaysia*.

Against this backdrop, one of the first major actions Seiyu management was spurred to by Wal-Mart advisors was a plan of cutting costs by cutting headcount. While reducing personnel costs is a classic way for U.S. firms to cut costs even in good times, *risutora* (restructuring) is a taboo here in Japan. Today, many people and companies are worried about the global credit crunch. Yet, mass job cuts are still viewed as detrimental to Japanese society. Recent articles in major newspapers as well as televisions spots on prime time news shows highlighting the difficulties facing laid-off workers attest to this fact.[36] Seiyu aimed at reducing the number of *seishain* by approximately one-quarter at the head office through inducing early retirement and converting other workers to part-time status.[37] No one was being fired, and no one was being forced out, the company was simply hoping to solicit takers.[38] As jobs cuts go, these seemed rather mild.

Surprisingly for Wal-Mart, and perhaps realizing the worst fears of Japanese executives, the jobs cuts did not go unnoticed. Workers who were forced out began to appear in the media complaining about how Seiyu had lost its way.[39] The Japanese media is typically more emotional than its American counterparts, and disgruntled employees found they had ample opportunities to air grievances. This not only created a less cooperative workforce (after all, if your job suddenly becomes expendable, pressing ahead with further restructuring can hardly be seen as in your interest), but also hurt the company's image. With a struggling supermarket chain and a new foreign owner, how the public perceives you is important. If the public is not supportive of your measures, they may also not be supportive of your

---

[36] For an example, see, "Teinenn made, machigae da" (Staying Until Retirement is a Mistake), *Yomiuri Shinbun*, Morning Edition 26 December 2008, which highlights a middle age worker who lost his job at IBM. Article translated by author.

[37] "The suuji: 22.78% hiritsu fuyasu patotaimu roudousya" (The Numbers: Ratio of Part-Time Workers to Rise to 22.78%), *Yomiuri Shinbun*, Tokyo Morning Edition, 18 January 2004. Article translated by author.

[38] *Ibid.*

[39] William J Holstein. Why Wal-Mart can't find happiness in Japan (27 July 2007). *Fortune.*

stores, and retail outlets are especially vulnerable to public perception problems.

THE JAPANESE RETAIL MARKET — AN ONGOING CHALLENGE

Japanese Consumers

After alienating workers, Wal-Mart then stepped on the toes of another group of powerful stakeholders in Japan: housewives. One of the reasons for Wal-Mart's spectacular success in the suburbs of America is the car society and the shopping habits it engenders. Suburban Americans will drive the car to the nearest strip mall or supercenter and stock up on goods and groceries for the week. They have the space in their homes to stock large quantities of goods as well as cars to transport heavy loads. In Japan, especially in urban areas, shopping is spread throughout the week and is often done by bicycle or on foot. For several items, especially fresh grains and vegetables, Japanese consumers go shopping on an average of once every other day.[40] Housewives who do not work often compare prices before they go out by looking at daily newspaper inserts called *chirashi* (see Fig. 1). In 2004, citing their Everyday Low Prices (one of Wal-Mart's slogans in the U.S.), Wal-Mart cut out the *chirashi*. In the U.S., consumers associate Wal-Mart with lower prices (15–20% lower) than the competition.[41] In Japan, consumers still wanted to see the deals in print; they did not trust Seiyu to deliver the lowest prices without some sort of authentication.[42] Without being able to compare prices, housewives were confused and simply went elsewhere.[43] After a marked drop in sales, Wal-Mart was forced to

---

[40] Yuko Aoyama. Why foreign retailers fail in Japan, Carrefour vs. Wal-Mart (paper presented at *Globalizing Retail* Surrey, United Kingdom, July 17–18, 2006). www.sorn.surry.ac.uk/research/groups/globalizingretailseminar/Aoyama.pdf.

[41] Ian Rowley. Japan isn't buying the Wal-Mart idea (28 February 2005). *Business Week*, Asian Business.

[42] *Ibid.*

[43] William J Holstein. Why Wal-Mart can't find happiness in Japan (27 July 2007). *Fortune.*

Figure 1. Japanese *chirashi*.

resurrect the *chirashi*. This is not merely a cautionary tale of the need to respect Japanese housewives. It is but one example of how Wal-Mart failed early on to understand the way Japanese shop.

INTRODUCING THE FAMOUS WAL-MART STRATEGY TO JAPAN

"We'll get the building blocks in place first — the systems, the financials, and the merchandising — and then we'll move towards the U.S. model". Greg Penner, CFO, Wal-Mart Japan (2004).[44]

Everyday Low Prices

Wal-Mart has thrived on a low-cost image since its inception. It is important to ask if this low-cost leadership strategy is fundamentally

---

[44] *Business Week*, May 2004.

sound here in Japan. Management slips and consumer misunderstandings may play a part in Wal-Mart's woes. Perhaps the most important question to ask is "will Everyday Low Prices work in Japan?"

Japan has often been called a mass luxury market. Louis Vuitton, the famous French purveyor of purses and fancy shoes, sells nearly one-third of its handbags here in Japan.[45] Japanese consumers have a taste for the luxurious, though it has also been shown that Japanese consumers are practically giddy about saving money on some goods. This fact must be mentioned with a caveat; though Japanese consumers like saving money, they are still picky about quality. They won't buy cheap goods, especially if the goods are perceived as an inferior substitute. As the old saying goes "*yasukarou, warukarou*" — if it is cheap, it is bad. In Japanese cuisine, how the food is presented is as important as what it tastes like, perhaps even more important because bad-looking food will not be consumed. Pricing is one aspect of presentation. This obviously carries over to groceries, but applies to other good as well. Wal-Mart carries a serious risk in Japan by being too cheap. Seiyu and her new partner are spending huge amounts of money to rebuild and renovate stores, making them more attractive to Japanese consumers, but they still have to convince them that they are getting a great deal, namely the best products for a price that they cannot believe. This has been a problem for the retailer. As then Seiyu president Masao Kiuchi lamented, "the lower price on *sashimi* (raw fish) doesn't mean that it's a few days old, but that Wal-Mart got a better price on it". Sadly, many Japanese consumers cannot help but be suspicious of items, especially food items, priced in the bargain range.

Problems Recreating Wal-Mart's Logistics Miracle

Wal-Mart must not only stock merchandise of only the highest quality for the lowest price, they must also contend with a bewildering

---

[45] Richard Katz. The myth of Louis Vuitton; too rich for their own good? (May 2003). *Oriental Economist.*

array of specialty goods. Each town and hamlet in Japan is known for a particular product, and consumers want this product from the town that made it famous. They also demand local produce be available and are willing to pay a higher price for it. Wal-Mart sources some products locally in the U.S. as well, but Americans are not so picky about local products as Japanese consumers. Food safety has recently become a hot topic in Japan — one of the scariest news stories of 2008 chosen by an online poll was tainted gyoza dumplings from China.[46] This only increases the demand for locally-produced food.

Food in Japan still changes with the seasons. In the U.S., seasonal foods are no longer such an important factor in shopping: you can more or less get what you want, when you want it. Japanese consumers vary their shopping habits significantly by what time of year it is. Certain fruits and vegetables are available only at certain times of the year, and the price of goods stocked year round can also vary significantly with agriculture production cycles.

Japan's distribution landscape is complicated by the sheer variety and variations in regional tastes of Japanese consumers, but Japan's distribution chain is also more complex. Whereas Wal-Mart has traditionally relied on buying directly from supplies in the U.S., this has proven to be a problem in Japan. First of all, Seiyu is not as predominant in the Japanese retail landscape as Wal-Mart is in the U.S. This makes it hard to secure special deals for merchandise in Japan. Also, there are many layers in the traditional Japanese supply chain.[47] Wal-Mart has attempted to push through some of these layers, cutting out some middlemen to reduce their costs. This has angered some suppliers.[48] Until Wal-Mart is able to bypass some of the numerous layers of the Japanese chain and consolidate their

---

[46] Business Media Makoto. Motomo kowai to kanjita nyuzu ha? (The news You felt was most frighting). http://bizmakoto.jp/makoto/articles/0809/29/news051.html. Translated by author.

[47] Masayoshi Maruyama. Japanese wholesale distribution: Its features and future. In *Japanese Distribution Strategy*, Michael R Czinkota and Masaaki Kotabe (eds.), pp. 19–22. London: Business Press.

[48] William J Holstein. Why Wal-Mart can't find happiness in Japan (27 July 2007). *Fortune.*

purchasing, they will not be able to be as efficient with their movement of merchandise.

Wal-Mart's efficiency of logistics has been one of their greatest assets in the U.S. The demand for seasonal and regional goods, coupled with Japan's more complex supply chain, have led to delays in duplicating Wal-Mart efficiency in Japan.[49] This has cost the company time and money.

A Tale of Two Discount Stores

Wal-Mart's core business is built around saving the consumer money by selling cheaper items than the store next door. We have just asked if this strategy is fundamentally flawed in Japan. But looking at a different discount retailer, Ikea, it seems that discount stores can in fact flourish in Louis Vuitton's biggest market. The similarities between Ikea and Wal-Mart are many. Both recently entered the Japanese market. Both concentrate on selling low-priced goods. Both take as many opportunities to cut costs as possible, for example, Ikea and Wal-Mart both use exposed lighting fixtures in their warehouse-sized stores. Both companies were told that their business model would not appeal to Japanese consumers.[50] In the case of Ikea, the business model was a huge success. Within a few years of returning to Japan, Ikea had made the country one of its top markets.[51] How can one discount retailer succeed so brilliantly while another does not? The answer can be found in image. Ikea has managed to be both cheap and have a cool, fashionable image.[52] Ikea is a Swedish company, and this in one of its main strengths. Though one of Ikea's most popular chairs may have been designed by a Japanese man, the furniture and accessories at Ikea are given a foreign, namely Northern European, flair.[53] This

---

[49] *Ibid.*

[50] Rolf Jensen, Presentation given at IKEA Japan, Funabashi Store. 16 December 2008.

[51] *Ibid.*

[52] David Pilling. Foreign investors: A tough nut to crack (13 March 2007). *Financial Times Online.*

[53] *Ibid.*

distinction appeals to Japanese consumers. Though the furniture may be cheap, it is designed in Sweden, and can therefore be considered fashionable. Wal-Mart is an American hypermart, selling mainly Japanese products. Sadly, this format does not have the same appeal as a hip Swedish discount retailer. In many ways, Carrefour, the French retail powerhouse, fell into the same trap. Instead of playing up its Euro roots, it tried selling cheap Japanese products to Japanese consumers. This strategy lacked appeal, and Japan turned into nothing more than a multi-million dollar misstep for the firm.

WAL-MART STRIKES BACK: THE KOLODZIESKI ERA

We have been harsh on Wal-Mart up to now. To their credit, Wal-Mart has stayed the course in Japan, believing that they can make Seiyu work. This is not simply stubbornness. Wal-Mart has shown in both Germany and South Korea that it knows when to quit. Wal-Mart has also shown that it knows how to adapt.[54] In Seiyu, Wal-Mart sees real opportunity. The company has not had full operational control for their entire sojourn at Seiyu. It was not until 2006 that the Japanese chairman of Seiyu stepped down and Wal-Mart was able to place their own man, Edward Kolodzieski, at the helm. Wal-Mart did not even decide to make the company a wholly-owned subsidiary until 2007. Looking at the facts, Wal-Mart has been in full control of Seiyu for a relatively short period of time. Since gaining a free hand at Seiyu in the last two years, Wal-Mart has moved aggressively to perform triage on Seiyu as the red numbers continue to add up.

Wal-Mart now has full control of the company and its executive leadership. Yet many of the problems outlined above remain. Questions still remain about Wal-Mart's understanding of the Japanese shopper and the Japanese market. Wal-Mart has raised

---

[54] One small example, in Canada, Wal-Mart's Super Centers are spelled as "Super Centre". Furthermore, in numerous markets, Wal-Mart has kept from making huge changes to acquisitions' names and logos.

eyebrows by pressing forward in re-making Seiyu in the American Wal-Mart's image and by adopting many radically different strategies from their rivals.[55]

Since taking full control of the company, Wal-Mart has continued to cut costs at Seiyu. In 2007, the company again solicited employees for early retirement.[56] In a move that may underscore the company's workforce issues, more employees opted for early retirement than were asked for. In 2008, Seiyu again announced job cuts, along with a plan to close about 20 stores aiming to cut costs and bring the retailer back into the black.[57] Although the company says that the cuts will help it return to long-term profitability, it remains to be seen if Wal-Mart is repeating past mistakes.

Wal-Mart is also looking for ways to cut costs that do not involve cutting jobs. The advanced global procurement systems SMART and Retail link that Wal-Mart uses to track inventory — which scour the globe for the cheapest wholesalers of goods and place orders automatically — continue to be phased in.[58] These systems have served Wal-Mart well in the past, and could radically change the way Seiyu does business. Furthermore, from 2008, Wal-Mart has announced that goods will now be centrally purchased at the home office in Tokyo.[59] Japanese retailers typically do not negotiate with wholesalers for purchases as a firm, but allow each unit to buy separately. This should give Wal-Mart more control over each store as well as more leverage with wholesalers. Ordering goods in this way could allow Seiyu the same kind of purchasing that Wal-Mart enjoys in the U.S., with comparable benefits. AEON, one of Seiyu's chief rivals, has also

---

[55] Seiyu adopts contrarian strategy (19 March 2007). *The Nikkei Weekly.*

[56] Seiyu: Soukitaisyoku 450nin Bosyuu (Seiyu seeks early retirement for 450 employees) (19 September 2007). *Mainichi Shinbun*, Tokyo Edition, Morning Edition Translated By Author.

[57] Analysis: Wal-Mart puts profit ahead of sales volume in Seiyu revamp (30 September 2008). *Nikkei Tuesday Morning Edition.*

[58] William J Holstein. Why Wal-Mart can't find happiness in Japan (27 July 2007). *Fortune.*

[59] Seiyu to centralize goods purchasing in '08 to cut costs (15 August 2007). *The Nikkei Wednesday Morning Edition.*

tried a similar strategy, using sheer size to go around middlemen.[60] Wal-Mart's chief in Japan said that local specialties would however not be ordered from the head office, but sourced by the local stores themselves, raising hopes that Wal-Mart is learning about Japanese consumer behavior.[61]

Wal-Mart continues to rebuild and re-model Seiyu stores, hoping to make them more attractive to Japanese consumers. However, many of the re-modeled stores look like Wal-Marts back in the States. It remains to be seen if this is a style that will appeal to picky Japanese consumers. Another big change at Seiyu reflecting the influence of Wal-Mart is the introduction of store-brand goods. As mentioned earlier, Wal-Mart is famous for their exclusive brands, like *Sam's American Choice Cola*, that are inexpensive and perceived as a good value by U.S. consumers. Seiyu is putting more and more Wal-Mart goods on their shelves in the hope of attracting price-conscious consumers.[62] Other Japanese retailers have also started down this path, for example Seven & I Holding and AEON have begun to offer many generic items like laundry detergent and snacks. Since Wal-Mart has used its private label brands all over the world, the firm should be clearly ahead of the game in developing its own brands. But will these brands fit Japanese tastes? Equally importantly, are Japanese consumers cost-conscious enough to buy generic brands for low prices? If they are, Seiyu could find itself on the leading edge of a huge growth opportunity. If they are mistaken about changing perceptions of generic household goods, they may wind up attracting less shoppers, not bringing in new ones. The Japanese economy, though still the second largest in the world, is not as affluent as it once was. Consumers may be willing to spend less and be more willing to

---

[60] Ian Rowley. Japan isn't buying the Wal-Mart idea (28 February 2005). *Business Week*, Asian Business.
[61] Seiyu to centralize goods purchasing in '08 to cut costs (15 August 2007). *The Nikkei Wednesday Morning Edition.*
[62] Seiyu to boost store-brand goods to lure bargain hunters (2 May 2008). *The Nikkei Friday Morning Edition.* Also, Seiyu to import 100 Wal-Mart store brand items by year's end (7 June 2008). *The Nikkei Saturday Morning Edition.*

accept cheaper substitutes, assuming they still meet a basic standard of quality.

Going back to *chirashi*, Wal-Mart has finally embraced the paper leaflets. Showing their continued desire to be the lowest priced retailer and to make sure that Everyday Low Prices survive in Japan, Seiyu has announced that they will now honor the *chirashi* of their competitors[63] — a marketing coup designed to make sure that when customers think of low prices, they think of Seiyu.

While competitors such as AEON are inviting more specialty retailers into their stores, Seiyu has done the opposite, focusing on making all the units in a store Seiyu owned.[64] When Wal-Mart officials first came to Seiyu, they were surprised about the pride of place given to in-store independent retailers, bakeries, bento shops and the like. Seiyu is moving to phase these out and bring in *Wakana* a Seiyu-exclusive brand.[65] AEON and others have gone the opposite direction, bringing in specialty retailers as an incentive to visit the store, along with using the rent these retailers pay to increase store revenue and make up for revenue lost to in-store competition.[66] Bringing in retailers has allowed some competitors, like Daiei for instance, to focus more on core products, in their case: groceries.

WHERE WAL-MART STANDS TODAY

Seiyu again failed to post a profit in 2008. Due to poor economic conditions, even AEON, the most successful of Seiyu's competitors, is not sure if it will post a loss or a slim profit.[67] Seiyu has noted

---

[63] "Seiyu 'tamise chirashi nebiki OK' supa- kakaku sennsou hakusya" (Spurring on the supermarket wars — Seiyu announces competitors' coupons are OK), Fuji Sankei Business i /Bloomberg Global Finance (12 May 2008). http://www.business-i.jp/article/200812040018a.nwc. Translated by author.

[64] Seiyu adopts contrarian strategy (19 March 2007). *The Nikkei Weekly.*

[65] *Ibid.*

[66] Seiyu adopts contrarian strategy (19 March 2007). *The Nikkei Weekly.*

[67] "AEON 2gatsu ki kessan yosou akaji ka kuroji ka wakaranai" (AEON unsure of profit or loss for two months) (8 January 2009). *Yomiuri Shimbun*, Tokyo Morning Edition.

some progress. Some stores are starting to show an increase in year on year sales.[68] Wal-Mart finally has their computer systems up and running at Seiyu. A new automated distribution center has just opened for the company, allowing it to distribute all types of goods from the same location.[69] There is a new CEO at the helm. However, the fact remains that Wal-Mart is about to embark on year seven of their tie-up with Seiyu and have still not made money from their investment. Wal-Mart is America's low price leader. They have worked hard to solidify this image in Japan as well, even going so far as to honor competitors' coupons. With the current financial troubles hitting consumers hard, Wal-Mart and their Everyday Low Prices should be in optimum position to gain on their rivals this year. We have seen Wal-Mart and Seiyu make mistakes and squander opportunities. The economic conditions of 2009 and 2010 seems to be giving the company a good chance to increase sales and market share, assuming they have learned from their mistakes. In a company that increasingly sees itself as a global entity, failure in Japan would be a huge blow. Staying the course in Japan for several more years before admitting defeat would be an even bigger blow. Perhaps Wal-Mart's success finally materializes across the Pacific. If not, Wal-Mart and Seiyu will be forced to make some serious decisions about their partnership.

QUESTIONS

1) Which market entry strategy did Wal-Mart choose to enter the Japanese market?
2) What challenges did Wal-Mart meet in Japan?
3) How does Japanese consumer behavior differ from Western consumer behavior?
4) Can private brand be internationalized?
5) Should Wal-Mart change its pricing policy?

---

[68] William J Holstein. Why Wal-Mart can't find happiness in Japan (27 July 2007). *Fortune.*
[69] *Ibid.*

6) What effect will economic downturn have on Wal-Mart's business in Japan?
7) Are there other American retailers that are successful overseas? Please name some and point out their international marketing strategies.
8) What future strategies should Wal-Mart apply in the Japanese market?

BIBLIOGRAPHY

AEON 2gatsu ki kessan yosou akaji ka kuroji ka wakaranai (AEON unsure of profit or loss for two months) (8 January 2009). *Yomiuri Shimbun, Tokyo Morning Edition.* (Japanese, translated by author).

Analysis: Wal-Mart puts profit ahead of sales volume in Seiyu revamp (30 September 2008) *Nikkei Tuesday Morning Edition.*

Aoyama, Y. Why foreign retailers fail in Japan, Carrefour vs. Wal-Mart. Paper presented at *Globalizing Retail* Surrey, United Kingdom, 17–18 July 2006. www.sorn.surry.ac.uk/research/groups/globalizingretailseminar/Aoyama.pdf.

Business Media Makoto. Motomo kowai to kanjita nyuzu ha? The news You felt was most frighting. http://bizmakoto.jp/makoto/articles/0809/29/news051.html. (Japanese, translated by author.)

Holstein, WJ. Why Wal-Mart can't find happiness in Japan (27 July 2007). *Fortune.*

Hopkins, J. Wal-Mart's influence grows. *USA Today.*

Katz, R. The myth of Louis Vuitton; too rich for their own good? May 2003 *Oriental Economist.*

Kumakura, T. Wal-Mart seeks full ownership of Seiyu; Business Asia by Bloomberg (23 October 2007). *International Herald Tribune,* Finance Section.

Maruyama, M. (2000). Japanese wholesale distribution: Its features and future. In *Japanese Distribution Strategy,* MR Czinkota and M Kotabe (ed.), pp. 19–22. London: Business Press.

Pilling, D. Foreign investors: A tough nut to crack (13 March 2007). *Financial Times Online.*

Rowley, I. Japan is not buying the Wal-Mart idea (28 February 2005). *Business Week*, Asian Business.

Seiyu adopts contrarian strategy (19 March 2007). *The Nikkei Weekly*.

Seiyu to boost store-brand goods to lure bargain hunters (2 May 2008). *The Nikkei Friday Morning Edition*.

Seiyu to centralize goods purchasing in '08 to cut costs (15 August 2007). *The Nikkei Wednesday Morning Edition*.

Seiyu to import 100 Wal-Mart store brand items by year's end (7 June 2008). *The Nikkei Saturday Morning Edition*.

Seiyu: Soukitaisyoku 450nin bosyuu (Seiyu seeks early retirement for 450 employees) (19 September 2007). *Mainichi Shinbun*, Tokyo Edition, Morning Edition. (Japanese, translated by author.)

Seiyu 'tamise chirashi nebiki OK' supa- kakaku sennsou hakusya (Spurring on the supermarket wars — Seiyu announces competitors' coupons are OK) (12 May 2008). *Fuji Sankei Business i/Bloomberg Global Finance*. (Japanese, translated by author.)

Smith, C. Wal-Mart stocks up on Seiyu (13 December 2002). *Daily Deal*, M&A section.

The secrets of Wal-Mart's success (14 June 1999). *BBC News*.

The suuji: 22.78% hiritsu fuyasu patotaimu roudousya (The numbers: Ratio of part-time workers to rise to 22.78%) (18 January 2004). *Yomiuri Shinbun Tokyo Morning Edition*. (Japanese, translated by author.)

Soble, J. Manager@work: If you must get sacked, then Japan's the place (27 October 2008). *The Edge Malaysia*.

Teinenn made, machigae da (Staying until retirement is a mistake) (26 December 2008). *Yomiuri Shinbun*, Morning Edition. (Japanese, translated by author.)

Troy, M. Wal-Mart invests in Japan, buys 6% share of Seiyu — brief article (25 March 2002). *DSN Retailing Today*.

Use of retail technology focuses on service (14 December 1995). *Discount Store News*.

Wal-Mart Corporate Website. History Timeline. http://walmartstores.com/AboutUs/297.aspx.

How eBay Got Outbid: Initial Failure and Market Re-entry in Japan

Julie Lafage

"We're in it for the marathon, not the sprint"

Margaret C. Whitman, President and Chief Executive
Office of eBay from March 1998 to March 2008

THE BIRTH OF eBAY

The online auction website eBay was launched as "AuctionWeb" in September 1995 by the French computer programmer Pierre Omidyar, as part of his online consulting company Echo Bay Technology Group. Due to the fact that the domain name EchoBay.com had been already taken, Omidyar chose the short version: www.eBay.com.

Pierre Omidyar believed that the auction business was a good and profitable marketing tool. Therefore, for him, everyone had the right to place a bid for an item starting at a minimum price. With his newly created low visual "AuctionWeb" website, he started to auction several categories, from books to electronics and computer appliances in order to attract different types of bidders. At first, the website was free of charge and had a slow users' traffic. The first item to be sold was a broken laser pointer at a rate of $13.83. Gradually, the traffic on "AuctionWeb" increased and by the end of 1995, the auctions got over 10,000 bids (eBay, 2008).

In 1996, the site had attracted 4400 subscribers. With the increase of hosting sellers, Pierre Omidyar decided to take a risk and charged sellers with a percentage of the final price sale. The hosting charge was widely accepted by the sellers' community and increased the profit of the company, which led to high revenues, reaching $165,000 by the end of the year (Sanderson, 2002). It was in 1997, after receiving $5 million in funding from the venture capital firm "Benchmark Capital" that the company changed its name to eBay.

During the summer of 1999, eBay went through its hardest moment, facing a 22 hour system crash, failing numerous auctions. However, management reaction was extremely positive to users, due to the fact that a large team of eBay employees contacted users to apologize for the huge inconvenience. As a result, users' trust in eBay has grown immensely. During that same year, eBay started to acquire several similar online auctions companies (USA Today, 2005). The year 1999 was also an important moment in eBay's expansion. Because of customers complaints due to the inconvenience of sending money orders or cashier's checks, eBay decided to acquire PayPal.com, offering online payments by credit cards. PayPal was a further insurance for customers who purchase on eBay. Indeed, customers could receive up to $200 compensation from PayPal in case of failure in receiving items ordered on eBay (Sanderson, 2002).

By the end of 2000, with eight million items auctioned and more than two million unique visitors per day, eBay became one of the most successful shopping websites online (Sanderson, 2002).

THE DEVELOPMENT OF eBAY

During 2000, eBay was already leader in several English-speaking countries such as Canada (150,000 daily listing), Australia (1.5 million daily listings) and the United Kingdom (100,000 daily listings). This successful expansion was particularly linked to the appointment of Meg Whitman as CEO of eBay at that time. Joining the company in 1998, Meg Whitman introduced several changes into eBay's strategy. By promoting PayPal to eBay's customers, she contributed to reducing transactions risks. She also promoted eBay outside the U.S. by acquiring and launching new websites (*Fortune*, 2004).

The largest and most significant acquisitions were between 2002 and 2005, when they acquired PayPal (online payments), Skype (Internet telephony), Shopping.com (online comparison shopping) and Rent.com (online apartment listing service). Increasing their existing revenues substantially, these acquisitions led to a 39% profit rise at the end of 2005 (eBay annual report, 2007).

The expansion of their revenue along the years allowed eBay to expand their business into additional countries apart from the U.S. Facing fierce competition in the U.S. from Amazon (online retailer) and Yahoo! Auctions (launched in 1998), eBay decided to expand its auction website abroad. Starting with Germany, the UK and Australia in 1999, eBay quickly became the leading company in auctions sales around the world. The international expansion was particularly promoted during the 1999–2002 period, when eBay entered Asia for the first time, launching activities in Taiwan and Korea (eBay website, 2008).

However, in order to achieve the same fame and profits as enjoyed in the U.S., there was the need to form joint ventures in some countries to reach sellers and buyers. Good examples are Taiwan and China, where there was the need to create joint ventures, respectively with NeoCom and Tom group's Tom online in order to reach the aimed target and compete against local competitors (*The Daily Deal*, 2008).

By progressively introducing standardized listing fees to all its international eBay websites, eBay is now promoting its new corporate strategy — the Cross-border trading where eBay's customers can sell and buy from all over the world (eBay website, 2008).

With more than 84.5 million active members worldwide in 2007, eBay is involved in 39 different markets including the U.S. It was reported by eBay that the total net revenue in 2007 increased 29% compared to the previous year with $7.672 billion.

Table 1.   History of eBay.

1995	Creation of "AuctionWeb" by Pierre Omidyar.
1997	"Auction web" changed for eBay
1998	Margaret C Whitman (Meg Withman) became eBay's CEO.
	eBay went public on NASDAQ.
1999	eBay started its expansion outside the U.S. market by entering in the UK, Germany and Australia.
	eBay introduced the fixed priced trading with its "Buy it now" option.
2000	eBay expanded in France, Austria, Canada and Taiwan.
	eBay acquired Half.com (site selling second-hand books, movies, music and games).
2001	International expansion in Korea, Italy, Ireland, New Zealand, Singapore and Switzerland.
2002	eBay acquired PayPal (online payment).
2003	eBay expanded to Hong Kong.
2004	Acquisition of Marketplaats.nl (classified advertising site) and Rent.com (online apartment listing service).
	Launched activity in Malaysia and Philippines.
2005	Acquisition of Shopping.com (online comparison shopping), Skype (Internet telephony), LoQuo and Gumtree (classified advertising).
	Launched activity in Poland and Sweden.
	Established ProStores (virtual store-front service), Kijiji (local classified advertising).
2007	Acquisition of StubHub.com (online ticketing site), StumbleUpon.com (research site).

Source: eBay website.

THE CORE BUSINESS OF eBAY

The three major businesses directed by eBay are "the eBay Marketplace" (about 70% of eBay net revenues in 2007), "PayPal" (approximately 25%) and "Skype" (around 5%). In consequence, the majority of eBay revenues come from listings and commissions on completed sales related to "the eBay marketplace in the U.S. and internationally" (eBay annual report, 2007).

The core business of eBay is its marketplace where eBay's customers buy and sell items through the website of eBay. The traditional format of the service is the auction listings where prices increase according to the demand. Most auction listings include a picture of the item, description and shipping costs. Buyers are able to see the bid history and can communicate with the sellers through e-mail. After the sale, buyers and sellers can leave feedback on the transaction. The new format introduced in 1999 is the "Buy it now" feature where customers can buy a fixed price item (Sanderson, 2002).

When Pierre Omidyar first introduced the idea to create a common exchange place such as eBay, the reaction was not optimistic. "People were skeptical that strangers would buy from strangers. But because it was such a quirky idea, it really kept others out of the market for a long time. By the time it was clear that this idea was working, it was almost too late to get in", commented Adam Cohen, author of "The Perfect Store", relating the story of eBay. In fact, analysts attributed the success of eBay to its first mover position and critical mass buyers and sellers (Sanderson, 2002).

The success is also linked to the strong brand image of eBay that created a safe environment for electronic commerce "by codifying and marketing the reputation of its buyers and sellers" mentioned Pitta Julie in the World Trade. The feedback mechanism is the key to reassuring consumers. Hence, eBay traders formed a real community based on trust (World Trade, 2003).

eBAY IN JAPAN

The Japanese site, www.ebayjapan.co.jp, was launched on February 28, 2000. The huge opportunity that the Japanese market represented at that time pushed eBay to develop its business in Japan. In fact, Japan was considered as the first largest Internet market in Asia and the second-largest Internet market in the world (*Business Week*, 2001).

However, six months prior to eBay's entry, Yahoo! Japan Auctions had developed an auction marketplace. In consequence, Yahoo! Japan Auctions was already well implanted in Japan when eBay entered the market. Two years after eBay's entry, eBay reported that Yahoo! Japan still had 95% of the online auction market compared to eBay Japan, which reached hardly 3% of the Japanese market (Japaninc.com, 2007).

Table 2.   Comparative data between Yahoo! Japan Auctions and eBay in the Japanese market in 2001.

Company	Yahoo! Japan Auctions	eBay Japan
Date of entry	September, 1999	February, 2000
Unique users	2,746,000	227,000
Time per visit	2.5 hours	9 min
Listings	2.2 million	3.500 (estimation)

Source: Business Week 2001, Nielsen/NetRatings Japan, Deutsche Banc Alex.Brown, company reports.

THE JAPANESE MARKET IN 2000/2001

However, Japan represented a profitable market for eBay. Indeed, Japan was the second-largest Internet market in the world. The Nomura General Research group reported that in September 1998, only 36.8% of Japanese declared having a PC at home. Two years later, in 2000, 54.3% of Japanese possessed a PC at home. In terms of Internet access, the increase is also clearly visible, passing from 10% to 20% of internet home users and from 20% to 30% of office users.

Moreover, another opportunity in Japan was the incredible success of e-commerce. According to the Ministry of Economy, Trade and Industry (METI) and the Electronic Commerce Promotion Council (ECom), the internet market of the B to C (Business to Consumers) increased from 0.5 to 11.6 billion Euros between 1998 and 2001. The C to C (consumers to consumers) is integrated in the B to C activity according to the ECom of Japan. Consequently, Japan started to develop its e-business activity in the late 1999.

The e-commerce in Japan was introduced by the American e-commerce website Amazon.com. This development arrived at the same time as the expansion of non-PC terminals such as I-mode. In 2000, e-commerce was already well-known and a new trend appeared: the "e-marketplace of C to C", where Yahoo! Auctions became the number one site (ECom, 2001).

The Cyber Business Case Bank (CBCB) and the Center for Cyber Community Infrastructure (CCCI) reported that in December 1999, the number of e-commerce sites in Japan achieved the highest peak value with 23,000 e-shops and decreased progressively in 2000 dropping back to 15,000. Competition in e-commerce was, consequently, particularly high (ECom, 2001).

A FIERCE COMPETITION

The specific business of eBay is based on the assumption that eBay does not have a lot of direct competitors in a particular market. However, this was not the case in Japan. In 2000, the Japanese auction market was mainly controlled by Yahoo! Japan Auctions when eBay decided to enter the market. Another domestic actor, Rakuten, was also developing its auction business during that time. Consequently, eBay faced stronger competition than expected.

YAHOO! JAPAN AUCTIONS

Yahoo! Japan is a joint venture between Yahoo! holding 41% and Softbank Corporation holding 33%. Yahoo! Japan Auctions developed its business for the first time in September 1999 (see Fig. 1). The idea came from the co-founder of Yahoo, Jerry Yang, who was first asked by Inoue Masahiro, CEO of Yahoo, to create an online auction website in Japan. After the launching, Inoue Masahiro solicited his 120 employees to list items for sale and in less than two years, Yahoo counted already 2.2 million items online (*Business Week*, 2001).

When Yahoo noticed eBay's entry, it decided to build up an aggressive marketing campaign in order to discourage its customers from visiting the eBay site. Consequently, it increased its active promotion to sellers and buyers by sending more emails and developing relationships with new website providers. In 2002, Yahoo was still controlling 95% of the auction market.

Figure 1.   Yahoo! Japan.

RAKUTEN

Founded in 1997 by Mikitani Hiroshi, Rakuten became the reference in terms of Japanese e-commerce. At its beginning, the website Rakuten-Ichiba (see Fig. 2) was composed of different shops. In this virtual gallery, it was possible to find a large number of products and services such as clothes, insurances, foods, etc; this was the first online shopping mall. In 1998, Rakuten initiated its first auction service, "Rakuten Super Auction", in relation to the website Rakuten-Ichiba.

In 2000, Rakuten expanded its market and created Rakuten Books thanks to a joint venture with Nippon Shuppan Hanbai Inc. Later, in 2002, it founded Rakuten Travel and it is only in 2005 that it started to really develop its online auction business with Rakuten Auctions. Rakuten Auctions was set up thanks to a joint venture with NTT Docomo, Inc. (Rakuten, 2008). Hence, Rakuten was an indirect competitor of eBay in the e-commerce environment.

OTHER COMPETITORS

In spite of the fact that there were only few direct competitors, eBay might consider several channels and companies as indirect

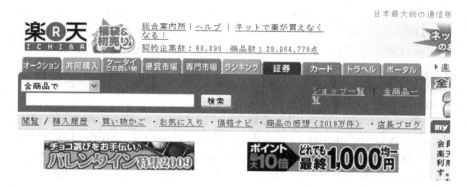

Figure 2. Rakuten-Ichiba.

competitors: online and offline retailers, outlets, import and export companies and antiques shops.

THE FAILURE OF eBAY IN JAPAN

Yahoo! Japan Auctions was the leader of the auction market when eBay developed its business in Japan. With 2,746,000 unique users, Yahoo! Auctions was the first mover. "Jerry Yang (co-founder of Yahoo) understood that it was critical to be first", commented Inoue Masahiro, the CEO of Yahoo Japan. Merle Okawara, the president and CEO of eBay Japan at that time, mentioned just before leaving the company, "When we arrived, the 800-pound gorilla was positioned" (*Business Week*, 2001).

Moreover, eBay decided to implement several practices that were new to the Japanese market. Thus, eBay charged commissions of 1.25% to 5% depending on what the customer buys. At that time, Yahoo! Japan Auctions did not charge any commission on sales (Japaninc, 2007).

Furthermore, when eBay entered the Japanese market, eBay asked its customers to submit credit card information on signup and its website offered payment by credit card. In 2001, customers of e-commerce were not yet up for buying on the Internet with credit cards, particularly young people who do not always own one.

In 2000, the most common payment method was still COD (Collect On Delivery where the payment is processed only when the delivery is done) with 47% and the post purchase bank or postal transfer with 44%. The credit card was ranked later with only 22% (ECom research, 2001). As a result, Japanese were not really used to paying by credit card (*Business Week*, 2001).

The team chosen to develop eBay in Japan was mainly set up by American or bilingual (English/Japanese) people. Merle Okawara was chosen to be CEO. Despite the fact that she was a talented business executive, she was "new to the internet" (*Business Week*, 2001).

In order to achieve interest among the Japanese population, eBay started to spread the word of its entry in Japan a long time before it actually entered (Japaninc, 2007). Yahoo! Auctions Japan replied to this threat immediately after by increasing its promotion and advertising campaigns. eBay, on the other hand, did not really advertise its entry and expected to develop its notoriety through word of mouth. Moreover, it also took eBay a long time to improve the website www.ebayjapan.co.jp in order to fit with the Japanese expectations (make it easier to understand and simpler to use) (*Business Week*, 2001).

Two years after eBay's entry, eBay mentioned that Yahoo! Japan still had 95% of the online auction market compared to eBay Japan which hardly reached 3% of the Japanese market. With this low rate of market penetration, eBay had not achieved its objective.

In March 2002, eBay decided to quit the Japanese market and thus, close the website, www.ebayjapan.co.jp, which reached about 25,000 listings at that time. The exit was consequently followed by the lay off of its 17 employees in Japan. After considering the options of acquisitions or partnerships with others players in the Japanese market, eBay chose to close its operations by explaining that "a partnership between eBay and Yahoo was too potent" (New York Times, 2002). In other words, eBay announced a possible return in the Japanese market thanks to a partnership with Yahoo. This failure urgently increased the need for eBay to look for new opportunities in Asia (*Fortune*, 2004). In the same year, eBay announced that it was planning on buying the Taiwanese auction site, NeoCom Technology, with its well-known website, ubid.com.tw/bid.com.tw. In fact, Taiwan represented Asia's third largest e-commerce market. "We will consider opportunities in the future for a return to Japan", Pursglove added (CNET News, 2002).

THE JAPANESE ONLINE AUCTION MARKET IN 2007

After the exit of eBay in 2002, the Japanese online auction market developed quite strongly. Its main players were still Yahoo! Japan Auctions and Rakuten. Different from Yahoo! Japan Auctions, which is the result of a joint venture between Yahoo! holding 41% and Softbank Corporation holding 33%, Yahoo! Auctions (not to be mixed up with Yahoo! Japan Auction) was created in 1998 in the U.S. to compete with eBay. Yahoo! Auctions was established in several countries such as Canada, the United Kingdom, Ireland, Singapore and Hong Kong. Despite these efforts, Yahoo! Auctions did not manage to repeat its success in Japan in other parts of the world.

Failing to compete with its main rival, eBay, Yahoo! Auctions decided to close its auctions in the U.S. and Canada on June 16, 2007. The UK and Ireland closed on June 28, 2007 and Singapore Yahoo! Auctions closed slightly later on September 22, 2008. France, Germany, Italy and Spain Yahoo! Auctions followed the same steps. Only Hong Kong and Japan and some other European countries such as Denmark are still working (Yahoo! Auctions, UK & Ireland website, 2008).

Missing the first mover advantage in the U.S. and Europe, Yahoo! wanted to focus on its profitable business (online travel, e-commerce) and abandon those that were faltering. "In Europe, for instance, Yahoo came late to the game and did not manage to attract enough exposure", explained an analyst of Jupiter Research in Paris (*New York Times*, 2008). This decision was also followed by an important measure. In certain countries, like the UK and Ireland for example, eBay's Auctions were promoted directly on the European website of Yahoo.

Yahoo! Japan Auctions, which do not entirely belong to Yahoo! Auctions had, at this time, the objective to develop its business abroad. However, Yahoo! Japan Auctions did not have the right to cross the border with the Yahoo! name. Thus, an international business outside Japan would not have been possible for Yahoo! Japan Auctions.

THE COMPETITION BETWEEN RAKUTEN AND YAHOO! JAPAN IN JAPAN

With a net profit of 17.18 billion in 2007, Yahoo! Japan had increased its revenue up to 29% compared to the last year. However, Yahoo! Japan competed with Rakuten in the online shopping mall business but still kept its dominant position in auction services (Nikkei, 2008).

Yahoo! Japan was facing a major problem of expansion. Based on a joint venture between Yahoo and Softbank Corporation, Yahoo! Japan was not allowed to use the Yahoo! brand outside Japan. Because of an expected slowdown in the domestic market, Yahoo! Japan decided to extend its business abroad (Nikkei Business Daily, 2007). With 1000 people working on the auctions' transactions, Rakuten had a much bigger team than Yahoo! Japan (100 people). It also had a larger range of activities (food delivery, auctions, etc.) than Yahoo! Japan. This led to a reactive marketing campaign against each other. However, Rakuten transactions were still lower than Yahoo! Japan with $6.6 million and $7.3 million for Yahoo! Japan in 2007 (Mr Mishima interview, 2008).

A parallel market of auctions was also visible in Japan in order to receive non-Japanese products. In other words, it was really common to see users "buying an item on eBay.com, bring it into Japan and then sell it at a higher price on Yahoo! Auctions Japan or Rakuten", commented Ken Mishima, director of eBay Japan's Business Development Unit (Mr Mishima interview, 2008). The schema explains the parallel market: Japanese buy items on ebay.com and sell those items later at a higher price on the Rakuten Auctions site or the Yahoo! Japan Auctions site (see Fig. 3).

Figure 3.   Parallel market of auctions.

JAPANESE ONLINE CONSUMER BEHAVIOR IN 2007

Japan counted 80 million Internet users in 2007, reaching 85% of households all over the country. Nikkei Business published in 2005 that 67% of Japanese used the Internet everyday. According to the Ministry of Internal Affairs and Communications (MIC), 90% of Japanese aged between 13–49 years old were surfing the Internet in 2005. Even if old people (between 65–69 years old) were less attracted, there were still 42% using Internet (Strategies, 2007).

Elderly Japanese were also representing new opportunities for e-commerce. Previously dominated by young or middle-aged consumers, e-commerce was now catching elderly people (60s and older). Home delivery and lower prices are the main advantages for them. In return, service loyalty is particularly high with elderly customers. Moreover, elderly people will certainly play an important role in the consumer market as 30% of Japan's population in 2030 will be people in their 60s and older according to a study by the National Institute of Population and Social Security Research (Nikkei Marketing Journal, 2008). Another important evolution in the Internet market is "the decline of the PC as an Internet access device and the continued increase of access by means of mobile devices". Indeed, Japan had more than 100 million mobile phone users in 2007 and "72.87 million cell phone customers accessed the Internet on their devices, compared with 78.13 million Japanese who browsed websites via PCs" as mentioned by the Communication Industry (*Nikkei Marketing Journal*, 2008). The mobile phone industry (shopping, music and games) counted for about 772.4 billion yen in 2005 and more than 1 trillion yen in 2006. Companies are now considering the mobile phone as "a way of stimulating consumer's appetite for buying" (Nikkei, 2007).

Amongst the most visited websites in Japan, Yahoo.co.jp was still the most popular website since its appearance. Yahoo.co.jp was the number one website in terms of time spent on it and unique visitors. The website, Rakuten.co.jp (e-commerce shopping site), was just behind Yahoo in terms of time spent and unique visitors (Strategies, 2007). Furthermore, a positive trend was that despite a stagnant economy in Japan, online sales were still expanding. Sales grew by 21.7% to 5.34 trillion yen in 2007 according to a study on electronic commerce presented by the Ministry of Economy, Trade and Industry. This trend can be justified by the fact that lower prices and home delivery offered by e-commerce makes a real difference in terms of cost savings (*Nikkei Weekly*, 2008).

The resistance to e-commerce has also considerably decreased thanks to the development of programs against fraud. 71% of Japanese believed that "they have not been infected by malware or spyware in the last six months". This highlights a high confidence and perceived safety of the Internet in Japan (*Telecom World Wire*, 2007). In conclusion, Japanese are less resistant to e-commerce and tend to buy more of their daily products online. For a large part of the population, "online shopping is becoming part of everyday life" (*Nikkei Marketing Journal*, 2008).

Competitors such as Yahoo! Japan, Rakuten and other e-commerce sites represent serious threats for eBay. Their abilities to offer various items fitting with the demands of the local market represent a real asset for attracting more customers. Their notoriety and market shares are also extremely difficult to overcome. The market's maturity is directly linked to the huge number of competitors in this market. Moreover, the power of Yahoo in terms of auctions is really important. Offering a portal with a large range of services represents a major advantage to catch the attention of customers.

By taking into account all the different aspects of the Japanese auction market, in 2007, eBay decided, after five years of absence, to announce its return to Japan.

QUESTIONS

1) Why is the online auction market in Japan so different from other countries?
2) Which strategies can eBay pursue to enter the market with more success this time?
3) Which adaptation will be necessary to succeed in the Japanese market?
4) Should they form an alliance with their competitors?

BIBLIOGRAPHY

Analysis: Easy-buy mobile phone shopping luring young consumers (4 June 2007). *The Nikkei*.

Clay, C (2004). An upstart takes on mighty eBay. *Fortune*, 150(10).

eBay website. http://www.ebay.com/ [November 2008].

eBay annual report (2007). http://www.ebay.com/.

Gaither, C. Technology briefing: Internet, eBay exits Japan for Taiwan (27 February 2002). *New York Times*.

Greg, L. (2007). Failed businesses in Japan. *Japaninc*, 73, 6–8.

Interview with Mr. Ken Mishima, director of the eBay Japan's Business Development Unit, 19 November 2008.

Julie, P. eBay's Growing up (February 2003). *World Trade*.

Kary, T. eBay exits Japan, moves into Taiwan (26 February 2002). *CNET News*.

Ken, B. How Yahoo! Japan beat eBay at its own game (6 April 2001). *Business Week*.

Koyanagi, T. Japan's Yahoo test global waters (10 December 2007). *The Nikkei Business Daily*.

Le Japon, laboratoire d'Internet (29 November 2007). *Strategies*.

Le Net du e-commerce au m-commerce (21 May 2003). *Le journal du Net*.

Maney, K. 10 years ago, eBay changed the world (21 March 2005). *USA Today*.

Orr, A. eBay looks for growth (6 October 2008). *The Daily Deal*.

Rakuten website. http://www.rakuten.co.jp/.

Rakuten website. http://auctions.yahoo.co.jp/.

Results of Internet confidence and safety survey (3 January 2007). *Telecom World Wire.*

Sanderson, I. (2002). Creating and Capturing Value. New York: Routledge.

Stagnant economy has yen-pinchers going online (27 October 2008). *The Nikkei weekly.*

Suzanne, K. Yahoo drops auctions in most of Europe (24 May 2008). *New York Times.*

The development of EC & its successful business models (31 October 2001). *The Electronic Commerce Promotion Council (ECOM).*

(Unknown author 2008). Elderly embrace online shopping (15 October 2008). *The Nikkei Marketing Journal.*

(Unknown author 2008). Advertisers to seek new audience metric for cell phone websites (19 September 2008). *Nihon Keizai Shimbun.*

Vente à distance grand public (June 2007). *Xerfi.*

Whitman, M. Sellers patricia (8 September 2004). *Fortune.*

Yahoo! Auctions, UK & Ireland website, http://uk.docs.yahoo.com/auctions/notice/.

Yahoo Japan Oct–Dec group net profit up 13% on strong ad demand (30 January 2008). *The Nikkei.*

Yahoo Japan sees eBay tie-up as key to overseas expansion (5 December 2007). *The Nikkei Business Daily.*

Nintendo — The 800-Pound Gorilla Returns

Greg Taylor

INTRODUCTION

At the turn of the millennium, Nintendo was facing a first; three strong rivals all vying for market dominance in the new "generation" of hardware. Leading the pack was incumbent Sony, whose Playstation 2 was succeeding its market-dominant Playstation (which had sold over 70 million units by 2000).[70] But former market leaders, Sega and Nintendo, along with newcomer Microsoft, were all poised to claim Sony's crown in the new hardware generation.

Sega, releasing its Dreamcast in 1999, had a year head-start on its competitors, but it was the first to drop out. In 2001, Sega left the console hardware business and refocused as a software-only company producing games for its former rivals' systems.[71] By 2003, Nintendo, while retaining a second place in Japan, had slid to third place world-wide. Nintendo posted its first loss warning in decades.[72] Rumors and

---

[70] Sony Computer Entertainment Inc. website. PlayStation cumulative production shipments of hardware (12 December 2007). http://www.scei.co.jp/corporate/data/bizdataps_e.html.

[71] Dennis McCauley. Sega emerges from dreamcast ashes (19 May 2001). *Wired* .

[72] Rob Fahey. Nintendo drops first half projections into loss (10 March 2003). *GamesIndustry.biz*.

speculation ran rampant that Nintendo would follow Sega and leave the hardware industry.[73]

Just four years later, worldwide sales of Nintendo's new system, the Wii, had surpassed both of its rivals (Microsoft and Sony) and reached 10 million units sold in its first year on the market.[74] Even producing 1.8 million units per month,[75] analysts predict that supply would not meet demand for the Wii until 2009.[76] The Nintendo DS (a hand-held system released in 2004) has sold over 40 million units worldwide,[77] and 20 million in Japan alone[78] (statistically, an average of one in six people in Japan own a DS). Suddenly, Nintendo's stock and profits are souring and it is once again king of the game industry.

THE VIDEO GAME INDUSTRY

In the 1970s, computer chips had become economical enough that companies like Magnivox, Atari and Coleco began marketing home video game systems. The first systems came with a fixed number of games built into the hardware itself. These systems had a limited market life-span and were marketed as a novelty item with reasonable

---

[73] Geoff Keighley. Is Nintendo playing the wrong game? (1 August 2003). *CNNMoney.* http://money.cnn.com/magazines/business2/business2_archive/2003/08/01/346319/index.htm.

[74] Ann Steffora Mutschler. Nintendo Wii trumps Xbox 360 in sales (24 August 2007). *Electronic News.* http://www.edn.com/index.asp?layout=article&articleid=CA6471657.

[75] Kris Graft. Interview: Wii triumphs in October (15 November 2007). *Next Generation.* http://www.next-gen.biz/index.php?option=com_content&task=view&id=7965&Itemid=2.

[76] John Gaudiosi. Games continue record pace (24 April 2007). *Home Media Magazine.* http://www.homemediamagazine.com/news/html/breaking_article.cfm?article_id=10568.

[77] Nintendo Co. website (2007). Consolidated sales by region. http://www.nintendo.co.jp/ir/en/library/historical_data/xls/consolidated_sales_e0708.xls.

[78] Anoop Gantayat. Twenty million DS systems in Japan (16 November 2007). *IGN.* http://au.ds.ign.com/articles/835/835823p1.html?RSSwhen2007-11-16_074300&RSSid=835823.

Figure 1.   The Atari 2600 (1977).

success. When Atari released a system (the 2600) (see Fig. 1) that was capable of playing software on cartridges,[79] the video game "industry" was truly born.[80]

With introduction of software, companies in the game industry adopted a "razor-blade" approach: "give the razors away and make money on the blades". The console hardware manufacturers generally made little profit on each unit sold — sometimes even took a loss — and made their profits on licensing fees charged for each unit of software sold for the system.

The industry developed upgrade cycles of roughly four to six years, which have been termed "generations" in industry parlance (see Tables 1 and 2). As the previous generation of hardware reaches market saturation and begins to wane, the various rival companies release a new generation of hardware and compete fiercely for market share.

The system-launch marketshare battle is of critical importance for the console manufacturers. Independent software publishers ("3rd party") prefer to develop their games for the "hottest" and largest install-base console. Futhermore, the end consumers want to buy the hardware with the best selection of games, both in quantitative and qualitative terms. Once a market-leader console is established, it

---

[79] Steven L Kent. (2001). The Battle For Home In *The Ultimate History of Video Games: From Pong to Pokemon*, 1st Ed. Three Rivers Press.

[80] Technically, the "Fairchild Channel F" was the first software-enabled console, but the Atari 2600 was the first to obtain wide-scale popularity.

Table 1.   Overview of relevant handheld consoles by generation.

Generation	Atari	Nintendo	Sega	Sony	Microsoft
2nd (~1976)	2600				
3rd (~1983)	7800	NES/ Famicom	Master System		
4th (~1989)		SNES/ Super Famicom	Genesis		
5th (~1994)	Jaguar	N64	Saturn	Playstation	
6th (~1999)		GameCube	Dreamcast	Playstation 2	Xbox
7th (~2005)		Wii		Playstation 3	Xbox 360

Table 2.   Overview of relevant[81] home consoles by generation.

Generation	Atari	Nintendo	Sega	Sony
1st (~1989)	Lynx	Game Boy	Game Gear	
2nd (~1998)		Game Boy Color		
3rd (~2001)		Game Boy Advance		
4th (~2004)		DS		Playstation Portable (PSP)

tends to gain further advantage as more software is developed for that system and late-adopter consumers react to the improved quality and selection of software.

Generational transitions constitute the primary points where companies can improve their market position. The console launch and two subsequent years usually determine its place for the following three or more years. Particularly successful consoles like the Playstation and Nintendo Famicom have enjoyed viable life spans of over 10 years. The only counters for post-launch market position movement are either a breakout hit game or a price reduction.

---

[81] Note a comprehensive list, limited to the systems by companies discussed in this case.

NINTENDO COMPANY HISTORY

The characters in which the name Nintendo is written in Japanese mean "entrust luck to the heavens". Founded by Fusajiro Yamauchi in 1889, Nintendo originally made traditional Hanafuda playing cards. The family business was passed down through the generations, father to son-in-law, as neither Fusajiro nor later Sekiryo had any sons.

At the age of 21, Hiroshi Yamauchi took over Nintendo in 1949 following the death of his grandfather. He led the company to several more years of success in the playing card business, highlighted by a 1959 deal with Disney to produce playing cards with Disney characters. In 1962, Nintendo was listed on the Osaka stock exchange and was renamed as Nintendo Company Ltd. (from the previous name Nintendo Playing Card Company). Yamauchi explored a number of additional business ventures, including a "love hotel" chain, manufacturing instant ramen, and a taxi company. Ultimately, the only successful expansion was into the toy industry in the early 1970s.

After spending the 1970s in the toy business with moderate success, Nintendo leveraged toy designer Gunpei Yokoi's electrical engineering background to move into the more lucrative electronic toy business. From electronic toys, Nintendo began producing video arcade machines in 1978.[82] With the booming popularity of arcade machines in North America in the late 1970s, Nintendo formed a subsidiary, Nintendo of America (in 1980), to market their machines in that region.

THE 800-POUND GORILLA

Nintendo's first break-out game was the arcade hit "Donkey Kong", released in 1981. It was designed by an apprentice designer Shigeru Miyamoto, who happened to be available when Nintendo of America (NOA) contacted its Japan office with a major problem — NOA had 2000 cabinets of the arcade game "Radarscope" sitting unsold in a warehouse and the subsidiary was bleeding money.

---

[82] David Sheff and Andy Eddy (1991). In Heaven's Hands. In *Game Over Press Start to Continue*. Cyberactive Media Group.

Radarscope had been a hit in Japan but was a difficult sell in the American market, where games of this type had already gone out of fashion.

Rather than attempting to fix Radarscope, Miyamoto designed a new game for the Radarscope hardware, where a portly carpenter had to save his captured girlfriend from a massive gorilla, "Donkey Kong". The carpenter was renamed from "Jumpman" to "Mario" in the American version, and the name ultimately stuck when the character reappeared in future games. Released in 1981, "Donkey Kong" was a huge success in North America and Japan and Nintendo began its rise to dominance.[83]

In 1983, Nintendo released its first home video game system in Japan, the Famicom (short for "Family Computer") (see Fig. 2). It used a similar processor to rival Atari's 2600, but featured additional chips to handle higher quality graphics and sound. The technology used in the Famicom was not cutting edge as it was designed for

Figure 2.   The original Famicom (1983).

---

[83] David Sheff and Andy Eddy (1999). *Game Over Press Start to Continue*, Cyberactive Media Group, pp. 103–111.

maximum price-performance with a target street price of 9,800[84] (it shipped at 14,800). This tendency to maximize cheaper technologies, rather than adopt cutting edge, has marked every console release in Nintendo history.

An American company with a Japanese name, Atari, was the market leader in America in the late 1970s and early 1980s, with its "Atari 2600" system. But the Atari 2600 saw only minimal success in Japan and the Nintendo Famicom was the first video game system to see mass-market adoption in that region. Driven by a stream of hit games, it sold millions of hardware units and single-handedly dominated the Japanese market.

In 1983, at the same time as the Famicom was storming Japan, the American video game industry crashed. The crash has been attributed to a number of high profile, massively overproduced, terrible games by market leader Atari. The most notable of these was the home version of the arcade hit "Pac-Man" and the game adaptation of the movie "E.T.". "E.T." has been repeatedly rated the "Worst Game of All Time"[85] in numerous polls in the decades since (though in some polls it rates 2nd or 3rd worst). And Atari manufactured more copies of "Pac Man" than there were Atari 2600s to play them on and famously buried millions of unsold cartridges in a Nevada desert.[86]

In 1984, Nintendo began preparing to bring its Famicom to the American market. Problem was, at this point there was nothing but rubble left. Nintendo of America (NOA) had to take aggressive measures to distance the Famicom from Atari and "video games". They renamed the system the "Nintendo Entertainment System" (NES), renamed game cartridges as "Game Paks" and redesigned the look of the system to a more "computer"-looking gray from its colorful

---

[84] David Sheff and Andy Eddy (1999). *Game Over Press Start to Continue*, Cyberactive Media Group, pp. 29–35.

[85] Emru Townsend. The 10 worst games of all time (23 October 2006). *PC World*. http://www.pcworld.com/article/id,127579-page,2-c,games/article.html.

[86] Steven L Kent. (2001). *The Ultimate History of Video Games: From Pong to Pokemon*, 1st Ed. Three Rivers Press.

Figure 3.   The "Nintendo Entertainment System" (NES) (1985).

plastic "toy"-like Japanese original (see Fig. 3). Through a combination of clever marketing and determination, the NES's New York City launch was a success, and it was released nation-wide in 1986.[87] Video games in America were reborn.

Nintendo attempted to avoid the mistakes that Atari had made and adopted strict quality and release control policies. Third party publishers were limited to five games per year maximum, and had to pass quality testing at Nintendo prior to release. Additionally, they kept tight controls on supply, ensuring that retailers never had excessive stock on hand. The goal of these measures was to ensure that the market was not flooded with poor-quality products like that which led to the collapse of Atari.[88]

The NES became even more popular in America than it was in Japan. The Famicom/NES sold over 60 million units worldwide,[89]

[87] David Sheff and Andy Eddy (1999). Enter the dragon. In *Game Over Press Start to Continue*, Cyberactive Media Group.

[88] David Sheff and Andy Eddy (1999). Game masters. In *Game Over Press Start to Continue*, Cyberactive Media Group.

[89] Nintendo Co. website (2007). Consolidated sales by region. http://www. nintendo.co.jp/ir/en/library/historical_data/xls/consolidated_sales_e0708.xls.

nearest rival Sega, sold 13 million of its Master System[90] and the top-selling game, "Super Mario Bros. 3" sold over 11 million copies.[91] In 1990, the video game industry's total sales were $4 billion, and Nintendo's total sales were $3.4 billion (or 85%);[92] Nintendo truly incarnated the spirit of the proverbial 800-pound gorilla.

THE HANDHELD MARKET

Nintendo branched out from the home market to create the first handheld video game system, the "Game Boy", in 1989 (see Fig. 4). The Game Boy, which only enjoyed a few months without competition, was soon faced with the Atari Lynx. The Atari Lynx boasted a powerful system capable of displaying rich colors and running complex games. The Game Boy was once again designed on a budget; lead designer Gumpei Yokoi opted for a black-and-white screen to boost battery life (35 hours on 4 AA batteries, where the Lynx ran for four hours on six AA batteries).[93] The Game Boy was launched at $109 and the Lynx at $189. With sales driven by the Russian puzzle game "Tetris", the Game Boy sold over 118 million units[94] and the Game Boy Tetris game sold 33 million copies.[95]

The Game Boy was originally marketed towards the usual Nintendo demographic, children aged eight to 12. However, Nintendo soon realized that they were seeing significant sales to

---

[90] Russel Carrol. Good enough (6 September 2005). *Game Tunnel.* http://www.gametunnel.com/articles.php?id=263.

[91] David Sheff and Andy Eddy (1999). *Game Over Press Start to Continue,* Cyberactive Media Group, p. 4.

[92] Eugene Provenzo (1991). *Video Kids: Making Sense of Nintendo.* Harvard University Press, p. 8.

[93] David Sheff and Andy Eddy (1999). *Game Over Press Start to Continue,* Cyberactive Media Group, pp. 294–295.

[94] Nintendo Co. website (2007). Consolidated sales by region. http://www.nintendo.co.jp/ir/en/library/historical_data/xls/consolidated_sales_e0708.xls.

[95] Nintendo Co. website. Did You Know? Ten Tetris Facts (12 December 2007). http://tgcontent.nintendo-europe.com/enGB/games_DS_TGP/tetris_ds/did_you_know.php.

Figure 4.   Nintendo Game Boy (1989).

adults, notably businessmen, who passed time on long business flights playing Tetris on their Game Boys. Nintendo quickly adjusted their marketing plans to target these unintended consumers, the combination of which led to the phenomenal success of the system.[96]

The Game Boy was succeeded with the Game Boy Color in 1998 and the Game Boy Advance in 2001. Each iteration of the Game Boy line was "backwards compatible", meaning they could play games of the previous systems. This allowed consumers to upgrade their hardware and still play all of their favorite games. This capability may well have been a key factor in maintaining its market dominance; since its introduction, Nintendo has never had a significant rival in the handheld sector until decades later, with Sony's PSP in 2004 (discussed later).

---

[96] David Sheff and Andy Eddy (1999). *Game Over Press Start to Continue*, Cyberactive Media Group, p. 295.

SEGA'S SURPRISE

The first faltering of the Nintendo empire came at the hands of rival Sega. With the introduction of the 16-bit Genesis in 1989, Sega spaw-ned the "next generation" of video games (the "fourth generation" as listed in the aforementioned Table 1) (see Fig. 5). Nintendo was slow to release a new system as it did not want to sabotage its lucrative Famicom market, holding out for the release of its own Super Famicom (known as the SNES in America) until two years later (1991). This two-year delay proved to be detrimental, but it was Nintendo's failure to respond to Sega's marketing campaign which accentuated the damage.

Sega aimed at an older audience, targeting the teen and young adult gamers who had grown up with the NES, but were not being actively targeted by Nintendo, which aimed its products primarily at the ages 8 to 12 demographic. With a markedly more powerful system, edgier games and a marketing slogan "Sega Does What Nintendon't" they made impressive gains in marketshare (see Fig. 6).[97] The Genesis sold 30 million units worldwide and the Nintendo Super Famicom sold 49 million.[98] Successive hardware

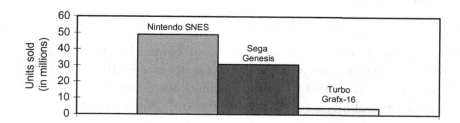

Figure 5. "Fourth generation" (~1989) console sales (in millions).

Source: VGChartz.com.

---

[97] David Sheff and Andy Eddy (1999). Sonic boom. In *Game Over Press Start to Continue*, Cyberactive Media Group.

[98] Nintendo Co. website (2007). Consolidated sales by region. http://www.nintendo.co.jp/ir/en/library/historical_data/xls/consolidated_sales_e0708.xls.

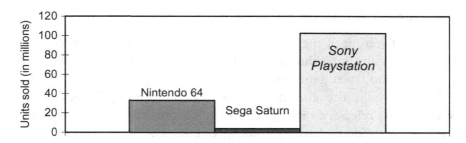

Figure 6. "Fifth generation" (~1994) console sales (in millions).
Source: VGChartz.com.

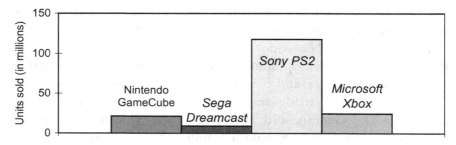

Figure 7. "Sixth generation" (~1999) console sales (in millions).
Source: VGChartz.com.

generations would see further decline of Nintendo's market share, from the Nintendo 64 in 1996 to the GameCube in 2001. By 2003, Nintendo ranked third worldwide behind Sony and Microsoft, and doubts on viability of a "next generation" Nintendo system ran rampant (see Fig. 7).

NINTENDO'S NEW (OLD) STRATEGY

Hiroshi Yamauchi retired from Nintendo in 2002, passing the reigns outside of the Yamauchi family for the first time in the company's 100-year history. Formerly a Nintendo affiliate at HAL

Laboratories, Satoru Iwata was noticed by Nintendo for saving HAL from bankruptcy and returning it to profitability, giving him the nickname of "Director of Problem-Solving".[99] Given Nintendo's precarious position in 2002, Yamauchi felt Iwata would be the best candidate to rejuvenate Nintendo's strategy and return it to market dominance[100] — a difficult challenge. In fact, the Nintendo Iwata inherited was relying heavily on its always-strong handheld division, whilst the GameCube home system was languishing in third place globally and company profits were declining.

Iwata, Miyamoto and the Nintendo R&D staff set to plan Nintendo's next generation of hardware. The past few generations of consoles had been an "arms race" in terms of raw power of the system. System launch marketing materials resembled sales pitches for personal computers: "X megabytes of this, Y bits of power, Z million triangles per second".

The next generation was no different; rivals Sony and Microsoft were clearly planning systems of immense power. Nintendo was already lagging behind in the power "arms race" and could not hope to compete on those terms so they defined new terms. For the successors to the handheld Game Boy Advance and GameCube home system, Nintendo would focus on the gaming experience itself, abandoning the power arms race and redefining what a game console should be.[101] This "new" strategy would revert to the one previously used before they began playing along in the arms race that competed with innovation and empowering the gaming experience.[102]

---

[99] Geoff Keighley. Is Nintendo playing the wrong game? (1 August 2003). *CNNMoney.*

[100] Nintendo's long-time president resigns (24 May 2002) *USA Today.*

[101] Nintendo Co. (2007). Annual Report 2004 — President's Message. http://www.nintendo.co.jp/ir/pdf/2004/annual0403e.pdf.

[102] Nintendo Co. (2007). Annual Report 2003 — President's Message. http://www.nintendo.co.jp/ir/pdf/2003/annual0303e.pdf.

THE DS GAMBLE

The first product of Iwata's new redefining gaming strategy was the DS (short for Dual Screen), released in 2004 (see Fig. 8).[103] The DS was a handheld system which had two color LCD screens, one of which could be drawn on using a stylus (a pen-shaped plastic pointer used with PDAs). The DS also featured a microphone which users could speak into and wireless network support using the PC industry standard 802.11b protocol. In addition to DS native games, it also was backward compatible with the entire Game Boy line.

The DS was initially distanced from the Game Boy line, Nintendo proclaimed it as not succeeding the Game Boy Advance but as being a third product line in itself.[104] They did not want to compromise their Game Boy line with an eventual failure scenario as it represented a primary source of income at that time. Once the DS proved successful,

Figure 8.   Nintendo DS Lite (2006).

[103] Figure 8 shows the "DS Lite" hardware revision, released in 2006. It featured a thinner, sleeker design, but was functionally identical to the DS.
[104] Todd Bishop. Nintendo to launch a new hand-held device (21 January 2004). *Seattle Post-Intelligencer.* http://seattlepi.nwsource.com/business/157413_nintendo21.html.

this position was reversed and the DS was acknowledged as the successor to the Game Boy Advance.[105]

Nintendo encouraged developers to utilize the unique capabilities of the system. The stylus has been used for everything from aiming a gun in a shooting game to chopping carrots in a cooking simulation, and even to performing surgical operations. The DS saw a number of break-out hits that would have been impossible without the system's unique capabilities. A wildly popular pet simulator, Nintendogs, allowed the user to interact with a virtual dog via voice command in the microphone and movement of the stylus. Japanese sales in particular were driven by "Brain Age", developed by Professor Ryuta Kawashima. It promised improved brain health via mathematical, linguistic and special puzzles. Nintendogs sold over six million copies, and Brain Age sold over five million copies worldwide.[106]

THE FUTURE BATTLE IN MINIATURE

Nintendo was not the only company to release a handheld game system in 2004. After over a decade of nearly complete domination of the handheld market, Nintendo faced competition it could not afford to ignore. With the Playstation and PS2, Sony had severely impacted Nintendo's market dominance in the home system sector (recall Figures 6 and 7 above). Sony sought to repeat its performance in the handheld market with a new system called the "Playstation Portable" (PSP).

In many ways, the DS versus Sony PSP battle was very reminiscent of the Game Boy versus Atari Lynx battle in 1989. The PSP had roughly the power of the PS2 home console system (a "6th generation" system) and the DS was roughly comparable to the N64 (a "5th generation" system) — a significant power differential. The PSP, like

---

[105] James Brightman. Harrison: Nintendo may 'retire' Game Boy (16 July 2007). *Game Daily.* http://www.gamedaily.com/articles/features/harrison-nintendo-may-retire-game-boy/70672/?biz=1.

[106] Nintendo Co. (2007). Annual Report 2007. http://www.nintendo.co.jp/ir/pdf/2007/annual0703e.pdf.

the Lynx, also had a significantly shorter battery life, only two hours compared to the DSs 10 hours per charge. It featured a larger screen, video and music playback capabilities and was marketed as an all-in-one multimedia device. The PSP was launched at $249, whereas the DS was launched in the same year at $149.

Like the battle with the Lynx, the lower-priced, more practical DS won the market share over the more premium PSP. However, the PSP versus DS battle also showed a preview of the upcoming battle of PS3 and Wii in the home console system market. The PSP was indicative of Sony's strategy with the forthcoming PS3: power and consolidation. The PSP was simultaneously competing with portable DVD players and iPod-like music players, in addition to its "primary" function as a game machine. All those additional features came at a price, a price Sony felt was justifiable for all the devices it could replace. The DS, on the other hand, was indicative of Nintendo's strategy for their upcoming Wii console. Rather than spreading its focus to encompass video and audio player, or pushing the power of the system to the cutting edge, Nintendo opted to focus the DS as purely a game machine. While the DS was not pushing the power front, it pushed the innovative control and interaction front. The new Nintendo strategy became clear: to change the way players experienced games.

GAMES FOR EVERYONE — "TOUCH GENERATIONS"

Nintendo's new strategy had two primary elements. First, they sought to change the way players interacted and experienced their games. Second, they sought to expand the market itself and reach out to people who had not played games before.

The first time Nintendo experienced an expansion of the market, it was at the hands of rival Sega, which targeted the older generation who was being ignored by Nintendo's kid-focused marketing. The failure of Nintendo to keep the "graduates" of the NES allowed them to be easy prey for Sega, which invited them to a system that promised a more teen-oriented game experience. Only a year later, Nintendo released the Game Boy and it was an unexpected hit with *adult* gamers. For an adult to play games in Japan at that time was often viewed as irresponsible. Adults were expected to adhere to the Japanese traditional value of *jyukyu*, which encouraged hard work, thriftiness and seriousness; eschewing leisure time amusements was seen as wasteful.[107] The idea that games could appeal to more than just children and teens was limited to the Game Boy and did not surface again until the DS and "Touch Generations" were introduced.

"Touch Generations" is the brand name given to a series of titles which started first on the DS but eventually found their way onto the GBA and Wii. The philosophy behind "Touch Generations" is to produce games and software targeted toward the non-traditional gamer.[108] Nintendogs and Brain Age were both released under the "Touch Generations" brand. "Touch Generations" software was very successful for Nintendo and spawned a whole gamut of unconventional software for the DS. It had everything from Brain Age clones, to study programs, dictionaries (with voice recognition and pronunciation guides), cookbooks, and yoga instruction software. As the "Touch Generations" brand developed, its way of thinking spread across the company and solidified Nintendo's strategy for the future, and directly influenced the development of the Wii, which was codenamed as "The Revolution".

VIVA THE REVOLUTION

When assigning the task of developing the successor to the GameCube, Iwata laid down a stack of three DVD cases before his R&D engineers.[109] He then told them to make the new system no larger than the stack. The first peak at the new console was at E3

---

[107] David Sheff and Andy Eddy (1999). *Game Over Press Start to Continue*, Cyberactive Media Group, pp. 292–293.

[108] Nintendo Co. (2007). Annual Report 2006 — Message From the President. http://www.nintendo.co.jp/ir/pdf/2006/annual0603e.pdf.

[109] Peter Cohen. E3: Nintendo revolution, Game Boy micro unveiled (May 2005). *Macworld*. http://www.macworld.com/news/2005/05/17/nintendo/index.php?pf=1.

(a major industry press event) in 2004; Iwata held up the form factor of their new machine with the mysterious code-name, "The Revolution". Details were scarce, but he promised the crowds that the Revolution was not an empty name, but the very mission of the console was to revolutionize gaming.

At that time, the DS had yet to show any of its eventual market power, and many industry pundits declared Nintendo as firmly off their rocker. After all, Sony and Microsoft were expounding the merits of their ultra-powerhouse systems, and Nintendo refused to give any performance specifications until within a year of the Revolution's release. When the specifications were finally released, it was in vague terms, not the nuts-and-bolts numbers the press were used to, such as "about twice as fast as the GameCube".[110] This put it roughly on par with the original Xbox in terms of power, and well behind the next generation system from Microsoft the "Xbox 360". Nintendo was ignored until they shocked the gaming world with the unveiling of the Revolution controller at E3 in 2005. The controller, not the console hardware itself, was the real revolution.

Game console controllers had undergone a button explosion over the years. The original Famicom (1983) had two buttons. Later, the Super Famicom (1991) added four more buttons for a total of six. The Nintendo 64 (1996) controller was truly boggling, it could be held in three separate ways, and featured a D-pad, an analog joystick, and eight buttons (see Fig. 9). When faced with the N64 controller for the first time, even seasoned gamers did not quite know how to hold it.

Nintendo designers were tasked with designing a controller that would not be intimidating and people would just naturally know how to use. The DS showed this thinking with the stylus control, which used the same movements and way of thinking as writing with a pen. The Revolution designers based its controller on a TV remote control.

---

[110] Steve Tilley. So you say you want a Revolution? (18 January 2006). *Calgary Sun*. http://www.calgarysun.com/cgi-bin/publish.cgi?p=119981&x=articles&s=hype.

Figure 9. The Nintendo 64 controller (1996).
It has plenty of buttons, but how do I hold it?

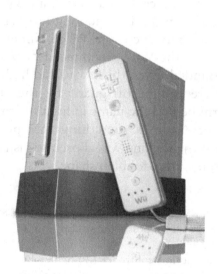

Figure 10. The Nintendo Wii with controller.

Usable with one hand, the Revolution controller (later dubbed the Wiimote) could be held just like a TV remote (see Fig. 10). It featured a direction pad, two buttons for the primary features and a few smaller secondary buttons. The remote, like the console itself, was designed with a very Apple-like industrial design: sleek, white and approachable.[111]

The approachable design was critical to their plans to expand the market to non-traditional gamers, but the Wiimote held other surprises that even the core gamer would appreciate. It contained gyroscopic sensors which could detect, with a high degree of precision, the movement of the controller in three dimensions. Players could twist, roll, shake, swing, and punch with the controller, and their movements could be detected and interpreted by the game software. It also had a sensor bar which allowed the Wiimote to act as a pointer on the screen. This acted like a mouse pointer for navigating the Revolution's main menus or integrated internet browser, and as a "zapper-like" aiming device for shooting games.[112]

After the unveiling of the controller, many industry insiders were still not convinced. It was criticized as "gimmicky"[113] and a "toy" that would not hold its ground in the long term against the powerhouse systems of Sony and Microsoft. When Nintendo later revealed the final system name, the Wii (pronounced "we"), the press were once again dumbfounded. Even those who had high expectations for the Revolution were caught off-guard by the strange name.[114] Nintendo stood firm behind the name in light of criticism as they felt it exemplified the console as something that people would play together ("we") and the spelling was chosen to visually integrate two distinctive controllers in the double-i shape.

---

[111] Danny Allen. A closer look at the Nintendo Wii (18 November 2006). *PC World.* http://www.washingtonpost.com/wp-dyn/content/article/2006/11/18/AR2006111800029_pf.html.

[112] Nintendo unveils revolution controller (20 September 2005). *Business Week.* http://www.businessweek.com/innovate/content/sep2005/id20050920_842519.htm.

[113] Marc McEntegart. Epic: Revolution console will be gimmicky, crappy, cheap (27 October 2005). *The Inquirer.* http://www.theinquirer.net/en/inquirer/news/2005/10/27/epic—revolution-console-will-be-gimmicky-crappy-cheap.

[114] Chris Morris. Nintendo goes 'Wii' ... (not a typo) (27 April 2006). *CNN Money.* http://money.cnn.com/2006/04/27/commentary/game_over/nintendo/?cnn=yes.

Even when all of the Wii's innovative features were unveiled, many game companies wrote off the Wii completely. Top third party publisher Electronic Arts CEO admitted in 2007 that the "Wii caught us flat-footed".[115] In spite of the runaway success of the system that was about to ensue, most third party publishers placed all their bets on the more traditional systems from rivals Microsoft and Sony (Xbox 360 and PS3).

THE WII'S COMPETITION

The GameCube's generation of hardware (the "6th" generation) saw two main competitors, Sony's PS2 and Microsoft's Xbox. The Xbox never caught on in Japan, only selling under half a million units, but sold 24 million units worldwide.[116] Market leader Sony's PS2 sold 117 million units[117] and Nintendo's GameCube sold 21 million,[118] placing it third in worldwide market share.

Microsoft was first to launch a "seventh" generation console in 2005, the Xbox 360. The Xbox 360 was launched with two configurations: the $299 core model and a more accessory-rich $399 model.[119] Sony launched along-side the Wii in 2006, also with two configurations priced at $499 and $599.[120] Both systems were

---

[115] Kris Graft. EA: Wii caught us flat-footed (26 July 2007). *Next Generation.* http://www.next-gen.biz/index.php?option=com_content&task=view&id=6580&Itemid=2.

[116] Microsoft Xbox website. Gamers catch their breath as Xbox 360 and Xbox live reinvent next-generation gaming (10 May 2006). http://www.xbox.com/zh-SG/community/news/2006/20060510.htm.

[117] Sony Computer Entertainment Inc. website. PlayStation 2 cumulative production shipments of hardware (12 December 2007). http://www.scei.co.jp/corporate/data/bizdataps2_e.html.

[118] Nintendo Co. website (2007). Consolidated sales by region. http://www.nintendo.co.jp/ir/en/library/historical_data/xls/consolidated_sales_e0708.xls.

[119] Todd Bishop. Xbox 360 launch price will be $399.99 (17 August 2005). *Seattle Post-Intelligencer.* http://seattlepi.nwsource.com/business/236918_msft17ww.asp.

[120] Chris Ayres. Sony launches PlayStation 3 (9 May 2006) *Times Online.* http://www.timesonline.co.uk/tol/news/world/us_and_americas/article714783.ece.

comparable in power (as exhibited by nearly identically performing games released on each platform),[121] but the Sony system
included a much larger media form-factor, the Blu-Ray disc, capable of storing up to 50 GB of data (compared to the 360's DVDs
at 9 GB).[122]

Both consoles were sold at a loss at launch, as Sony and Microsoft
battled for market share using a loss-leader strategy. Each Xbox 360
was sold at an estimated $126 loss,[123] though as of 2007, due to pro-
duction improvements, the console was no longer sold at a loss.[124]
The higher-end PS3 was estimated at $840 by iSuppli,[125] a $240 loss
on each unit (up to $400 in Japan, where the PS3 was sold at a lower
price).

The loss-leader strategy was not new to Microsoft. Their games
division had been operating at a constant loss since its inception,
reaching over $4 billion by the 360's launch in 2005. However, in
2007, with the launch of the anticipated Halo 3 title, the Xbox division posted its first profit.[126] Much of the high sticker price and
per-unit losses of the PS3 were attributed to its inclusion of the
cutting-edge Blu-Ray disc technology. Sony-backed Blu-Ray was in
a format war for the high-definition video format to succeed the

---

[121] Levi Buchanan. With consoles, it's all about the games (19 December 2006).
MSNBC.com. http://today.msnbc.msn.com/id/16273891/.

[122] Danny Allen. Sony's packed PlayStation 3: The nitty-gritty details (15
November 2006). *PC World.* http://www.pcworld.com/article/id,127857-page,4-c,
gameconsoles/article.html.

[123] Arik Hesseldahl. Microsoft's red-ink game (22 November 2005). *BusinessWeek.*
http://www.businessweek.com/technology/content/nov2005/tc20051122_
410710.htm.

[124] Eric Bangeman. Sony taking a bit hit on each PS3; Xbox 360 in the black
(16 November 2006). *Ars Technica.* http://arstechnica.com/news.ars/post/
20061116-8239.html.

[125] PlayStation 3 offers supercomputer performance at PC pricing, iSuppli's tear-
down analysis reveals (16 November 2006). *iSuppli.* http://www.isuppli.com/
news/default.asp?id=6919.

[126] James Brightman. Xbox division posts $165 million profit in Q1 (25 October 2007).
Game Daily. http://www.gamedaily.com/articles/features/xbox-division-posts-
165-million-profit-in-q1/71095/?biz=1.

DVD with rival format HD-DVD.[127] As each PS3 was a Blu-Ray player, the per-unit loss of the PS3 was justified as an attempt to gain market share not just in the video game sector but also in the high definition video sector. Both Microsoft and Sony designed their consoles as a multi-media centerpiece for the living room, not just as a video game console.[128]

THE WII

The Wii was launched in 2006 with a very unconventional game as its poster child. "Wii Sports" was a whimsical collection of sports mini-games, which showcased the motion-sensing and pointing capabilities of the controller. Advertisements showed people of all ages, genders and ethnic groups playing "Wii Sports" with their family and friends. The advertising campaign was the culmination of the demographic experiments they began with Touch Generations on the DS. Nintendo was not targeting the established gamer with the Wii; Nintendo was targeting non-gamers with a system designed specifically for the non-traditional gamer.

The Wii was launched within a few weeks of the PS3, at $249 in North America, bundled with "Wii Sports" and 25,000 in Japan,[129] with Wii Sports sold separately at 4,000. The Wii was half the price of the low-end PS3. Both the Wii and PS3 were sold out after being launched. However, Wii shortages continued throughout its first year on the market,[130] and the PS3 was readily available within three months after launch.

---

[127] Danny Allen. Sony's packed PlayStation 3: The nitty-gritty details (15 November 2006). *PC World.* http://www.pcworld.com/article/id,127857-page,4-c, gameconsoles/article.html.

[128] Dean Takahashi. Gaming consoles go head-to-head as entertainment centers (8 November 2006). *PCMag.com/Fox News.* http://www.foxnews.com/story/0,2933,228227,00.html.

[129] Kathleen Sanders and Matt Casamassina. US Wii price, launch date revealed. (13 September 2006). *IGN.* http://wii.ign.com/articles/732/732669p1.html.

[130] Rhys Blakely. Wii shortage to cost $1.3bn to Nintendo in short term. (17 December 2007). *Times Online.* http://business.timesonline.co.uk/tol/business/industry_sectors/technology/article3062612.ece.

In early 2007, Nintendo's market-expansion strategy was paying dividends. The Wii was a hit in a most unconventional place — retirement homes.[131] Retirees were holding "Wii Sports" tournaments in bowling, golfing and baseball home-run derbies.[132] Like the DS, the Wii was seeing a number of unusual games, including updated versions of the DS cooking and surgery games. Wii was sold swiftly and 3rd party publishers, most of which had only released a few token titles for the Wii, began shifting their development to target the new system.[133]

In a surprise announcement, Square/Enix declared the Nintendo DS as the target for the 9th entry in the Japan's top-selling "Dragon Quest" series — a defection from Sony consoles (previous entries of the game were on the PS1 and PS2).[134] In a similar announcement, Capcom changed the target for the third "Monster Hunter" game from the PS3 to the Wii.[135]

In late 2007, Nintendo was set to launch the second wave, led by flagship title Super Mario Galaxy for its core fans and another Wii innovation: "Wii Fit".[136] "Wii Fit" is an exercise program for the Wii, complete with a balance board accessory that can detect weight, body fat percentage, and position on the board. In a similar advertising campaign to "Wii Sports", Nintendo took aim at a new set of non-gamers.

---

[131] Dave Wischnowsky. Wii bowling knocks over retirement home (16 February 2007). *Chicago Tribune*. http://www.chicagotribune.com/news/local/chi-070216 nintendo,1,609357.story.

[132] Kevin Reece. Grandpa and grandma get their game on with the Wii (25 December 2007). *Khou.com*. http://www.khou.com/news/local/houstonmetro/stories/khou071224_tnt_seniorswii.4aa768ec.html.

[133] Michael White. Electronic arts plays catch-up after shrug-off of Wii (update1) (9 April 2007). *Bloomberg*. http://www.bloomberg.com/apps/news?pid=20601087&sid=amWmy6_JG16U&refer=home.

[134] Reuters. Nintendo rides strong DS sales to 40% profit boost (25 January 2007). *FoxNews.com*. http://www.foxnews.com/story/0,2933,246866,00.html.

[135] Emma Boyes. Monster Hunter 3 now Wii-exclusive (10 October 2007). *GameSpot UK*. http://www.gamespot.com/news/6180675.html.

[136] Brandon Sheffield. E3: Miyamoto talks super mario galaxy, Wii Fit (13 July 2007). *Gamasutra*. http://www.gamasutra.com/php-bin/news_index.php?story=14676.

DOUBTS ON SUSTAINABILITY

After reclaiming the top spot in home consoles with the Wii and the DS handheld selling even stronger, it seems that Nintendo can do no wrong. In 1989, with the release of Super Mario Bros. 3, Nintendo was looking just as unconquerable; yet, the years that followed saw a slow decline as Nintendo failed to maintain its momentum. In 2007, Nintendo CEO, Iwata, stated that he was determined to avoid a return to arrogance (referring to the company's historical loss of the market at the hands of rivals, Sega and Sony).[137] At the same time that Nintendo's market value briefly topped Sony's (*all* of Sony, not just the games division),[138] there was a worrying buzz among third party developers. As reported by Nikkei Business Daily, anonymous developers were worried about committing resources to the Wii, citing that its success could be a fad and third party titles were selling significantly less units than Nintendo's first party games.[139]

These concerns are not unfounded. A report by leading Japanese game magazine Famitsu found that 67% of respondents had not used their Wii recently.[140] And of the top-selling Wii games, the seven top-sellers were Nintendo first party titles (see Table 3).

After a year on the market, the Wii's "attach rate" (or "tie rate", the number of games sold per console) in North America (reported by NPD Group) was 3.44, compared to the PS3's 3.58 and the Xbox

---

[137] Frank Caron. Nintendo president wary of a return to arrogance (5 September 2007). *Ars Technica*. http://arstechnica.com/journals/thumbs.ars/2007/09/05/nintendo-president-wary-of-a-return-to-arrogance.

[138] Kiyoshi Takenaka. Nintendo market value at $85 billion thanks to Wii (15 October 2007). *Reuters UK*. http://uk.reuters.com/article/ousiv/idUKTKB-00289220071015.

[139] Rob Burman. Developers 'nervous' about making Wii games. (11 October 2007). *IGN UK/Famitsu*. http://uk.wii.ign.com/articles/826/826558p1.html.

[140] David Hinkle. 67% of Wii owners haven't touched the console recently (16 October 2007). *Wiifanboy/Famitsu*. http://www.nintendowiifanboy.com/2007/10/16/67-of-wii-owners-havent-touched-the-console-recently/.

Table 3.   Top-selling Wii games (in millions) as of 26 November 2007.

Name	Publisher	Japan	America	Others	Total
Wii Sports[1]	Nintendo	2.23	6.28	3.52	12.03
Wii Play[2]	Nintendo	1.79	2.94	2.16	6.89
Legend of Zelda: Twilight Princess	Nintendo	0.56	2.05	1.24	3.89
Mario Party 8	Nintendo	0.91	1.39	0.41	2.71
Wario Ware: Smooth Moves	Nintendo	0.54	0.75	0.70	1.99
Super Paper Mario	Nintendo	0.52	0.84	0.34	1.70
Super Mario Galaxy	Nintendo	0.38	0.75	0.21	1.34
Rayman Raving Rabbids	Ubisoft	0.02	0.62	0.48	1.12
Red Steel	Ubisoft	0.04	0.45	0.54	1.03
Resident Evil 4: Wii Edition	Capcom	0.14	0.55	0.33	1.02

[1] Wii Sports is bundled with the Wii in all regions except Japan.
[2] Wii Play is bundled with a Wiimote controller, at a cost of $10 more than a Wiimote without the game.
Source: VGChartz.com.

360's 6.59.[141] The Xbox 360's attach rate is significant, as the console sold only slightly fewer units than the Wii, but with almost double the number of software units.

The high Xbox 360 attach rate can be attributed to its focus on the "core" gamer, who expects higher-end graphics and games. Core gamers tend to purchase more games individually than the "casual" or non-traditional gamer that the Wii (and DS) targets.[142] But if successfully captured, the non-traditional gamer market is much larger. The top-selling PC game of all time is "The Sims" and it took the title from the previous top-seller "Myst". Both of these games are aimed at a casual gamer audience and sold

[141] Alexander Sliwinski. 360 leads hardware to software ratio, Wii and PS3 trail with similar ratios (31 October 2007). Joystiq. http://www.joystiq.com/ 2007/10/31/360-leads-hardware-to-software-ratio-wii-and-ps3-trail-with-sim/.
[142] Jeremy Reimer. The dark side of console attach rates (22 November 2006). Ars Technica. http://arstechnica.com/news.ars/post/20061122-8273.html.

millions more copies than the most popular core gamer focused titles.[143]

NOA Vice President George Harrison admitted in an interview that they may "lose some purists" (core gamers) when attempting to expand the market.[144] While Nintendo has released a number of purist-oriented titles from the Mario, Metroid and Zelda franchises, concerns remain whether the Wii will capture enough of the core gamer market to sustain the console should the casual market wane.[145]

The form of the successor console to the Wii is also in question. Having broken from the traditional power arms race in the Wii (which is comparable in power to the previous generation's Xbox), where does Nintendo go from here? If it releases a console on par with the Xbox 360 or PS3, even with a Wiimote style control, it will have a difficult time in the market competing with Microsoft and Sony's *next* offerings. For Nintendo, banking both its handheld and home console lines on the "Touch Generations" philosophy, everything depends on capturing this expanded market for the long term.

QUESTIONS

1) Which aspects made Nintendo such a successful company?
2) Why is the company considered innovative?
3) How can the company develop a long term strategy to sustain their competitive advantage?

IMAGE REFERENCES

Figure 1 — Atari 2600, taken by 'joho345' 2007, 17 October 2007, public domain http://en.wikipedia.org/wiki/Image:Atari2600a.JPG.

---

[143] Trey Walker. The Sims overtakes Myst (12 March 2002). *GameSpot*. http://www.gamespot.com/pc/strategy/starcraft/news.html?page=1&sid=2857556.

[144] James Brightman. Harrison: Wii hardware revision not out of the question (23 July 2007). *Game Daily*. http://www.gamedaily.com/articles/features/harrison-wii-hardware-revision-not-out-of-the-question/70703/?biz=1.

[145] Kris Graft. E3: Is Nintendo abandoning the hardcore? (12 July 2007). *Next Generation*. http://www.next-gen.biz/index.php?option=com_content&task=view&id=6413&Itemid=2.

Figure 2 — Nintendo Famicom, taken by 'Shizhao', 13 July 2005, GNU Free Documentation License http://en.wikipedia.org/wiki/Image: Famicom.jpg.

Figure 3 — Nintendo Entertainment System, promotional material, Copyright Nintendo Co. http://cybernetnews.com/wp-content/uploads/2007/09/nes-console.jpg.

Figure 4 — Nintendo Game Boy, taken by 'Boffy b', 26 March 2006, public domain http://en.wikipedia.org/wiki/Image:Gameboy.jpg.

Figure 5 — Nintendo DS Lite, taken by Estoy Aquí, 13 July 2007, Creative Commons Attribution 2.5 http://en.wikipedia.org/wiki/Image: DSLite_white_trans.png.

NTT DoCoMo: Beyond i-mode and FOMA

Kaoru Kusuma

"DoCoMo is our flag bearer."

Hiroyuki Arai, Director,
Parliament Telecom Policymaking Committee

"Having evolved from an analog mobile phone provider to the premiere brand in digital mobile communications in Japan, we are now leading the transition of the mobile phone from a means of communication into a vital "lifestyle infrastructure"."

Masao Nakamura, President and
Chief Executive Officer, NTT DoCoMo

INTRODUCTION

Ever since mobile phones were first introduced in the 1980s, they have become an integral part of people's daily lives. This is especially true in Japan where users continually demand increased mobile functionality. Mobile service providers, in turn, are eager to meet this rising demand.

There are several mobile service providers in Japan. The privatization of government-owned Nippon Telegraph and Telephone (NTT) in 1985 marked the turning point of Japan's telecommunication market, leading to the birth of other telecommunication companies such

81

as KDD, DDI, IDO (later merged as KDDI Corp.) and J-Phone (later known as Softbank Corp.).[1] This marked the beginning of the long-running competition among the mobile phone carriers within an undifferentiated mobile phone market.

Following NTT's privatization, NTT DoCoMo was established as its subsidiary to take over its mobile communication business. NTT DoCoMo has been investing greatly in its research and development sector. As such, it was always the first mobile carrier to introduce revolutionary products such as i-mode[146] and FOMA.[147] While NTT DoCoMo has emerged as the market leader in Japan's cellular phone market, it also faced several problems. After its success with the revolutionary mobile internet service i-mode, NTT DoCoMo has taken aggressive moves for global expansion. NTT DoCoMo began investing in foreign mobile carriers such as Hutchison Telecom, AT&T Wireless, KPN and KTF in 1999. These moves showed little success as foreign mobile phone market peculiarities were drastically different from that of Japan's. As a result, NTT DoCoMo was forced to write-off some of its foreign investments and the company registered one of the biggest corporate losses in Japan in the year 2002.[2]

NTT DoCoMo announced that it would launch its third generation (3G) phones under the brand name FOMA in May 2001. However, this initial launch date had to be postponed by six months due to technical problems with its 3G network. This delay proved to be disadvantageous as 3G customers began feeling disenchanted with the 3G services provided by NTT DoCoMo. Furthermore, in April 2002, Japan's second largest mobile phone operator, KDDI Corp.,

---

[146] i-mode: The first instantly accessible mobile internet in the world, which made the internet available on the phone without the need to dial-up. With this service, subscribers were able to perform many internet functions such as exchanging e-mails, getting maps and train schedules, buying movie tickets, downloading ring tones and games and even making online purchases.

[147] FOMA: "Freedom of Mobile Multimedia Access" is the brand name of the third generation (3G) mobile phones, which focused on value-added multimedia services such as video calls, video call conferencing, improved music and video downloads.

launched its 3G service and it became more popular than the 3G service provided by NTT DoCoMo.[3]

In November 2006, the mobile number portability system, which made it possible for customers to switch mobile phone operators while retaining the number used with their previous operator, was implemented. This intensified the competition among the mobile phone operators in this already saturated market. Japan's third largest mobile phone carrier, Softbank Mobile, move to offer rock-bottom rates has led DoCoMo and KDDI to halve their monthly basic charges.

COMPANY HISTORY

NTT DoCoMo is Japan's leading mobile communications company. Its history can be traced back to 1949, when the Ministry of Communication in Japan was split into the Ministry of Telecommunications (MTEL) and Ministry of Posts (MPosts). MTEL became a public corporation in 1952 and was renamed as Nippon Telegraph and Telephone (NTT). Until the 1970s, NTT held a monopoly. In a bid to break NTT's monopoly, the Ministry of International Trade and Industry (MITI) pressured the Japanese government to privatize NTT. NTT was eventually privatized in April 1985 and this marked the turning point for the Japanese telecommunications industry. Local as well as foreign players such as Vodafone K.K. began entering the Japanese telecommunication market during this time.[4]

Following the privatization of NTT, NTT Mobile Communications Network Inc., was established as its subsidiary in July 1992. It was later renamed as NTT DoCoMo, which stands for "**Do Com**munications over the **Mo**bile Network", in the year 2000. DoCoMo also shares the same pronunciation as the Japanese word *dokomo*, which means "everywhere". The majority (67%) of NTT DoCoMo's shares are owned by NTT. NTT DoCoMo was first listed on the Tokyo Stock Exchange in October 1998. It is also listed in the London (NDCM) and New York (DCM) Stock Exchange.[5]

NTT DoCoMo took over the wireless communication business from NTT. It was primarily involved in offering various wireless communication devices and services. Among the wide range of wireless services offered by NTT DoCoMo then were pagers, mobile phones, satellite phones, car phones, maritime phones, and in-flight phones. The company also developed the personal digital cellular (PDC)[148] system in 1993 and began providing digital mobile services based on this system. In July 1995, an alternative mobile phone system, the personal handyphone system (PHS)[149] was developed. When it was first launched, the PHS subscription rate increased drastically as PHS has the advantage of low cost, long battery life, compact and lightweight terminals and relatively fast data transmission rate (64 KB/s compared to PDC's 9.6 KB/s). NTT DoCoMo found itself competing with its parent company, NTT Personal Group that was offering the PHS service. To resolve this problem, NTT DoCoMo took over the PHS business from its parent group in December 1998. Due to the production of improved and more advanced PDC cellular phone terminals, the PHS subscription base dwindled rapidly in the late 90s. NTT DoCoMo has since announced that it is stopping its PHS service by December 2007.[4]

In the early 1990s, NTT DoCoMo faced tough competition with the entry of foreign players such as Motorola into the Japanese cellular phone market. Shortly after NTT DoCoMo was formed, the company registered a drastic decline in sales in 1992–1994. In order to sustain its position in the market, the company stopped renting out handsets to customers in October 1993. Instead, the company launched its own handsets and encouraged its customers to purchase these handsets rather than renting them in April 1994. With the introduction of attractive handsets as well as customized service packages, NTT DoCoMo's subscription base grew rapidly. Further

---

[148] Personal digital cellular (PDC): The PDC is a system for the second generation mobile phone technology in Japan. In the 1990s, it is the predominant system used in Japan.
[149] Personal handyphone system (PHS): PHS is essentially a cordless phone with the capability to handover from one cell to another. PHS cells are small, and has a much smaller transmission range than personal digital cellular (PDC) or global system for mobile communications (GSM).

growth in its subscription base was observed in December 1996 when NTT DoCoMo eliminated the initial subscription fees for its services after the Ministry of Posts and Telecommunication deregulated its procedure for amending mobile phone charges from permission to simple notification. By 1997, NTT DoCoMo emerged as the market leader in Japan's telecommunication market.[4]

However, during the same period, the then-president (CEO) of NTT DoCoMo, Kouji Oboshi, sensed that there was little differentiation between the products offered by the various mobile phone carriers in Japan. He foresaw that the demand for new mobile phones would soon peak unless new mobile phones with value-added capabilities and services were developed. He believed that the future laid in non-voice (or data) communications. Following Mr Oboshi's initiation, NTT DoCoMo began focusing heavily on research and development (R&D), concentrating specifically on the non-voice communications area.[2]

I-MODE: A MOBILE REVOLUTION

To develop the revolutionary non-voice communication service, the mobile data service taskforce, Gateway Business Department (GBD), was developed in January 1997. Mr. Keiichi Enoki, an electrical engineer in NTT, was appointed as its head. In February 1999, Mr. Enoki and his team launched the revolutionary product, i-mode — NTT DoCoMo's mobile internet. i-mode was the first instantly accessible mobile internet in the world, which made the internet available on the phone without the need to dial-up. With this service, subscribers were able to perform many internet functions such as exchanging e-mails, getting maps and train schedules, buying movie tickets, downloading ring tones or games or even making online purchases. With the launch of i-mode, the mobile phone market dynamics changed drastically overnight. In addition, i-mode led to a phenomenal growth in NTT DoCoMo's subscriber base, and i-mode quickly became the service that NTT DoCoMo became famous for worldwide. After the launch of i-mode, NTT DoCoMo foresaw the prospects of global expansion. NTT DoCoMo started investing in foreign carriers such as Hutchison Telecom, AT&T Wireless, KPN and KTF. Nevertheless, there was little success in foreign investments made by NTT DoCoMo during this time.[2]

Following the huge success of i-mode in the Japanese market, NTT DoCoMo continued to develop and launched more revolutionary products in order to sustain its position as Japan's cellular phone market leader. In late 1999, shortly after the introduction of i-mode, NTT DoCoMo announced its plans to develop the third generation (3G) mobile phones, which focused on value-added multimedia services. With 3G mobile phones, users were able to make video calls as well as download ring tones and videos to their mobile phone terminals at faster speed. The 3G service was given the brand name "FOMA" or "Freedom of Mobile Multimedia Access" and it is based on the International Telecommunication Union (ITU) standard W-CDMA (Wideband CDMA).[150] Seeing the 3G service as a strategy to establish itself as a global mobile service provider, NTT DoCoMo tried once again to break into foreign markets through strategic alliances with mobile and multimedia service providers in the Asia-Pacific and Europe. Although it was a little more successful than NTT DoCoMo's first global expansion drive in 1999, its success remained limited.[2]

In recent years, NTT DoCoMo has also taken moves to provide fourth generation (4G) services to the Japanese market. The 4G mobile phones has lifestyle applications such as wallet-in-mobile-phone service known as "*osaifu keitai*" and NTT DoCoMo hoped that this service would boost its subscriber base in the highly competitive and almost-saturated mobile phone market. By September 2007, NTT DoCoMo held more than half (53.4%) of Japan's cellular phone market share and had 52.9 million subscribers. The other main Japanese mobile phone operators, KDDI and Softbank (previously known as J-Phone of Vodafone) owned 29.5% and 17.2% of the market share respectively.[1]

---

[150] CDMA: A second generation (2G) telecommunications standard that uses the digital radio system "code division multiple access". It is used by the mobile phones in Japan.

JAPAN'S UBIQUITOUS MOBILE AGE

Japan's mobile journey began with car phones, which were introduced by the NTT in 1979. After its privatization, NTT began offering portable mobile phone rental services in 1987. Rapid development of mobile communications in Japan occurred in the mid 1990s. During this time, the pager, which is an electronic device that displayed the caller's number, was launched. It was initially designed for businessmen. However, this was quickly adopted as an important means of communication among high school students.[4]

In April 1994, customer ownership of handsets was introduced. Handsets were beginning to be sold to individual customers, rather than making them available on a rental basis. At the same time, the Ministry of Posts and Telecommunications deregulated its procedure for amending mobile phone call charges from permission to simple notification. This accelerated the growth of mobile phone subscriber base greatly as mobile operators could reduce their call charges more easily and efficiently. In addition, mobile operators introduced attractive handsets and customized tariff packages and this led to further phenomenal growth in new mobile subscriptions.[4]

When *keitai* (Japanese for cellular mobile phone) was first launched in Japan, it was targeted for business professionals and was considered a luxury item. However, *keitais* quickly gained popularity among the non-business professionals. Japan now has one of the highest mobile phone penetration rates in the world. In addition, it ranked third in the world in terms of overall mobile subscribers after China and the United States.[4]

Great progress in mobile phone functionality was further seen in the late 90s and early 2000s. Mobile internet (i-mode) was first made available to the Japanese market and it immediately became popular, especially among teenagers and young adults. Specially-designed handsets that were internet-enabled were launched in Japan and they were used by customers to check their e-mails or other information services such as internet banking and ticket reservation. Today, Japan has made mobile internet services an integral part of mobile phone ownership. In fact, the country boasts the highest total number and percentage of mobile internet users in the world. The number of mobile internet users even outnumbers that of personal computers internet users.[4]

At almost the same time as the launch of mobile internet, multimedia functions were made available on handsets. Users were able to download and play music files, take photographs and view graphic images. They could also send multimedia messages (MMS) to each other. These value-added services were meant to change the function of the 2G mobile phones to not just be the usual call-enabled handsets. In 1999, the introduction of the colored LCD screen and camera-installed handsets created another boost in mobile phone subscriptions. Game interface, video viewing and mobile television features were also added into mobile phone headsets in order to cater to Japan's growing demand for functionality.[4]

The third generation phone (3G) was released in 2000 and this featured twin-camera-installed handsets that allow users to communicate via video calls. This marked a significant change to the mobile phone industry. Today, lifestyle applications such as wallet phones or *osaifu keitai* have been launched to meet the increasing demand for functionality in the saturated Japanese mobile phone market.

A fictional story: A day in the life of 22-year old Kyoko and her keitai

Kyoko, a 22 year-old woman, works at an office in the city. Kyoko wakes up at 6.30 AM to the sound of her mobile phone. She checks her *keitai* immediately for new mails: 10 e-mails from friends/family and five spam messages. Her best friend, Noriko, suggests a new movie tonight. Her new boyfriend, Takeshi, asks for a date over the weekend. Her sister, Kaori, currently studying in the USA, asks for easy Japanese recipes. Her mother in her hometown is asking how she is. Her father on a business trip wants to know what souvenirs she would like. After acquiring a mobile phone, she has had more contact with her father and he is so happy that he continues to subsidize her mobile bills. Kyoko then starts her commute to work.

During her time on the train, she replies to most of her messages. She interrupted her mobile game, after she received a call. Before she boarded the train, however, she had set her mobile to "manner mode" so that it didn't ring. Her mobile also has a sticky film covering, an accessory for the LCD display. This film covering is recently a popular item to avoid snooping by others, especially in the very crowded trains. It means that mobile screens can only be viewed by the person who is facing the phone directly, and not by people on either side of the phone. Kyoko heard from her friends that a new ring tone of a popular Japanese song has just been released, so she immediately downloads it to her mobile phone for a small fee. Kyoko works as a secretary for a worldwide trading company. Typically, she sits in front of her PC in the office, but she communicates with her friends only through her mobile phone, because she doesn't have a computer at home.

After her day at work, she goes shopping and replaces her mobile phone with a newer model, one that has a very secure system with fingerprint identification. Now, she can assign different fingers for accessing different data: for instance, the right forefinger for Noriko's folder, the left middle finger for Takeshi's folder and so on. Another attractive function that Kyoko enjoys is mobile chatting: this allows a series of messages to be exchanged in the form of near real-time dialog similar to Internet chatting software. She did end up going to the movie with Noriko, after buying both tickets electronically through her keitai. She did not find the new movie interesting. So in the theatre, she wrote a few more e-mails and sent pictures to friends with her new mobile handset....

Source: ITU, http://www.itu.int/osg/spu/ni/futuremobile/general/casestudies/JapancaseLS.pdf.

CHARACTERISTICS OF THE JAPANESE MOBILE MARKET

One of the most distinguishing aspects of the Japanese mobile industry is that it is operator-led. Equipment manufacturers and operators work in closely-knit groups and supply the market with handsets and portable devices in a coordinated effort. The mobile operator retains ownership of the handset. As such, the operator's brand is dominant rather than that of the manufacturer. The three largest mobile operators in Japan today are NTT DoCoMo, KDDI Corp. and Softbank Corp.

Unlike the Western mobile industry, Japanese mobile operators, and not the manufacturers, play a leading role in research and development activities. They also maintain a close relationship with the manufacturers in order to ensure further innovation and service take-up. This close knit relationship between the manufacturers and operators in Japan accounts for the sophistication and availability of handset technology and take-up of value-added services.[4]

The high adoption rate of new technologies in Japan could be due to cultural factors. Japanese consumers are informed and demanding. They carefully choose technology for its innovative quality, functionality, and value for money. In a highly homogeneous society like Japan, consumers tend to be keen on having the latest gadgets, in order not to be outdone by their neighbors and friends. Hence, it is not surprising that high-tech, value-added phones are a hit in the Japanese market. Japan is also famous for developments in miniaturization and product packaging. The three main mobile phone operators, NTT DoCoMo, KDDI and Softbank continuously strive to produce compact, lightweight mobile phone terminals with attractive look and design to meet the Japanese market's preferences. This is aided by Japan's success in miniaturization and robotics, specifically in the area of mini chips, semiconductors and memory cards.

Japan is one of the countries that have seen successful penetration of mobile internet. Few countries have known similar success.

For example, Wireless Application Protocol (WAP)[151] in Europe suffered from low transmission speeds and paucity of content, causing users to be disenchanted. On the other hand, Japan witnessed phenomenal growth in mobile internet usage and subscribers and continued to introduce a wide array of mobile internet services. This success could be attributed to the low PC and internet penetration in Japan.[6] When mobile internet (i-mode) was launched in 1999, not many people in Japan had access to PCs. Moreover, subscribers in Japan prefer to send and receive e-mails through their mobile phones rather than through fixed-line internet-enabled PCs. Furthermore, some analysts have also attributed mobile internet growth to the large number of long-distance commuters using public transport in Japan.[4]

As Japan stepped into an ubiquitous age, mobile phones are no longer seen as luxury goods. Mobile phones soon became fashion accessories for the consumers, especially among high school students and young working adults. Other companies have been quick to produce a wide variety of colorful tags and stickers that can be used to personalize mobile phones, in line with the latest trend and fashion of the day. Mobile phone operators too have taken the heed and produced several handsets that allow users to change their outlook by switching phone covers. Handsets of different colors such as candy pink or blue or winter white were also produced to appeal to different markets. With this culture, it is of no wonder that Japanese consumers change their handsets frequently (approximately once a year). Another interesting note on mobile phone usage in Japan is the portability and proximity of the device to the human user. According to Mobile Content Forum,[152]

---

[151] Wireless Application Protocol (WAP): WAP is an open international standard for applications that use wireless communication. Its principal application is to enable access to the Internet from a mobile phone or PDA. WAP is the protocol used worldwide. It is different from Japan's i-mode, which uses cHTML based on wCDMA.

[152] Mobile Content Forum conducts surveys in order to enable companies within and outside of Japan to keep up with the latest developments and exchange information with the top players in the world's number one mobile data market. Its members include the three major mobile carriers in Japan.

70% of Japanese mobile phone users keep their mobile within one meter of their body during the daytime, and 40% during the night. As such, the mobile phone is seen as "an extension of one's physical self, intrinsically linked to identity and accessibility". [4]

The commercial success of the launch of mobile internet has many social ramifications in Japan. The use of mobile e-mail has altered the ways in which people in Japan interact, conduct their lives, and coordinate themselves in time and space. This is especially true among the youth since penetration of mobile phones among teenagers in Japan is remarkably high (over 80% on average and 95% among teenage girls). Nowadays, Japanese mobile subscribers do not set up precise locations or times for meetings in advance. This is in contrast to the past whereby people had to stick to preset time and locations for meetings decided long ahead of time. It is also worth noting that youths in Japan spend more time on exchanging mobile text messages than on voice or video call. This is probably because of the strict observation of mobile etiquette in Japan. Although no government regulation has been passed, the use of mobile phones is prohibited on trains (Japan Rail Railway system and Tokyo subway system), and also in most restaurants. Mobile phone owners are expected to turn their mobile phones to "manner mode", which means that mobile phones will vibrate instead of ringing in times of incoming calls and messages.[4]

The use of mobile text messaging service has also given rise to another form of writing among the youth in Japan. This form of writing is known as "*Galmoji*", which involves the creation of Japanese characters from other types of characters such as "&" or "><". *Galmoji* is used as a type of personal mobile signature, giving the user a sense of identity. In addition, in order to save on text message charges, youths adopted a truncated abbreviated language when creating and sending text messages. This allowed the Japanese to be less formal with each other. Another ramification of the *keitai* culture is the rise of the "*oyayubisoku*", which is literally translated as "the thumb tribe". It consists of youths who are able to type mobile phone messages by moving their thumbs at an extraordinary speed, often without even looking at the handset. These trends continue to amaze Western scholars. There is no doubt that the use of high-tech mobile phones in Japan has certainly been changing the way Japanese interact and socialize.[4]

THE OTHER PLAYERS: COMPETITION IN THE JAPANESE MOBILE MARKET

KDDI

KDDI is Japan's second largest cellular operator with almost a 30.0% cellular phone market share. It was formed through the merger of DDI Corp., KDD Corp., and IDO Corp. in 2000. KDDI is the only domestic company that provides both mobile communication service and broadband service. KDDI is extremely successful for its 3G service, CDMA 2000 1x, launched in April 2002. Although this 3G service was released later than NTT DoCoMo's 3G service FOMA, it outshines FOMA at the infant stage of 3G technology and KDDI gained substantial customers' satisfaction and trusts after its launch. KDDI is currently taking measures to convert all of its services to CDMA 2000 1x service.

KDDI also enjoyed an increase in the number of subscribers after the mobile number portability (MNP) system was introduced in Japan in November 2006. KDDI aims to become a "ubiquitous solution company" which provides high value-added solutions. As such, aggressive improvement of communications environment in preparation for the coming ubiquitous network society is underway at KDDI.[7]

Softbank Mobile Corp

Softbank Mobile Corp. is the Japanese subsidiary company of a mobile phone operator Softbank Corp. It was previously known as Vodafone K.K. or J-Phone. Softbank Mobile Corp. has operations in broadband, fixed-line telecommunications, e-Commerce, internet, broadmedia technology services, finance, media and marketing, and other businesses. Softbank Corp. also has various partnerships in Japanese subsidiaries of foreign companies such as Yahoo! and E*Trade.

Since the introduction of the mobile number portability (MNP) system, Softbank saw the MNP as a great opportunity to target a larger share of the mobile telephone market. It began its aggressive marketing strategies, offering low-priced or discounted packages and incentives such as the white and double white plan. It also invested heavily on advertising. Hollywood celebrities such as Cameron Diaz and Brad Pitt were roped in as ambassadors to help promote Softbank Mobile services. In addition, posters were seen at almost every corner of Japan such as in trains, train stations and along shopping streets. It has been reported that Softbank has successfully won its rivals in attracting more subscribers after the introduction of MNP. Softbank Mobile Corp. is also working to improve its services.[8]

WHAT MAKES DOCOMO TICK: THE SUCCESS STORY OF I-MODE

i-mode is the mobile internet service provided by Japan's leading telecommunication company, NTT DoCoMo. It is the first mobile internet launched in the world. It made the internet available on the phone without the need to dial-up. With this service, subscribers were able to perform many internet functions such as exchanging e-mails, getting maps and train schedules, buying movie tickets, downloading ring tones or games and even making online purchases. Its instant success contributed to phenomenal growth in NTT DoCoMo's subscriber base. By early 2001, barely two years after the launch of i-mode, Japan accounted for 60% (18.1 million) of the total number of mobile internet subscribers in the world. In addition, by February 2002, NTT DoCoMo held 62% of Japan's mobile phone market share, with 40 million people subscribed to i-mode. The success story of i-mode has given NTT DoCoMo a strong brand name, especially in the Japanese market whereby customers dubbed NTT DoCoMo as the "trend-setter" of the mobile phone industry.[6]

The birth of i-mode was not accidental. In 1997, then-president of NTT DoCoMo, Mr. Kouji Oboshi, foresaw that the growth of voice communications would taper off in the near future unless a new cutting-edge non-voice communications service was developed.

Hence, he initiated the formation of the mobile data service task-force, Gateway Business Department (GBD), which functions to develop data communication service for NTT DoCoMo. Mr. Keiichi Enoki was appointed as the head of this organization.[6]

One interesting feature of the GBD is that it began with ten staff recruited from both within and outside the parent organization. This is unusual for a Japanese institution. By recruiting expertises from within and outside NTT, GBD allowed new innovations and new flow of knowledge to occur within the organization. After its formation, GBD began its intensive research and development (R&D) process for a new data communication service, i-mode. Its initial goals were to "develop a network that could deliver the content, develop the mobile phones that could receive the content, and bring on board the internet service providers to design the content that attract the end-user customers" [2]. During the initial phase of development, Mr. Enoki and his team faced many objections from within NTT DoCoMo itself. However, rather than running away from conflicts, Mr. Enoki persuaded NTT that providing mobile internet (i-mode) was a viable idea. Having convinced NTT DoCoMo leaders, GBD carefully structured strategies that contributed to the explosive growth of i-mode.[6]

The first strategy is a "portal strategy", which involved developing new, useful content for the i-mode service. The second strategy, "terminal strategy", aimed to develop new i-mode-compatible mobile phone terminals or handsets with the add-on features. The last strategy, "platform strategy", aimed to develop i-mode-compatible platforms other than mobile phones. These strategies proved to be the "secret ingredient" for the phenomenal growth in the i-mode subscriber base. For example, having the "portal strategy" in mind, NTT DoCoMo opted for partnerships instead of rental relationships with Internet Service Providers (ISPs). This meant that NTT DoCoMo worked with the ISPs to provide good-quality web contents. By doing so, NTT DoCoMo shared the risks and profits with the ISPs. In addition, NTT DoCoMo adopted a win-win billing system in which NTT DoCoMo takes a 9% commission out of the service charges from the websites offered in i-mode. This gives the Internet

Content Providers (ICPs) the incentives to create better content, which in turn benefit end-users, i.e., i-mode subscribers.[9]

NTT DoCoMo's "internet way of thinking" also contributed to i-mode's success. Unlike the mobile phone companies in Europe, which provided the Wireless Application Protocol (WAP) technology, NTT DoCoMo chose internet technology for its mobile internet service. This meant that websites found in the i-mode service came in c-HTML format, a compressed version of the predominant internet language, Hypertext Markup Language (HTML). This is in contrast to the WAP technology, which requires websites to be written in Wireless Markup Language (WML). The fact that i-mode adopts the c-HTML format allow ICPs to quickly convert their existing websites on the World Wide Web to the c-HTML format for i-mode users by minor programming changes. Hence, i-mode customers get to enjoy a wide variety of choices of over 100,000 websites that were made available by NTT DoCoMo.[6]

Another reason for i-mode's success is its revolutionary billing system. Unlike most other internet services that charges users based on the amount of time they are connected to the internet, NTT DoCoMo applied the DoPa billing system that charges data communications in packets. This means that i-mode users are charged according to the volume of data they sent or received and not on the amount of time they spent on the internet. This billing system was adopted from the America Online (AOL) pricing model. Under this billing system, i-mode subscribers are not charged for the time taken to compose e-mail messages, i.e., they can take ten minutes or two hours to write an e-mail without being penalized for being connected to the internet. Rather, the customers are billed according to the length (or volume) of the e-mail sent. In this respect, the packet billing system creates an incentive for i-mode users.[6]

The third reason for i-mode's success was NTT DoCoMo's clever marketing strategy. NTT DoCoMo kept the expectations for i-mode service low by purposely eliminating the terms "internet" or "web" during i-mode promotional campaigns for two reasons. The first was to differentiate the service from web and WAP services across the world. The second was to position i-mode as "a simple, usable and fun-to-use service" [5]. In addition, during the initial launch of i-mode service, i-mode was first marketed to teenagers and young users. This was because the company realized that there was greater penetration of mobile phone users among youths of age 25 years and below. The group of people tended to be more attracted to value-added contents such as e-mails and video games. These teenagers and young people later went on as catalysts in spreading i-mode compatible phones to the mainstream market.[4]

One of the biggest factors that contribute to i-mode's success is Japan's low PC penetration and high mobile phone penetration rate. The fact that there was still low PC penetration in Japan in early 1999 worked towards NTT DoCoMo's i-mode advantage. i-mode service, in turn, offers the advantage of providing "always-on" mobile internet service in which users are connected anywhere, anytime. Another important factor for the success of i-mode was the development of easy-to-use, well-designed i-mode compatible handsets — "terminal strategy". Without these handsets, i-mode would probably not become so popular so quickly. In conjunction to the launch of the i-mode service, NTT DoCoMo released new phone models that had larger screens and one button specially dedicated for i-mode. These new phone models allowed users to quickly access i-mode by pressing a single button. This attractive, user-friendliness of handsets contributed greatly to users' satisfaction. Finally, the rapid uptake of i-mode technology could also be attributed to NTT DoCoMo's strong brand name. NTT DoCoMo's affiliations with NTT, which used to be Japan's monopoly telecommunication service provider, provided NTT DoCoMo with the infrastructure to provide the i-mode network. It also gave NTT DoCoMo a strong brand position within Japan.[9]

Following the launch of i-mode by NTT DoCoMo in February 1999, other mobile operators also began offering mobile internet services later in the same year; KDDI group launched EZweb (based on the WAP protocol) while J-Phone group launched J-sky. Despite the fierce competition from KDDI and J-Phone, NTT DoCoMo's i-mode remained the most popular among the three mobile internet systems and the company obtained the lion's share of the mobile phone market. i-mode subscribers grew from four million in February 2000 to 20 million in March 2001, and then to 30 million in December 2001 and finally to 40.5 million in March 2004. This was 59.3% of all cellular subscriptions in Japan. The growth of i-mode was so huge that NTT DoCoMo suffered 16 disruptions in its i-mode service by April 2000.[2]

NTT DOCOMO'S GLOBAL EXPANSION DRIVE

With i-mode's success, NTT DoCoMo went on to take a first shot for global expansion in the form of investments in foreign carriers such as Hutchison Telecom, AT&T Wireless, KPN and KTF in 1999 (please refer to Exhibit 2 for the list of NTT DoCoMo's key acquisitions in 2000). In the words of IDO Corp. Senior Adviser, Takeo Tsukada remarked that, "DoCoMo is like a huge sumo wrestler overpowering the market. There is nowhere left for it to go but overseas". Beginning in 1999, NTT DoCoMo was aggressively involved in a drive for overseas expansion. The company soon found itself in a host of problems for this global expansion drive.[2]

NTT DoCoMo's global expansion drive began by introducing the company's highly successful mobile internet service i-mode to foreign markets in places such as Europe and Hong Kong in 2001. However, given the different peculiarities of foreign markets, the adoption rate of the i-mode service in foreign markets was poor. This could be due to non-existing infrastructure that led to NTT DoCoMo's portal, terminal, and platform strategies not being applicable to foreign markets. For one, i-mode could not succeed due to its incompatibility with the digital transmission standard used worldwide (the global system for mobile communications (GSM) system compared to Japan's CDMA system). In addition, the necessary infrastructure for i-mode transmission may also be absent in foreign markets such as the American and European markets.[2]

Second, few i-mode compatible mobile phones or terminals were made available to the overseas market. The western cellular phone market was also less developed than the Japanese mobile phone market. Users in the western market, for example, were less prone to paying for value-added services such as mobile internet since PC penetration rate was much higher in the western market. It was even harder to convince foreign customers to purchase i-mode compatible, made-in-Japan handsets since they were already used to strong mobile phone brands such as Nokia or Sony Ericsson.[6]

NTT DoCoMo completed the acquisition of a 16% stake in AT&T, the United States of America's leading mobile phone service provider, in January 2001. This was, by far, the company's biggest overseas investment. However, in early 2001, wireless stocks were plummeting across the world. Due to its poor performance in overseas investments, NTT DoCoMo had to write-off the value of its various other investments during early 2002. By May 2002, NTT DoCoMo recorded a net loss of 116.19 billion yen and a goodwill write-off of 624.6 billion yen for the fiscal year ending March 2002. This was one of the biggest corporate losses in Japan (Exhibit 3). In addition, NTT DoCoMo's management had to face the wrath of its shareholders in July 2002. NTT DoCoMo reacted by announcing that its management would shoulder the burden of the losses, starting with the cutting of salaries of its top executives by 10–20% for a year.[2]

Despite the little success in global expansion, NTT DoCoMo continues to invest in overseas wireless services. While investments in some foreign markets might show little hopes in establishing the company as a regional mobile phone service provider, NTT DoCoMo continue to suffer losses from its foreign investments. In 2003, NTT DoCoMo had to refuse its partner, KPN Mobile and Hutchison's request to pump in more capitals to help relieve their financial crisis. And in November 2007, NTT DoCoMo had to liquidate its French unit.[10]

MOVING FORWARD: 3G TECHNOLOGY

NTT DoCoMo felt a need to create new revolutionary technology to maintain its market leader position in Japan's cellular phone market. In early 2001, the company announced the development of "Freedom of Mobile Multimedia Access (FOMA)", a 3G service that provides video calls and faster-speed music and video downloads. FOMA was scheduled to be launched in May 2001. With this launch, NTT DoCoMo planned to re-enter the global arena with its 3G service. As an analyst, Mitsuyama Nahoko pointed out that "3G is offering DoCoMo the first global stage that Japan can enter. The company's international thrust could act as a wedge, forcing open new markets for its parent NTT as well as for Japanese cell phone manufacturers like Sony and Matsushita, which have done well domestically but have struggled to gain ground abroad against Nokia and Ericsson".[2]

However, even within the home Japanese market itself, FOMA was not doing well. NTT DoCoMo was experiencing a lot of problems launching FOMA. The initial launch date of May 2001 had to be postponed by six months. While NTT DoCoMo spokesperson claimed that this delay was necessary for the company to conduct further testing to ensure that technical problems and service disruption would not occur again, such as that of the i-mode case. Analysts, however, pointed out that the reason behind the postponement of service was due to NTT DoCoMo experiencing some technical problems with its 3G networks, and that it had bought time to rectify those mistakes. Nevertheless, the FOMA service was still provided to a small group of people involved in the trial phase.[2]

Unlike the marketing strategy NTT DoCoMo employed for its i-mode service, the company opted for a high profile promotional drive for its 3G FOMA service. However, the postponement of the 3G FOMA service proved to be disadvantageous for NTT DoCoMo. By June 2001, there were reports that the initial enthusiasm over the 3G technology was dying down across the world. Investors began losing interest in 3G services and stocks of companies foraying into 3G services fell drastically. Adding to the problems, NTT DoCoMo faced severe criticisms from its customers who were provided with FOMA services as a part of the trial. This was mainly because the initial 3G FOMA-enabled DoCoMo phones developed had very short battery life, and crashed easily. There was also limited network coverage at the time of launch. In addition, the value-added function, the videophone function, was not as good as they were promised to be. Apart from this, many customers complained of hackers manipulating FOMA-enabled phones. It was reported that during the trial phase, a customer would get an email attachment, which caused the phone to automatically call another phone number, and then forward the email to other mobile users. On account of such complaints, DoCoMo was forced to recall over 1,500 FOMA-enabled handsets in late June 2001.[2]

Although NTT DoCoMo was the first to introduce the 3G service in Japan, it was unable to reap first-mover advantage. In April 2002, KDDI launched its version of 3G service CDMA 2000 1x. Though slower than FOMA, it gained more than one million subscribers in the first three months. The reason why KDDI's 3G service was more popular than NTT DoCoMo's was because its technology upgrade was in sync with technology standards worldwide and did not require rebuilding of a whole system, as required by FOMA or i-mode. In November 2003, KDDI went on to introduce its packet service CDMA 2000 1x ED-VO service under the brand name "WIN". In line with its name, this service was extremely popular because it enhanced delivery times for its traditional mobile internet services. KDDI's subscriber base grew rapidly after its introduction of 3G services and the company now boasts the largest 3G penetration (almost 90% of its subscribers are 3G subscribers) in Japan. KDDI has since continued to provide enhanced services such as the EZ flat, a flat-rate billing system which allow users to have unlimited access to EZweb services for a fixed monthly rate of 4,200 yen. This was the first flat-rate billing system introduced in Japan. The third leading mobile phone operator in Japan, J-Phone, also introduced its 3G service IMT-2000 in June 2002 and proved successful in the market.[2]

Despite NTT DoCoMo's efforts to resolve technical errors with the 3G network, FOMA had yet to make profits even in late 2002, while competitors KDDI and J-phone's 3G services were doing rather well. In fact, the growth of FOMA subscribers was not observed till early 2004. To attract subscribers, NTT DoCoMo had to offer heavy discounts on FOMA handsets and services.

During this period, the company also began offering free global roaming to its FOMA customers to retain its existing customers and to lure new customers. According to the company sources, such discounts and free offerings took a heavy toll on the company's revenues.[11]

To add on to NTT DoCoMo's problems, the company faced difficulties in convincing its partner wireless companies in other countries to adopt its technology. Reportedly, its partners were reluctant to spend huge amounts in upgrading their wireless networks as they feared that DoCoMo's products and services might not attract as many customers in their countries as expected. The main reason for foreign customers' lack of interests in 3G technology was the need to purchase costly 3G-enabled handsets just to have faster service and to view pictures and videos. More than a year after FOMA was launched, NTT DoCoMo decided to focus on increasing profits by reducing its promotional expenditure on 3G services. The company began focusing on offering better phones with good battery life and on enhancing the quality of its content through better content partnerships. In addition, it also provided affordable subscription packages for FOMA users. With these improvements, NTT DoCoMo began seeing the rise in the number of FOMA subscribers. Nevertheless, the number of FOMA subscribers was still below the targeted number of the fiscal year 2002–2003. By April 2003, NTT DoCoMo was reported to be bouncing back to profitability on account of its successful launches of a new FOMA-enabled handset that had a rotating liquid crystal screen and a good battery life of over 250 hours.[2]

Almost at the same time, NTT DoCoMo attempted to focus once again on providing value-added services for its 2G technology after experiencing sticky problems with its 3G technology. This "return to 'basics'" strategy helped NTT DoCoMo to regain its position as one of Japan's most profitable companies. Some of the examples of value-added 2G services provided during this period were "wrist-watch with phone" and the 2G camera phones (collaboration project with Sony, Sharp, Fujitsu and Mitsubishi), which offer a fingerprint-authentication feature.[2]

However, despite turning the company back to a profitable position, NTT DoCoMo was not free of problems. In April 2003, the Japanese Government passed the Local Taxes Amendment Law, which removed a loophole in the accounting rules. With this rule in place, NTT DoCoMo continued to record a drop in its profits for the fiscal year 2002–2003.[2]

The close-to-saturation Japan's wireless phone market was also posing a severe threat to the company's growth. This was made worse by the introduction of the mobile number portability (MNP) system, which is a system that allows customers to switch mobile phone operators while retaining the number used with their previous operator. This intensified the competition among the mobile phone operators in the already-saturated market.

THE MOBILE NUMBER PORTABILITY (MNP) SYSTEM AND A PRICE BATTLE

The mobile number portability (MNP) system in Japan was implemented on October 24, 2006. Under this system, mobile phone subscribers are able to change cellular phone carriers without changing their phone numbers. However, mobile e-mail addresses are still subject to change.

The introduction of the MNP system came as a result of a study done on MNP by the Ministry of Internal Affairs and Communications (MIC) in June 2002. Based on the results of the research, MIC conducted a workshop on number portability rules for mobile phone service in late 2003. The workshop suggested implementing the MNP system in Japan in the fiscal year 2006 so as to increase customers' convenience as well as to promote competition among mobile phone carriers. On May 28, 2004, the MIC announced guidelines concerning MNP introduction in October 2006. This gave all mobile phone service providers two years to prepare for the MNP system.[1] Since its introduction, MNP has intensified competition among the cellular phone operators. In the words of NTT DoCoMo senior vice president, Bunya Kumagai, "Introduction of MNP will undoubtedly enhance customer convenience by allowing customers to change operators without changing their mobile phone numbers. On the other hand, mobile operators will more than ever be put to the test to demonstrate the overall appeal of their services. However, we believe that this test is a good opportunity to review our services from the customer's viewpoint and to further cellular phone market".[11]

Mobile phone competitors started preparing for the MNP through providing more attractive packages and offering more value-added services, mostly focusing on lifestyle infrastructure services. One month before the implementation of the MNP system, KDDI announced on August 9, 2006 that a service fee of 5000 yen (USD 45.62)[153] will be charged to its existing customers who switched to other carriers under the MNP system. This was KDDI's measure to deter its customers from switching to rival carriers. KDDI also worked to enhance its "Complete Music Download" or the *Chaku-Uta* (literally translated as having songs everywhere) service.[7]

NTT DoCoMo's solution to reducing customer abandonment rate was to provide customer-oriented billing plans, enhance FOMA services, and offer packet flat rate plan applications for FOMA-i-mode users. It also emphasizes on the loss of members preferential service "DoCoMo Premier Club" membership points for current NTT DoCoMo subscribers should they switch carriers. The membership points entitle NTT DoCoMo customers loyalty discounts for services offered by the carrier. NTT DoCoMo also worked to improve its lifestyle infrastructure services, especially the *osaifu keitai* or wallet-in-cellular phone service. *Osaifu Keitai* allows users to have the convenience of installing credit cards (DCMX) or train ticket passes (Mobile Suica) into their mobile handsets. It was developed by NTT DoCoMo as a pressing need to create a new revenue model in the nearly saturated cellular phone market.[11]

Faced with stiff competitions from its rivals, NTT DoCoMo developed similar packages to that of its rivals. For example,

---

[153] As of 2008 January 10, exchange rate: 109.6003 yen = 1 USD.

KDDI's enhancement in its *Chaku-Uta* (music download) service spurred NTT DoCoMo to provide flat-rate music download service with its 903 series terminals. However, despite efforts to retain its customers, NTT DoCoMo suffered from a loss of market share as customers defected to rivals, including KDDI and Softbank Mobile (see Fig. 1).[11]

Softbank Mobile was the most aggressive in attracting new customers as it sees the MNP as an opportunity to increase its market share. It began offering packages at rock-bottom prices, a move that led KDDI and NTT DoCoMo to halve their package prices. Softbank also added new services such as "push to talk" and full browser services in order to catch up with its rivals in service enhancement.[8] It also began an aggressive marketing campaign, hiring Hollywood celebrities such as Cameron Diaz and Brad Pitt as ambassadors to the company. Softbank's aggressive low-cost price plans and marketing blitz paid off as the company was reported to have won its two rivals in attracting more subscribers for seven consecutive months.[12]

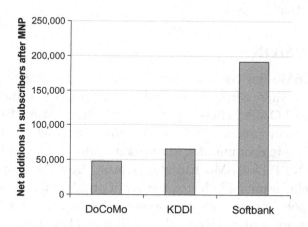

Figure 1. According to data released by the Telecommunications Carriers Association, Softbank Mobile added a net 191,600 subscribers in November, while KDDI gained a net 65,400 subscribers with its 'au' and 'tu-ka' services. On other hand, NTT DoCoMo added a net 48,200 subscribers. [As of September 2007].

Table 1.

	Average amount spent per month by each customer (in yen) as of September 2007
Softbank	4,800
KDDI	6,400
DoCoMo	6,550

In response to the MNP system, NTT DoCoMo and KDDI added new plans that eliminated rebates on new handsets but charged lower calling rates. The wide variety of plans offered might have appeared too complex to customers, who apparently preferred a Softbank Mobile plan with a monthly base fee of just 980 yen (see Table 1).[12]

Ever since the MNP system was implemented, NTT DoCoMo suffered a reduction in the mobile phone market share (6% decrease since its peak at 60% in 2001) and a profit plunge of 21% as users defected to rivals including KDDI and Softbank Mobile. NTT DoCoMo had predicted that the loss in the number of subscribers would eventually cease.

CONCLUSION

NTT DoCoMo has come a long way since its privatization in April 1985. It has successfully innovated revolutionary products such as i-mode and FOMA. These products had since changed the global mobile telecommunication market dynamics drastically. Indeed, NTT DoCoMo is a telecommunication market leader in Japan.

While NTT DoCoMo had always been the "flag bearer" of the Japanese cellular phone industry, it was not problem-free. For example, its initial global expansion drive showed little success. Its 3G service FOMA was not well-received either until much later (three years after its launch). Last but not least, the implementation of the mobile number portability system caused many of its customers to defect to rival companies, which offered cheaper price plans. It is highly likely that NTT DoCoMo will continue to face stiff competitions from rival companies locally and globally.

Today, the telecommunication market is becoming more and more saturated. Mobile phone service providers are pressed to generate new revenue models in a highly undifferentiated cellular phone market. It remains to be seen what NTT DoCoMo would come up with next to maintain its market leader position.

QUESTIONS

1) What are the particularities of the Japanese mobile phone market?
2) How do Japanese mobile users differ from users in other markets?
3) How can NTT DoCoMo defend and strengthen its dominant position?
4) Which strategies should the company develop for further growth?
5) How did the latest developments in the mobile industry affect NTT DoCoMo?

BIBLIOGRAPHY

1. InfoCom Research, Inc. (2007). Information & Communications in Japan 2007.
2. Radhika, AN (2003). DoCoMo — The Japanese wireless telecom leader. *ICMR Case Collection*, 1–19.
3. Middleton, J (2001). DoCoMo deluged by 3G customer complaints. *IT Week*.
4. Srivasta, L (2004). Shaping the future mobile information society: The case of Japan. *ITU/MIC Workshop*, 1–59.
5. NTT DoCoMo. http://en.wikipedia.org/wiki/NTT_DoCoMo.
6. Krishnamurthy, S (2001). NTT DoCoMo's i-mode phone: A case study, 1–40.
7. KDDI Corp. official website. www.kddi.com.
8. Softbank Mobile Corp. official website. http://www.softbankmobile.co.jp/corporate/en/index.html.
9. Kodama, M (2003). Strategic community-based theory of firms: Case study of NTT DoCoMo. *Pergamon*.
10. NTT DoCoMo announces liquidation of French subsidiary and establishment of representative office in Paris (November 2007). *NTT DoCoMo Press Release Article*.

11. Annual report 2006: The mobile phone as the key to daily life. NTT DoCoMo, 1–116.
12. Negishi, M. Japan's Softbank beats rivals in Nov (7 December 2007). *Reuters.*

APPENDIX 1: LIST OF SOME OF THE KEY ACQUISITIONS OF NTT DOCOMO DURING ITS FIRST GLOBAL EXPANSION DRIVE

- **Hutchison Whampoa — Hong Kong**
  In December 1999, DoCoMo acquired a 19% stake and in May 2000, Hong Kong became the second place in the world where i-mode is available.

- **Dutch KPN Mobile — Europe**
  In May 2000, NTT DoCoMo bought a 15% stake and they will be setting up Europe's first i-mode service.

- **Telecom Italia Mobile (TIM) — Italy**
  TIM has had a joint alliance with NTT DoCoMo since 1997 (with no exchange of equity), exchanging engineers.

- **AT&T Wireless — United States**
  In November 2000, they bought a 20% stake for $9.8 billion and have their sites on establishing the first 3G i-mode networks here in 2003–2004.

- **SK Telekom — South Korea's biggest mobile provider**
  In July 2000, DoCoMo purchased a 10% stake for $3 billion.

- **KG Telecom — Taiwan**
  NTT DoCoMo has acquired a 20% stake in KG Telecom. The firms are to jointly provide wireless broadband services in Taiwan.

- **Tele Sudeste Celular Participacoes — Brazil**
  DoCoMo acquired a 7% stake in this Brazilian company.

Source: www.nttdocomo.com.

Xbox in the Land of the Rising Sun

Ali AL Dahmen

INTRODUCTION

Microsoft's game division has been in the headlines ever since its release of the Xbox video game system on 15 November, 2001.[154] The system was more powerful than its competition's, and it sported quite a few AAA titles. Facing competitors such as Nintendo and Sony, Microsoft was able to secure a second position in the *Console Wars* save for one market: Japan. Here the Xbox was trumped even by Nintendo's GameCube, whose sales were dismal outside of Japan.[155]

Eight years later, learning from its last home console successes and failures, Microsoft released a second console which has been extremely successful in North America and Europe. Somehow, it is still flailing in the Land of the Rising Sun. This time, Nintendo took the number one spot worldwide, with Microsoft and Sony trailing behind. Microsoft has made a bit of headway with hit games like Blue Dragon and Lost Odyssey, but it does not seem to be enough to keep the Xbox 360 afloat in Japan.[156]

---

[154] Xbox hardware: The complete history of Xbox, ComputerAndVideoGames.com.
[155] Charts Index, VGChartz.com.
[156] *Ibid.*

MICROSOFT — A SOFTWARE GIANT

Microsoft is a company that hardly needs introduction. Bill Gates founded the company with a single product, the Altair Basic. Since then, they have become large enough to be accused of monopolistic activities which resulted in an antitrust suit in America and Europe as well as class action lawsuits targeting various product lines (including the Xbox line).[157] The growth has been almost dumbfounding. Microsoft now offers the dominant home operating system, consumer electronics lines, licensing, support services, online tie-ins and a business division. Each product line has seen different levels of success, but with an annual income of $17.6 billion in 2008,[158] it is clear that things have changed since the 70s. The Microsoft Office and Windows products are company flagships although in recent years, they have seen competition from Apple as well as free products such as OpenOffice and Linux. Some critics point to poor design, while others see poor marketing as the cause for the loss of market share.[159] There is also a great deal of bad press swirling, especially when all of the security holes found in its software are taken into consideration.[160] Despite these concerns, Microsoft continues to be the market leader in the PC market, which is inline with Bill Gates' vision for the company: "Microsoft was founded based on my vision of a personal computer on every desk and in every home. We've never wavered from that vision".[161] But Microsoft is, and has always been, a technology company; thus it must move with innovation in order to compete. It is also not limited by its most popular products. In recent years, it has released its own smartphone (the Zune) to compete with Apple's iPhone, a search engine (Bing) to counter Google and the Xbox series to compete with Sony's Playstation. This is not, however,

---

[157] Antitrust settlement fact sheet; Consumer class action settlement information; EU slaps record fine on Microsoft, Tech News on ZDNet.

[158] MSFT annual report 2008.

[159] The Microsoft marketing myth, Columns by PC Magazine.

[160] Microsoft security holes hit record High, CBS News.

[161] Making Microsoft safe for capitalism, NYTimes.com

the beginning of Microsoft's involvement with the video game industry. That story begins in 1983.

FUN WITH GAMING

The story of Microsoft's experience in the video game industry begins in 1983[162] with a computer hardware standard called MSX (see Fig. 1). MSX was an initiative started by Microsoft as an attempt to create standards for computer hardware producers. That is, manufacturers would be able to make devices that could plug into computers and provide additional functionalities, not unlike the widespread USB standard that was invented later. The format was initially a success in Japan, but was not met as favorably in North America and Europe. Despite its somewhat mitigated success, the MSX gave Microsoft first-hand experience in creating development tools for a machine that could be used to run games. Development tools are very important in the video game console market because this set of software allows developers to program games or applications to fit the hardware.

Microsoft's first attempt at video game software was actually a collection called the Microsoft Entertainment Pack, first released in

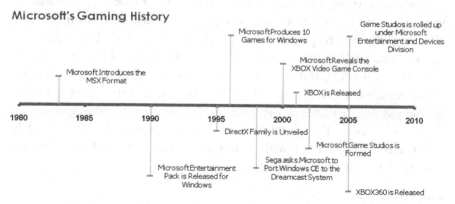

Figure 1. **A brief history of Microsoft's experience with *gaming*.**

---

[162] MSX history.

1990s.[163] The disk included thrilling titles such as Chess, Rodent's Revenge and Tetris. What made this pack unique is that it was designed to run on Windows only, as opposed to MS-DOS. This was seen by many as an early tie-in, encouraging consumers to switch to Windows. Over the years, Microsoft produced many more video games that ran on both MS-DOS and Windows, some of the best known being Microsoft Flight Simulator, Age of Empires and MechWarrior.

The next gaming-related activity undertaken by Microsoft coincided with the release of Windows '95.[164] This was the beginning of the DirectX family. DirectX allowed game developers to access the computer's hardware directly. This in turn would support better graphics and sound, or in short, a better gaming experience. This was seen as an attempt to create a media-rich operating system and attract more game developers. This attempt paid off and even led to an increased number of games produced by Microsoft; until this point, the company had only produced a handful of computer games. In 1996 alone, Microsoft produced ten video games for the Windows operating system.

Microsoft's continued to benefit from the DirectX platform for years to come. In 1998, the company was even approached by Sega who wanted to use a version of Windows on their video game console: the Sega Dreamcast.[165] Over the next two years, Microsoft worked closely with Sega to port Windows CE, and therefore DirectX, onto the Dreamcast. There were very few games produced for the console that used DirectX, but in the process, Microsoft gained invaluable experience with video game consoles. After a disagreement over the online gaming features of the Dreamcast, Microsoft and Sega discontinued relations. To the outside world, it seemed that Microsoft's short-lived involvement with video game consoles had come to an end; this was far from the truth.

---

[163] Microsoft entertainment pack for Windows for Windows 3.x, MobyGames.
[164] What is DirectX?, Developer.com.
[165] Inclusion of Windows CE operating system inclusion of Windows CE operating system.

INSIDE THE BIG BLACK BOX

In March 1999, Microsoft executives began discussing the potential for entering the video game industry.[166] In that same month, a team headed by Seamus Blackley sent a formal proposal to Bill Gates for the development of a video game console. By July of that year, the Xbox console received corporate approval. The team responsible for the launch, headed by Rick Thompson, was born.[167] The next couple of years would be spent on meeting with developers, designing the hardware, promoting the would-be console, and keeping a close eye on Sony. The world received it first glimpse of what was to come at the 2000 Game Developers Conference. Here, Bill Gates introduced the X-box (later changed to Xbox) as stronger and faster than others in the market. It also sported a number of powerful features, such as internet capabilities right out of the box. Initial reactions seemed neutral; the system was certainly powerful, but there were a limited number of games in development for the console.[168] From this point onward, Microsoft began working more closely with game developers, and in somewhat of a gamble, it purchased a small developer called Bungie. The biggest reason cited for the purchase was to acquire rights to Halo, a game that would later help lead XBox sales.[169]

THE XBOX — A LESSON IN FAILURE

15 November, 2001 saw the official launch of the Xbox in North America. Sony already had a 20-month lead by releasing the PS2 in March of 2000. This was a big concern for Microsoft, so the launch was seen as critical. Within a week, over 625,000[170] Xbox consoles had been sold in North America, almost double the number of Playstation 2 consoles sold during the same period. This was despite

---

[166] Microsoft explores a new territory: Fun, NYTimes.com.
[167] A brief history of the Xbox — Launch — Kotaku.
[168] Microsoft takes the mystery out of Xbox, CNET News.
[169] Microsoft buys Bungie in home gaming bid, CNN.com — Technology.
[170] Charts Index, VGChartz.com.

Table 1.   Current generation sales as of January 2010.

	Current Generation		
	Microsoft — Xbox 360	Sony — Playstation 3	Nintendo — Wii
Worldwide	37,510,285	32,173,905	66,392,161
Japan	1,244,201	4,683,737	9,799,610

Table 2.   6th generation lifetime sales.

	6th Generation		
	Microsoft — Xbox	Sony — Playstation 2	Nintendo — Gamecube
Worldwide	24,189,847	134,302,434	21,515,337
Japan	477,809	23,030,602	4,024,279

the high price tag ($299).[171] The launch appeared to be a success, but the battle was just beginning. Halo, the number one selling point for the console, was not a success in Japan. Consequently, it is no wonder that sales were so low for that region.

For the next five years, Microsoft would have to overcome fierce competition from Sony and Nintendo, and deal with issues in Japan. Despite its best efforts, Microsoft was only able to sell 477,809 units in Japan. This is compared to Sony's 23 million.[172] (Additional sales figures can be found in Tables 1 and 2 above). To say that the Xbox was a failure in Japan would be an understatement. The Xbox was discontinued in 2006, only months after Microsoft's next home console, the Xbox 360, was released.

GAMING IN JAPAN

The apparent failure in Japan left many at Microsoft Game Studios scratching their heads. How could the console that held up so well in

---

[171] Xbox hardware: The complete history of Xbox, ComputerAndVideoGames.com.
[172] Charts Index, VGChartz.com.

Europe and the Americas be such a blatant failure in Japan? This question would have to be answered and the problems addressed before the launch of their next console, the Xbox 360.

It appeared that whatever made the Xbox so successful in the West did not apply to the Japanese market. Even Halo, which received game of the year awards from more than a dozen publications, was not well received.[173] This revelation called for a close look at the gaming preferences of Japanese consumers.

The infinitely subjective nature of taste also applies to the video game industry: there exist clear regional preferences regarding gaming genres. In America, the most popular genres are sport, action, and shooting. Japanese tastes are quite different, with the highest selling segments being role-playing, puzzle, fighters, and adventure games.[174] Without high-quality games in these three categories, it seemed Microsoft would be hard-pressed to convince the Japanese market that the Xbox was worth their money.

Hironobu Sakaguchi, the creator of the Final Fantasy series, then entered. (Final Fantasy is a role-playing game series created in 1987 that has previously known tremendous success on previous Nintendo platforms). The brand included 13 titles considered part of the main series, two official movie releases, countless spinoffs, and lucrative merchandizing opportunities.[175] Sakaguchi had created the series when he was working for Square (now Square-Enix). Microsoft hired him to produce two games for the Xbox 360: Blue Dragon and Lost Odyssey.[176] The result? Microsoft released a version of the Xbox 360 that came bundled with Blue Dragon in 7 December, 2006 and all 10,000 units were sold out in a single day.[177] In the following December, Lost Odyssey sold 54,000 units upon release.[178] These

[173] Halo: Combat Evolved — Awards, Xbox.com.
[174] Methods to Market Mario.pdf.
[175] A complete history of Final Fantasy, MegaGames pc.
[176] Xbox 360 aspires to break Japan, BBC News — Technology.
[177] Xbox 360 blue dragon bundles sell out in Japan news.
[178] Wii fit top in Japan; Lost Odyssey sales solid, Videogame News, GAMER — The UK's Leading Videogames Resource.

are very impressive numbers, especially when considering the small number of Xbox 360s in Japan. Another headline that seemed promising was an agreement with Square Enix to release Final Fantasy 13 simultaneously with the Xbox 360 and PS3. Many Xbox owners were jubilant, since this would bring one of the all-time bestselling role-playing series to the Xbox. That promise was short-lived, however, when it was later learned that the Xbox 360 version would not be released in Japan.[179] What seemed like a promising start was cut short by Microsoft's inability to secure the series release on its system where it seemed most needed.

The release of the new system also allowed Microsoft to reconsider one area where they had received a great deal of criticism: design. In an article released by the Design Management Institute, Jonathan Hayes of the Xbox redesign team detailed the efforts made to conform to the Japanese market. The issue of design with the original Xbox was, in essence, a lack of design. Microsoft's Xbox was created to be the most powerful console at the time, using mostly non-proprietary components that were assembled very much like the inside of a normal PC. As a result, the console itself was large, clunky and arguably, ugly.[180] This might not have been a huge sticking point in the West, but Japan is a market where design counts. It did not help that Microsoft was going against electronics giant Sony, which has design down to an art. Incidentally, when it came to the controller, Microsoft did make a design decision directed at the Japanese market. While the rest of the world dealt with the large ("Duke") controller. This smaller controller was created for users with smaller hands, and eventually made its way to the United States.

Microsoft recognized design as an integral part of the brand, and an important element for success in Japan. Don Hall, brand director for the Xbox states that the "'Xbox1' was about proving that Microsoft could build a viable gaming platform; Xbox 360 is

---

[179] Final Fantasy XIII hits Japan, Xbox 360 News at GameSpot.
[180] Reconceptualizing the Xbox platform.pdf.

about doing it *right*".[181] As a result, the design team was completely reorganized, and five design teams from three continents were consulted — two were from Japan. The result was a much more appealing console and controller that did not sacrifice functionality.

Microsoft addressed two of its biggest criticisms for failure in Japan with the release of its new console, the Xbox 360. Now that it saw its internal weaknesses, it would have to consider its future in Japan, especially when faced with big names like Sony and Nintendo.

AN AMERICAN BRAND IN A FOREIGN LAND

Japan is the home of the home console (video game consoles), and has always held the most powerful players. Nintendo and Sony both hail from Japan, as does the once great Sega. The Playstation's dominance worldwide cannot be ignored, but in Japan, it is stifling. Nintendo should not be taken lightly either. While its sales have been on the decline in Japan, the Wii still has an install base of nearly nine million units. That is compared with Playstation 3's four million and the Xbox 360's 1.2 million.[182]

Microsoft, as a console producer, was a big unknown in Japan until the release of the XBOX console. However, its poor sales in Japan did little to put confidence in Japanese consumers or game producers. As Jonathan Hayes, design director for the Xbox puts it: "Think of someone from California considering a Japanese surfboard".[183] Japan is already home to the two largest video game powerhouses in the world, why would they put their faith (and money) into a foreign product that has failed to perform in the past? Disappointed customers, after all, are far more difficult to recruit than ignorant ones.

One effort on Microsoft's part is to match or beat Sony on price. Price cuts are frequent and usually fall in line with an announcement

---

[181] *Ibid.*

[182] Charts Index, VGChartz.com.

[183] Reconceptualizing the Xbox platform.pdf.

by Sony, or to promote a new "hit" game.[184] It has even released limited configurations of the Xbox 360 in Japan. Configurations of the console are differences in features as well as bundled accessories. In America, the most expensive version of the Xbox is the Elite 250 GB version, retailing for $399.[185] This version was not released in Japan. Instead, a cheaper version was introduced.

THE FUTURE

The future of the Xbox in Japan is still unclear. Consoles are still available from major online retailers in the country, but are disappearing from shops, even in major electronics hubs such as Akihabara. This points to a lack of confidence that Microsoft can or will do anything to turn around the consoles' current direction. There have been hints that the Japanese market is not essential to Microsoft's actual sales figures, but that it holds strategic importance.[186] There are even rumors that Microsoft has labeled Japan as a "lost cause" and may not release its next console in Japan.[187]

Then again, a new console release could be an opportunity to do Japan right. After all, Nintendo was able to turn its position around with a new release. During the last generation of consoles, it held a third place position overall (with the GameCube).[188] Picking a new

Table 3.   Size of the gaming market in Japan and North America.[189]

	Size of gaming market in $Bil
Japan	6.5
North America	21.33

---

[184] Microsoft cuts Japan price for Xbox.
[185] Announced, dated for Japan — Elite — Kotaku.
[186] Reconceptualizing the Xbox platform.pdf.
[187] Methods to Market Mario.pdf.
[188] N-Sider.com: Nintendo GameCube.
[189] Game consoles wars: Xbox 360 vs. PS3 vs. Wii; In 2009, Japanese game market shrinkage continued — Japan — Kotaku.

direction for its current console, the Wii, Nintendo was able to seize the number one position, with its competitors lagging far behind. Will Microsoft be able to replicate this success with the next generation of game consoles? Or is it doomed to fail in the Land of the Rising Sun?

QUESTIONS

1) Which aspects hindered Microsoft from being successful in Japan?
2) What should a successful strategy for the Japanese market look like?

BIBLIOGRAPHY

A brief history of the Xbox — Launch — Kotaku. http://kotaku.com/164683/a-brief-history-of-the-xbox.

A complete history of final fantasy — megaGames pc. http://www.megagames.com/news/html/pc/acompletehistoryoffinalfantasy.shtml.

Announced, dated for Japan — Elite — Kotaku. http://kotaku.com/275081/announced-dated-for-japan.

Antitrust settlement fact sheet. http://www.microsoft.com/presspass/legal/01-17-06AntitrustFS.mspx.

Charts Index on VGChartz.com. http://www.vgchartz.com/chartsindex.php.

Charts Index on VGChartz.com. http://www.vgchartz.com/chartsindex.php.

Consumer Class Action Settlement Information. http://www.microsoft.com/about/legal/consumersettlements/default.mspx.

EU slaps record fine on Microsoft. *ZDNet.*

Final fantasy XIII hits Japan (17 December). *Xbox 360 News at GameSpot.*

Game consoles wars: Xbox 360 vs. PS3 vs. Wii. http://www.wikinvest.com/concept/Game_Consoles_Wars:_Xbox_360_vs._PS3_vs._Wii.

Halo: Combat evolved — Awards. http://www.xbox.com/en-US/games/h/halo/awards.htm.

In 2009, Japanese game market shrinkage continued — Japan — Kotaku. http://kotaku.com/5440306/in-2009-japanese-game-market-shrinkage-continued.

Inclusion of Windows CE operating system. http://www.microsoft.com/presspass/press/1998/May98/Segagmpr.mspx.

Making Microsoft Safe for Capitalism — *NYTimes.com.*"

Methods to market mario. http://www.geoffreymcook.com/articles/methods_to_market_mario.pdf.

Microsoft cuts Japan price for Xbox. http://www.digitaltrends.com/gaming/microsoft-cuts-japan-price-for-xbox/.

Microsoft entertainment pack for Windows for Windows 3.x MobyGames. http://www.mobygames.com/game/microsoft-entertainment-pack-for-windows.

Microsoft explores a new territory: Fun *NYTimes.com.*

Microsoft security holes hit record high *CBS News.*

Microsoft takes the mystery out of Xbox — *CNET News.*

Microsoft buys Bungie in home gaming bid (22 June 2000). *CNN.*

MSFT annual report 2008. http://www.microsoft.com/msft/reports/ar08/10k_fr_inc.html.

MSX history. http://www.msx.org/MSX-history.Kazuhiko-Nishi-Tilburg-2001-lecture.articlepage4.html.

N-Sider.com: Nintendo GameCube. http://www.n-sider.com/hardware-view.php?hardwareid=11.

Reconceptualizing the Xbox Platform.pdf. http://www.dmi.org/dmi/html/members/05164HAY10.pdf.

The Microsoft marketing myth PC Magazine. http://www.pcmag.com/article2/0,2817,1754192,00.asp.

What is DirectX? Developer.com. http://www.developer.com/open/article.php/968461/What-is-DirectX.htm.

Wii fit top in Japan; lost odyssey sales solid GAMER — The UK's Leading Videogames Resource. http://www.gamer.tm/news.php?id=1871.

Xbox 360 blue dragon bundles sell out in Japan news. http://www.totalvideogames.com/Blue-Dragon/news/Xbox-360-Blue Dragon-Bundles-Sell-Out-In-Japan-10309.html.

Xbox hardware: The complete history of Xbox ComputerAnd VideoGames.com. http://www.computerandvideogames.com/article.php?id=131066.

Xbox 360 aspires to break Japan. *BBC News.*

Big Gulps and Big Business: Seven-Eleven Japan and the New Keiretsu

Paul Gaspari

INTRODUCTION

It was his first day in Tokyo as an English teacher. He had just gotten off a long flight from the U.S. and wanted nothing more than to arrive at his apartment and rest for the night. When he finally made it into the city, he realized his stomach was growling. He looked around the train station for a place to eat, and saw a familiar convenience store logo that beckoned him to enter.

When he entered the store, he was amazed at how different and yet familiar everything seemed. There were rows and rows of different kinds of bread, aisles stacked with household goods, and a huge variety of beverages in the refrigerated sections. Customers were being treated like royalty and everyone who walked in was greeted with a loud welcome from the store's staff. He grabbed a Japanese "bentou"-style lunchbox and went looking for a Slurpee or Big Gulp but could not find one. In their places were hi-tech copy machines, faxes, ATMs, and customers paying for their purchases with their own Seven Eleven credit cards.

After buying a self-contained meal inside a small plastic container, the English teacher walked outside the store. He stopped and noticed for the first time that along that very street was several other convenience stores. Suddenly, the teacher realized just how far he was from home.

A convenience store is, quite literally, a store that is meant to provide "convenience" to local residents within its vicinity. In America, parts of Asia and several countries in Europe, convenience stores act as places where customers can usually grab a quick snack, a magazine, and some daily household good. The history of the convenience store has its origins with the 7-Eleven chain of stores in the U.S. but has since evolved to include many different brands in different locations around the world. Each of these stores and the products they offer change depending on the country where they are located.

As familiar as the brand's logo may be to the English teacher and others who come from the U.S. to Japan, Seven-Eleven Japan is a much bigger enterprise than its American counterpart. Convenience stores in Japan, known as *conbini*, are designed to provide total customer convenience for the Japanese shopper. They are therefore tailored to easily meet most of the daily needs of their customers. In terms of convenience products, their product lines range from food, to magazines, stationary items, household daily needs, and even articles of clothing. The services that they offer include the payment of utility and healthcare bills, shipping, and purchase tickets for events.

The Japanese convenience store has become "... a part of local community life" and plays "... a vital role in Japanese society" (Betros, 2007). Estimates now say that more than 90% of Japanese citizens live just within a five-minute walk from a convenience store (McCaughn, 2007). They have even been designated as safety stations by the Japanese government to go to in the event of an emergency (Betros, 2007). In order to achieve this level of dependency with Japanese society, the convenience store has had to undergo several changes when it was brought to Japan over 30 years ago. However, its primary mission of providing convenience services to its patrons has never changed from the corporation's humble beginnings in the U.S.

7-ELEVEN: THEN AND NOW

Origins of the 7-Eleven Company

There are few brands in the U.S. as long-lasting as 7-Eleven (see Fig. 1). The original U.S. company that came to be known as Seven Eleven

Figure 1. The 7-Eleven brand logo.

Inc. was founded in 1927 in Dallas, Texas, as the Southland Ice Company. The concept of selling convenience items was originally proposed by John Jefferson Green, an employee of the Company. He approached his supervisor and one of Southland's founders, Joe C Thompson, with the idea of selling "convenience" food like milk and eggs from the back of one of the company's ice docks (Dubovoj).

This was at a time in the U.S. when refrigerators were sparse, car owners were few, and people generally went to sleep early at night. Those who lived outside the city in particular did not have too many shopping choices and were limited to moving about during daylight hours.

Once the crowds started gathering on a daily basis for Green's goods, the idea of selling more convenience products was embraced by the rest of the company. Stores were developed around Texas by Southland called "Tote'm Stores", named for a signature Native American totem pole placed in front of every store. The name also symbolized the fact that patrons could easily "tote" their goods back to their homes (Dubovoj, 2007).

In 1946, Southland officially began to call this brand of stores "7-Elevens", since many were now operating from 7 am to 11 pm every day of the week (Dubovoj, 2007). Southland was growing as a company through the success of its 7-Eleven stores. In 1963, Southland purchased 100 SpeeDee Marts (an early convenience store chain) and converted them to franchises of 7-Eleven. This exposed them to the "franchise" concept for the first time and they soon began selling 7-Eleven stores as franchises to others (Dubovoj, 2007). Stores

Figure 2.   The Slurpee and Big Gulp, two of 7-Eleven's most well-known original products in the United States.

began sprouting up outside the state of Texas and around the rest of the U.S.

Besides food items, 7-Eleven stores sell a variety of products such as magazines, coffee, tobacco, etc. They also developed original products such as the flavored crushed-ice drink called a Slurpee, and the Big Gulp, which is a one liter container filled with sodas (see Fig. 2).

In addition to its more than 7,100 locations in North America (United States and Canada), there are now over 31,400 7-Eleven stores in about 20 different territories (Exhibit 1). Its worldwide success, however, is nothing compared to the way that this convenience store business revolutionized Japan.

The "Japan-ization" of the Convenience Store

In 1973, Toshifumi Suzuki was a young executive of the Ito-Yokado Corporation in Japan. Ito-Yokado was a growing supermarket chain looking to branch into other industries. While in the U.S. to work out the details of a licensing agreement with Denny's, Mr. Suzuki stopped in a 7-Eleven store (Tanner, 1992). Impressed by the business model and realizing its potential in Japan (where many businessmen work long hours and could benefit from "convenience" stores), Suzuki brought the concept back to his country through an area licensing agreement with the Southland Corporation. This licensing

Country	Number of stores
United States	584 (directly operated by Seven-Eleven)
United States (Franchises and Licenses)	4800
Canada	457
Mexico	1180
Japan	12753
Australia	397
Sweden	191
Taiwan	4735
China (Hong Kong, Shenzhen, Guangzhou & Macau)	1680
Singapore	493
Philippines	469
Malaysia	1115
Norway	177
South Korea	2282
Thailand	5409
Denmark	126
Beijing, PRC	93
Shanghai, PRC	20
Indonesia	5

Source: 7-11 Around the World. Seven-Eleven Japan Co. Ltd. [1 January 2010]. http://corp.7-eleven.com/AboutUs/InternationalLicensing/tabid/115/Default.aspx.

Exhibit 1. Total number of 7-Eleven convenience stores worldwide (as of 2010).

agreement would allow Ito-Yokado to have complete control over the product in Japan while still using the 7-Eleven name and the U.S. company's organizational tools (Dubovoj, 2007). As a result, a new subsidiary company was established by Ito-Yokado for this venture; the name of the brand would be changed from "7-Eleven" to "Seven-Eleven Japan" (SEJ) with Suzuki as its head.

Suzuki quickly went to work adapting the brand to the Japanese market. He kept the company's familiar logo and storefront design but made some specific changes to better suit the Japanese market.

Figure 3.   Japanese *bentou* and *onigiri*.

Various Japanese-style meal services and other items would be offered within each store location. The Slurpee, an American stable, was tried for a limited time but was not successful and soon discontinued. In its place would be distinctly Japanese food like *bentou*, self-contained meals, and *onigiri*, which were balls of rice usually wrapped in seaweed (see Fig. 3).

In addition to making changes with the product offerings, Suzuki imported several of 7-Eleven's management tools and adapted them to his own needs. In 1982, he took 7-Eleven's original computer system primarily used for inventory control in the U.S. and turned it into an advanced point-of-sale (POS) stock monitoring system (Tanner, 1992). The system improved the speed of the checkout process and allowed each convenience store to record customer data such as the time and type of item purchased (Tanner, 1992).

Every item sold in the store was given a bar code that would convey this information. Cash registers would scan this information as well as profile the customer by age range and gender. All of this information would then be sent to computers at company headquarters and suppliers to be used in market research, product development, and inventory control (Exhibit 2). These databases were all linked together in order for SEJ to better target their customers for sales promotions and accurately predict the number of products sold in a store each day. By knowing the shopping habits of their customers for any given store, SEJ would be able to eliminate unsold stock and cut down on storage and shipping costs. This led to the development of a sophisticated "just-in-time" (JIT) model.

The JIT system works in conjunction with the POS system to make purchase orders. Inventory is grouped according to certain

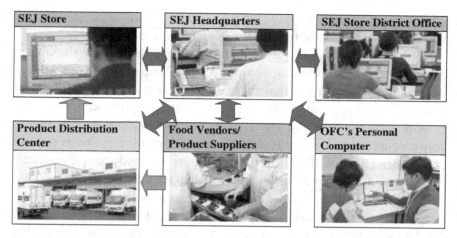

Source: Seven & i Holdings, Seven-Eleven Corporate Profile, p. 8–9, translated by Paul Gaspari.

All customers, products, promotional, and sales data are linked amongst several different sources. A store's computer sends sales information to SEJ Headquarters, which in turn passes that information to the Product Distribution Center and the Food Vendors/Product Suppliers.

Food Vendors/Product Suppliers send their freshly-made products and inventory to Product Distribution Centers, which are responsible for the shipping of items to SEJ store. Product Distribution Centers make several deliveries of fresh food and other inventory to several stores within a given territory.

SEJ Headquarters also sends sales and promotional data to a SEJ store's computer, Store District Offices in charge of multiple stores within a district, and the OFC's computer. The OFC and the regional Store District Office work together with SEJ store to maximize profits and find new ways to make the JIT inventory work more efficiently.

Exhibit 2.   Network of product and sales data.

periods within the day and shipped from warehouses according to their assigned period. Store managers must accurately predict what time and how much of a certain item will sell on a given day. They are able to make these predictions based on geographic data (retrieved from a store's cash registers) as well as weather reports sent directly to a store manager's computer. Any food not sold before its period expires and is discarded. According to SEJ, unsold food is trashed for a total of nine times per day (Betros, 2007). This is done in order to keep a high standard of freshness within each store.

Other products in the store include magazines, books, stationary, cosmetic goods, deodorant, shampoo, toilet paper, and even underwear. Convenience stores may carry dress shirts and ties to cater to the needs of the businessman who has stayed out all night and needs to be at work early the next day. The average number of items present in any convenience store is roughly 2,500 with about 100 new items on sale every week (Betros, 2007). Items are routinely introduced, tested, and discontinued in order to make additional room for new products.

Additional services at convenience stores in Japan include shipping and postal services, fax, photocopy, ATM machines, and even machines for tickets to concerts, movies, and theme parks. Stores also allow customers to pay for utility bills such as telephone, electricity, gas, and even health insurance.

In addition to product changes, land and store space posed a problem for SEJ. Land property in Japan is expensive ("Japan: Land Values Rise", 2007). In order to maximize space in the conveniences store, store layouts are strategically built to maximize total space. Display cases for food products in stores are sometimes mobile and can be moved during the day to adapt to the eating schedules of customers. For instance, when customers are on their way to work in the morning, more bread products are on shelves for breakfast. In the afternoon, the bread shelves can be moved to make room for additional refrigerated shelves with ice cream for people who want a snack after lunch.

By working with its "sister" companies within the Ito-Yokado group, SEJ developed a strong relationship with vendors and suppliers. Many of these vendors only produce products for SEJ and are shipped several times a day from warehouses in the suburbs to convenience stores around Japan.

In order to keep inventory and re-stocking costs low, SEJ employs an "area dominance strategy", which places several convenience stores all within the same area. These convenience stores interact with company headquarters through an operational field counselor (OFC). The OFC reports on the current situation of stores within his or her given territory to a regional store district office, which in turn relays that information to company headquarters (Exhibit 2). OFCs also attend weekly meetings at headquarters on special promotions and relay important information to the stores in their territory.

All of these adaptations to the brand brought almost immediate success to Ito-Yokado's new company. Seven-Eleven Japan convenience stores grew from just 15 in 1974 to over 12,700 in 2009 (Exhibit 3), thanks in part to a strong emphasis on franchise selling,

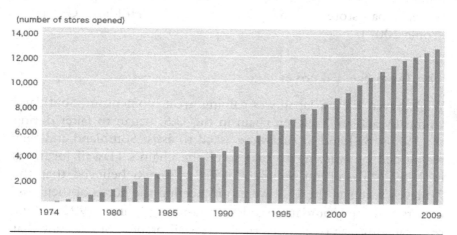

Year	Total stores	Year	Total stores	Year	Total stores
1974	15	1986	2,964	1998	7,732
1975	69	1987	3,304	1999	8,153
1976	199	1988	3,653	2000	8,602
1977	375	1989	3,954	2001	9,06
1978	591	1990	4,27	2002	9,69
1979	801	1991	4,629	2003	10,303
1980	1,04	1992	5,058	2004	10,826
1981	1,306	1993	5,475	2005	11,31
1982	1,643	1994	5,905	2006	11,735
1983	2,001	1995	6,373	2007	12,034
1984	2,299	1996	6,875	2008	12,298
1985	2,651	1997	7,314	2009	12,753

Source: Total Stores and Total Number of Stores. Seven & i Holdings [1 September 2010]. http://www.sej.co.jp/english/company/s_growth.html.

Exhibit 3.   SEJ store growth in Japan.

and also resulted in Suzuki's appointment as President of Ito-Yokado in 1992 (Tanner, 1992). Several of Suzuki's innovations, such as the POS stock monitoring system, were transferred to other groups within the Ito-Yokado Corporation. Suzuki had revolutionized Japan's retail sector and brought the franchising concept to the country ("Toshifumi Suzuki Profile"). Total store sales now exceed 2,700 billion yen from the country's many locations (Exhibit 4 and Exhibit 5). Currently, about 14 million customers shop at a Seven-Eleven Japan store on a daily basis (Seven & i Holdings Corporate Profile 2007).

The Japanese Takeover

While Seven-Eleven Japan was gaining great momentum, Southland Company and its 7-Eleven chain in the U.S. began to falter during the 1980s. SEJ and Suzuki were asked to assist Southland and they responded by offering to take over the chain's Hawaii locations in 1989 ("Toshifumi Suzuki Profile"). Suzuki believed that the 7-Eleven stores in the U.S. were not meeting the needs of their customers and using outdated modes of business (Tanner, 1992). While re-organizing the operations of the Hawaii branch, Suzuki saw that the amount of inventory present within each store was as much as three times the average of a store in Japan. Stores in Japan usually had a floor space of 100 square meters and had daily sales of 650,000 yen. In contrast, U.S. stores had about 170 square meters of floor space but daily sales of only 400,000 yen (Tanner). Hawaii stores were overhauled and given the company's complex POS system to combat the inventory problem.

By 1990, Southland's 7-11 U.S. convenience stores were rapidly losing money due to poor management and excess inventory. The company defaulted on $1.8 billion in publicly traded debt and had to file for bankruptcy (Dubovoj, 2007). At this point, Seven-Eleven Japan's parent company Ito-Yokado invested $430 million into the U.S. 7-Eleven chain. This investment gave Ito-Yokado a 70% stake in Southland and would allow them to make structural changes in order to improve profit margins ("Toshifumi Suzuki Profile"). In 1994, SEJ

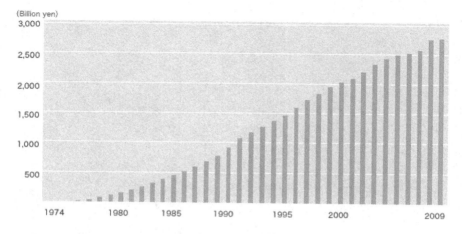

Year	Total sales	Year	Total sales	Year	Total sales
1974	0.7	1986	521.9	1998	1,848.1
1975	4,80	1987	599.1	1999	1,963.9
1976	17,40	1988	686.3	2000	2,046.6
1977	39.8	1989	780.3	2001	2,114.0
1978	72.5	1990	931.9	2002	2,213.2
1979	109.8	1991	1,081.8	2003	2,343.1
1980	153.6	1992	1,194.9	2004	2,440.8
1981	202.1	1993	1,281.9	2005	2,498.7
1982	256.5	1994	1,392.3	2006	2,533.5
1983	319.0	1995	1,477.1	2007	2,574.3
1984	386.7	1996	1,609.0	2008	2,762.5
1985	453.6	1997	1,740.9	2009	2,784.9

Source: Total Stores and Total Number of Stores. Seven & i Holdings [1 September 2010]. http://www.sej.co.jp/english/company/s_growth.html.

Exhibit 4. Total SEJ store sales in billion yen.

closed 1,180 stores, performed a massive remodeling effort, changed their merchandise mix, and did away with "insult pricing", or markups on each item that customers would have to pay in exchange for the convenience of shopping at the store (Tanner, 1992). Most importantly, SEJ transferred their POS system to the U.S. in order to better control each store's inventory levels.

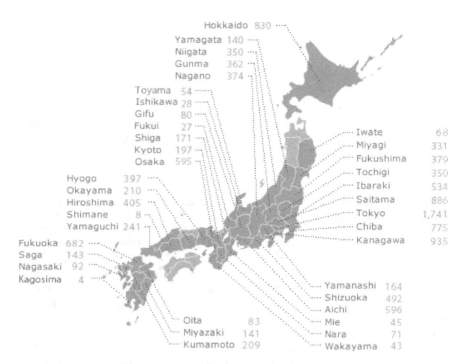

Geographical Store Expansion 13,233 stores

Hokkaido 830

Yamagata 140
Niigata 350
Gunma 362
Nagano 374

Toyama 54
Ishikawa 28
Gifu 80
Fukui 27
Shiga 171
Kyoto 197
Osaka 595

Hyogo 397
Okayama 210
Hiroshima 405
Shimane 8
Yamaguchi 241

Fukuoka 682
Saga 143
Nagasaki 92
Kagosima 4

Iwate 68
Miyagi 331
Fukushima 379
Tochigi 350
Ibaraki 534
Saitama 886
Tokyo 1,741
Chiba 775
Kanagawa 935

Yamanashi 164
Shizuoka 492
Aichi 596
Mie 45
Nara 71
Wakayama 43

Oita 83
Miyazaki 141
Kumamoto 209

Source: Number of Stores in each administrative division. Seven & i Holdings [1 September 2010]. http://www.sej.co.jp/company/en/n_stores.html.

Exhibit 5.   SEJ store locations in Japan.

After these changes, 7-Eleven stores in the United States were once again turning a profit. The Southland Corporation, with its newfound success, decided in 1999 to change its name to 7-Eleven, Inc. SEJ would continue to play a larger and larger role in the U.S. 7-Eleven until 2005, when it purchased the remaining stock, thereby becoming the sole owner, and set its sights on making the brand as important to Americans as it is to the Japanese.

SEJ's growth is no accident. The company originally utilized the resources of its parent, Ito-Yokado, to transform a store of convenience in the U.S. into a necessary part of daily Japanese life — the *conbini*. In turn, the SEJ Company experienced unprecedented growth. This ultimately resulted in the business group's name being changed from the Ito-Yokado Corporation to Seven & i Holdings. In order to understand the connection between SEJ's growth and its existence as a subsidiary company, one must first take a look at the history of doing business in Japan.

THE CORPORATE ENVIRONMENT OF JAPAN AND THE KEIRETSU BUSINESS SYSTEM

Much like other Japanese companies, Seven-Eleven Japan had originally belonged to a parent company, the Ito-Yokado Corporation. SEJ's success led to the success of the whole Ito-Yokado Group. Over the years, the Group went on to purchase other businesses in a variety of industries. A complete timeline of the Ito-Yokado Group and Seven & i Holdings is in Exhibit 6.

Month	Year	Event
Apr.	1958	Yokado Co. Ltd. was incorporated.
Mar.	1971	Company name was changed to Ito-Yokado Co. Ltd.
Sept.	1972	Ito-Yokado was listed on the Tokyo Stock Exchange (TSE), second section.
Mar.	1973	Business tie-up with York-Benimaru Co. Ltd.
July	1973	Ito-Yokado moved to the first section of the TSE.
Nov.	1973	York-Seven Co. Ltd. was established under a license agreement with the largest U.S. convenience store chain operator, The Southland Corporation.
Nov.	1973	Denny's Japan Co. Ltd. was established under a license agreement with the US-based restaurant chain, Denny's Inc.
July	1977	Ito-Yokado registered American Depositary Receipts (ADRs) on NASDAQ.
Jan.	1978	York-Seven name was changed to Seven-Eleven Japan Co. Ltd.

Exhibit 6.   Timeline of the Ito-Yokado Group/Seven & i Holdings Group.

Month	Year	Event
Aug.	1981	Seven-Eleven Japan was listed on the first section of the TSE.
Aug.	1984	York-Benimaru was listed on the first section of the TSE.
July	1986	Ito-Yokado's ADRs were transferred from NASDAQ small-cap listing to the National Market System.
Aug.	1986	Denny's Japan was listed on the first section of the TSE.
Mar.	1991	Through IYG Holding Company, Seven-Eleven Japan and Ito-Yokado acquired major interest of The Southland Corporation.
Dec.	1996	Chengdu Ito-Yokado Co. Ltd. was established in Chengdu, Sichuan, China.
Sept.	1997	Hua Tang Yokado Commercial Co. Ltd. was established in Beijing, China.
Apr.	1999	The Southland Corporation name was changed to 7-Eleven Inc.
July	2000	7-Eleven Inc. shares were transferred from NASDAQ to NYSE.
Apr.	2001	IYBank Co. Ltd. was established.
Oct.	2001	IY Card Service Co. Ltd. was established.
May	2003	Ito-Yokado abolished the registration of ADRs on NASDAQ.
Jan.	2004	Seven-Eleven (Beijing) Co. Ltd. was established in Beijing, China.
Nov.	2004	Beijing Wang fu jing Yokado Commercial Co. Ltd. was established in Beijing, China.
Sept.	2005	Seven & i Holdings Co. Ltd. was established and listed on TSE, first section.
Oct.	2005	IYBank name was changed to Seven Bank Ltd.
Nov.	2005	7-Eleven Inc. was converted into a wholly-owned subsidiary.
June	2006	Millennium Retailing Inc. became a wholly-owned subsidiary through a stock-for-stock exchange.
July	2006	Cancelled 427,509,908 shares of treasury stock.
Sept.	2006	York-Benimaru became a wholly-owned subsidiary through a stock-for-stock exchange.
Jan.	2007	Seven & i Food Systems Co. Ltd. was established.
Mar.	2007	The Loft Co. Ltd. became a subsidiary.
June	2007	Seven Cash Works Co. Ltd. was established.

Source: Seven & i Holdings Corporate Outline.

Exhibit 6.   (*Continued*).

Mergers and acquisitions are very common in Japan as several large companies control many different industries. Companies utilize their relationships with other firms to prosper in the market. This is seen in the concept of the *keiretsu* (meaning a "line of connections"), a special type of business group existing primarily in Japan.

For several centuries, the nature of one's relationships to others has been an important aspect of Japanese society. Relationships and personal connections are highly valued. Even the Japanese language is structured around one's relationship to others. This connection between others and the networks that one forges are of particular importance in Japan's business world.

Following the end of the Tokugawa Shogunate, which ruled Japan for roughly three centuries, the Meiji Restoration (1868) began a new era of modernization and commerce for the island nation. Relationships would play a key role in the development of the country's industries. Businesses worked closely together and as companies formed, they would buy stock into one another.

By World War I, several *zaibatsu* companies controlled many of Japan's industries. The *zaibatsu* were large, family-owned companies that were vertically integrated and revolved around a financing bank. These large companies wielded a great deal of economic and political power, utilizing their connections with one another and their ties to various banks to further their common goals. It was not until the U.S. Occupation following World War II (1945–1952) that the *zaibatsu* system was ultimately dissolved.

After the dissolution of the *zaibatsu* system, the *keiretsu* system of holding companies emerged in its wake. Scholars describe a *keiretsu* as the "ultimate form of teamwork" (Herbig). Unlike the *zaibatsu* organizations which were structured around family relationships, the *keiretsu* revolved mostly around shares of stock and the company's relationships to financing banks (Melville, 1999). Several companies exist within any given *keiretsu* group, all of which are connected to one another through horizontal and vertical cooperation. This relationship brings about a coordinated effort to increase the growth of the principal company and namesake of the *keiretsu* group. These companies can access the resources and capital of the entire group as well as the banks associated with them in order to undergo long-term research and development (Herbig). The *keiretsu*, much like its *zaibatsu* predecessor in the late 19th century, was instrumental in Japan's modernization and growth in the years following World War II.

Two types of *keiretsu* exist: a vertical *keiretsu* where one controlling company receives supplies from and has direct say over the smaller companies in the group in a pyramid-like, top-down structure; and a horizontal *keiretsu*, where company integration is across various industries with a bank providing financial support ("Keiretsu") (see Table 1). *Keiretsu* firms would play an important role during Japan's economic growth in the years after World War II up until the early 1990s when Japan's "bubble economy" began to implode.

Keiretsu are often considered to be a barrier to free trade by some Western companies. Some critics point to the fact that many *keiretsu*, and Japanese companies in general, partake in a practice of buying large shares of each other's stock, a practice known as cross-shareholding (Miller 16). This was done following World War II as a way of keeping foreign direct investment out of Japan. Larger Japanese companies would support weaker ones financially rather than risk being bought out by foreign firms. This helped give foreigners the impression that Japan was very much a closed society with tight networks that were nearly impossible to breach into.

Critics felt that the *keiretsu* created entry barriers by engaging in anti-competitive practices (Herbig). Japanese firms in a *keiretsu*

Table 1. The two types of keiretsu: horizontal and vertical.

Horizontal Keiretsu (*kinyuu keiretsu*)
Affiliated 'brother and sister' companies spanning different industries.

Vertical Keiretsu

Manufacturing Keiretsu (sangyou keiretsu). Assembled parts move up to the 'parent' through a pyramid of supply companies.	*Distribution Keiretsu (ryuutsuu keiretsu).* The 'parent' sends finished goods down through a pyramid of distributors to retailers.

Source: Melville, Ian. Marketing in Japan: 12.

procure bids from one another within the group. Some critics of the *keiretsu* refer to Article 23 of the General Agreement on Tariffs and Trade (GATT), which stipulates that all countries must provide the same access and benefits to foreign firms in its country (Herbig). Due to the practice of cross-shareholding and of tight networks in general, foreign firms felt that Japan was not abiding by the GATT.

The complaints of foreign companies, coupled with the end of the "bubble economy", led to the phasing out of the *keiretsu* and to more innovation within the Japanese business group system. Many companies in Japan, however, have managed to develop and maintain ties with other business groups without actually buying one another's stock. As the economy recovers, these ties become stronger as different holdings groups merge and acquire various businesses. Once again, the practice of cross-shareholding is playing an important role in Japanese business.

A new form of *keiretsu* is now emerging as holdings groups emerge concurrently with the improvement of the Japanese economy. This new *keiretsu* combines features of the old vertical-style and horizontal-style structures, and companies across different industries (the horizontal *keiretsu*) promote one specific group brand (the vertical *keiretsu*). This type of *keiretsu* exists in a format where a group of companies across different industries uses one specific brand image. This holdings group system is becoming the new *keiretsu* for the 21st century in Japan. Over the years, Seven-Eleven Japan became very dominant in its industry, partially through channeling the resources of its original holding group, the Ito-Yokado Corporation. Its brand image has since gone on to consume all the brands within the Ito-Yokado Corporation, thus creating the need to push the formerly American brand to the forefront of the entire business group.

Transformation of the Ito-Yokado Group into Seven & i Holdings

Supported by the strength of the SEJ brand within the Ito-Yokado Group, the entire business group began to prosper. Ito-Yokado was able to expand and acquire other properties. In December of 2006, the company spent $1.1 billion to buy a 65% stake of Millennium Retailing, owners of the Seibu and Sogo department store chain. This acquisition has transformed Seven & i Holdings into the largest retailing organization in Japan with combined sales of $36 billion (Brady). Eventually, the decision was made by Suzuki, now Chairman of the entire Group, to merge all of these business groups under the new name of Seven & i Holdings, a name derived from his original company. This was done, they claim, in order to create, "a New, Comprehensive Lifestyle Industry" and to better serve the needs of their customers (Seven & i Holdings Annual Report 12).

Seven & i Holdings debuted in September of 2005. All companies within the group were listed separately on the Tokyo Stock Exchange prior to the debut but are now found under the single name of Seven & I Holdings ("Financial Data"). The Seven & i Holdings Group currently includes the following different types of businesses: Convenience Store Operations, Superstore Operations, Supermarkets, Department Store Operations, Restaurant Operations, Financial Services, IS/IT Services, and other areas (Exhibit 6). By attempting to merge several types of businesses under one specific brand, Seven & i Holdings is seeking to overlap resources amongst each business group that will drive the consumer to utilize all the brands in their shopping experiences.

For the moment, the decision to create the Seven and i Holdings Group has been successful (Exhibit 7). Just as the original 7-Eleven brand changed to meet the needs of Japanese society, Japanese society is also showing signs of change. There are many issues that exist in Japan that could stop the momentum of this new Holdings Group. Given that branding is an important aspect in marketing, Seven & i Holdings believes that integration with the Seven-Eleven Japan brand can boost the sales of the other business units within the Group. As a result, Seven and i Holdings is investing much in the areas of advertising, technology, and research to integrate all these various business groups under one brand.

Convenience Store Operations

Seven-Eleven Japan Co. Ltd.	Operates convenience stores by franchise system in Japan	11,735 locations
7-Eleven Inc.	Operates convenience stores by franchise system in North America and licenses the operation of Seven-Eleven stores to area licensees worldwide	6,050 locations
Seven-Eleven (Hawaii) Inc.	Operates convenience stores in the state of Hawaii, U.S.A.	54 locations
Seven-Eleven (Beijing) Co. Ltd.	Operates convenience stores in Beijing, China	50 locations

Superstore Operations

Ito-Yokado Co. Ltd.	Operates superstores handling apparel, household goods, and food in Japan	174 locations
Hua Tang Yokado Commercial Co. Ltd.	Operates superstores handling apparel, household goods, and food in Beijing, China	6 locations
Chengdu Ito-Yokado Co. Ltd.	Operates superstores handling apparel, household goods, and food in Chengdu, China	2 locations

Departmental Store Operations

Sogo Co. Ltd.	Operates departmental stores mainly in the Kansai (Eastern) area, Japan	12 locations
The Seibu Department Stores Ltd.	Operates departmental stores mainly in the Kanto (Western) area, Japan	16 locations

Supermarket Operations

York-Benimaru Co. Ltd.	Operates supermarkets, mainly in the Tohoku (Northern) area, Japan	128 locations

Restaurant Operations

Denny's Japan Co. Ltd.	Operates family restaurants in Japan	585 locations

Exhibit 7. Business units of Seven & i Holdings and their locations.

Financial Services

| Seven Bank Ltd. | Offers financial services mainly through ATMs placed at domestic group stores such as Seven-Eleven | n/a |
| IY Card Service Co. Ltd. | Engages in credit card business and issuance and management of electronic money | n/a |

Source: Seven & i Holdings Corporate Outline.

Exhibit 7.   (*Continued*).

Integration within Seven & i Holdings

According to their 2007 Annual Report, the decision to merge all brands under a single name was done to better meet the needs of Seven & i Holding's customers. According to an interview with current Seven & i Holdings President, Noritoshi Murata, the Group feels it needs to, "... continually reinvent... in response to customer needs..." (Seven & i Holdings Annual Report 10).

In order to be successful as a *keiretsu*-style firm, Seven & i Holdings is looking into various ways to provide assistance in fostering cooperation amongst brands and corporate integration. Top managers at the Holdings Group level are responsible for the entire group's long-term management strategies. Individual businesses will be responsible for gaining profit and growth, but their decisions will ultimately be influenced by the management of the Holdings Group (Seven & i Holdings Annual Report 9).

Since Suzuki brought over the computer system from 7-Eleven in America, computer and database integration has been a priority for the business. An elaborate computer integration system has been developed which will allow all brands in the Group to use the same POS system to aid in customer growth. Existing shipping and warehouses will also be slowly integrated to reduce costs.

This point card is symbolic of the Group's desire for total integration. The Group touts it as the world's Computer databases

Figure 4. The "Nanaco" point card.

will be accessible by all brands in the Group and will capture consumer spending habits and collect vital market research data. This data collection will be accomplished using a credit/point card known as the Nanaco card this is created just for brand integration (see Fig. 4).

The point card is the first prepaid and postpaid electronic money system on a single card (Seven & i Holdings Annual Report 15). The card, issued by the Holding Company's credit division, IY Card Service, will act as both a credit card and debit card across business units in the Group. Seven & i Holdings is also pursuing partnerships with other companies outside the group to allow for payment using the Nanaco card. To encourage customers to use the card, customers will be able to accumulate points that they can exchange for payment on products within the entire group of businesses.

The Nanaco card is an important step for the brand's integration. Convenience stores are almost a necessary part of daily living in Japan, and Seven-Eleven Japan controls the market by a wide margin. The Nanaco card has the potential to drive customers from the convenience stores into the departmental stores, shopping malls, and restaurants of the other brands within the Group in order to use and collect points.

Using data collected from the Nanaco point card, Seven & i Holdings will be able to develop accurate profiles on their customers and their spending habits. With this information, they will be able to create special and original products and customize their existing product inventories to match the seasonal tastes of their customers.

BECOMING THE "NEW KEIRETSU" — CHALLENGES WITH INTEGRATING THE SEVEN & I HOLDINGS GROUP

Although integration is seen as an answer to a rapidly-changing and diverse market, problems can arise because some of these business units are vastly different. The Loft, one of their new properties, is a departmental store that targets younger generations with its "hip" take on common household items. A customer who shops at The Loft would not be as likely to visit the Seibu Department Store, which targets middle-aged and older housewives. These two departmental store businesses are also very different from the Denny's Restaurant chain, which is also different from the convenience store business. By trying to integrate all of these units in order to develop the so-called "new, comprehensive lifestyle industry", the danger exists for Seven & i Holdings to dilute the brand power of each individual business unit.

In addition to their brands in Japan, Seven & i Holdings has the most franchise agreements with convenience stores around the world. In particular, they have been aggressive in developing their United States 7-Eleven chain since making them a wholly-owned subsidiary. In July of 2007, they proposed to build an additional 1,000 stores that would increase their total stores in the U.S. to 7,000. They hope that with the new stores and better integrated software from Seven & i Holdings in Japan, they can achieve sales in the U.S. of $10 billion by the year 2010 (Seven & i Holdings 2007 Co. Ltd.).

But their U.S. brand and others overseas may be affected by changes and issues that can arise in those specific countries. Seven & i Holdings is also experiencing competition in their own native Japan. While trying to leverage the Group's abilities as a whole, some brands may suffer as a result of integration. While they are number one in the convenience store market, they are not the leaders in their other industries.

The convenience store industry, the lynchpin of the Seven & i Holdings brand, also contains several challenges. SEJ's top rivals are Lawson (8,603 stores), Family Mart (7,083 stores), and AM/PM (1,251 stores). These stores are trying to differentiate themselves in the Convenience Store market by experimenting with different kinds of food, atmosphere, and product tie-ins. Lawson, for example, is developing Lawson Plus stores, which specifically target retirees and the aging while Family Mart is working with a CD/DVD rental store chain to develop a point card system (Betros). Besides competition from other convenience store chains, SEJ is also facing more competition from supermarkets, drugstores, and cheaper discounted stores (Betros).

Another problem that exists for Seven & i Holdings is under-pinned by the dynamics of change within the Japanese society. Japan is currently the world's fastest aging society. By 2055, nearly 40% of its population will be aged 65 and older (Sano). The total population itself is expected to shrink down to 90 million people in 2055 from the current population of 127 million. There will be fewer workers in society, which could affect the business model of all companies within the Holdings Group. According to Seven & i Holdings, office workers and students account for the majority of a convenience store's sales. Until a few years ago, 70% of a convenience store's shoppers were in their 20s and 30s. That figure is now around 50% (Betros).

In their Annual Report, Seven & i Holdings specifically mentions that they are concerned about the future and of changing domestic trends such as fewer children per family and an aging population (Seven & i Holdings Annual Report 12). As Japanese society ages, the population will be less mobile and confined to the suburbs, which would hurt many stores in metropolitan areas. Product preferences also change with age, which could adversely affect SEJ's suppliers. This aging population could also affect individual brands within the business group. Younger consumers who frequent the Loft may "graduate" to shopping at the more conservative Seibu Department Store. Since each group within Seven & i Holdings is responsible for its own sales, competition may develop within the Holdings Group as a result of these changing demographics and will affect how the Holdings Group ultimately allocates its various resources.

Other problems exist with an aging population, such as the changing nature of the work force. Japan, in an effort to keep a young work force, may make immigration easier for people from other countries. These immigrants will bring with them their own consumer habits and preferences, which can also affect the individual businesses within the Group.

Recently, Seven & i Holdings also started a banking division called Seven Bank. This new division has entered into a joint venture with Toyota Financial Services Corporation called Seven Cash Works Co. Ltd (Seven & i Holdings Annual Report 35). Seven & i Holdings is not an experienced player in the banking sector. They may not be able to handle the intense banking industry in Japan and may waste some of the resources of the Holdings Group should the banking venture be unsuccessful.

CONCLUSION

Seven & i Holdings has come a long way since selling milk and bread from the back of an ice company's loading dock in a small Texas town. The company became international through its agreement with Seven-Eleven Japan, a part of a larger Japanese business group. This brand became so strong in Japan that it ultimately purchased 7-Eleven in the U.S. and took over the entire group, resulting in the name being changed to Seven & i Holdings.

Seven & i Holdings, while maintaining certain aspects of a traditional *keiretsu* system, is re-inventing itself by pushing all companies within the group under one brand name. As a large international company, Seven & i Holdings has various obstacles to its continued growth both worldwide and at home in Japan. Their name change can affect the unique brand image within their individual businesses. They are also now more reliant on issues in other countries as well as their own country's changing population structure. In order to continue its growth, Seven & i Holdings needs to solidify existing strategies and implement new ones to reduce risk across all their businesses.

QUESTIONS

1) What adaptations were necessary to make convenience stores appealing to Japanese consumers?
2) What is a keiretsu and how has it transformed over the past decades?
3) Why did the company choose the keiretsu form? Discuss advantages and disadvantages.
4) How can Seven-Eleven Japan stay competitive?
5) What are the challenges of the retail market in Japan?

BIBLIOGRAPHY

Betros, C. At Your Convenience (21 December 2007). *Metropolis*, 12 – 15.

Brady, R. Japanese spree (9 January 2006). *Business Week* 44.

Dubovoj, S. (2007) 7-Eleven. David E. Salamie (ed.) http://www.answers. com.

Financial data. Ito-Yokado Corporation. http://www.itoyokado.co.jp/ company/investors/index_e.htm.

Herbig, P. Lecture #23: The Role of the Keiretsu in Japan's Economy. http://www.geocities.com/Athens/Delphi/9158/kwujmktg23.html.

Japan: Land values rise (2 August 2007). *The New York Times.*

Keiretsu. TheEverythingJapaneseGuide. http://www.japanese123.com/ keiretsu.htm.

McCaughn, D. Does your brand bore the Japanese? Blame 7-Eleven (13 August 2007). *Advertising Age.*

Melville, I. (1999). *Marketing in Japan.* Oxford: Butterworth Heinemann.

Sano, H. Tokyo's neon lights to dim as Japan ages (5 November 2007). *Reuters.*

Seven Eleven Japan. http://www.sej.co.jp/index.html.

Seven & i Holdings Co. Ltd. http://www.7andi.com/en.

Seven & I Holdings annual report. Seven & i Holdings Co. Ltd. http:// www.7andi.com/en.

Seven & i Holdings corporate profile. Seven & i Holdings Co. Ltd. http://www.sej.co.jp/corp/company/yokogao.html.

7-Eleven: Products & Services. http://www.7-eleven.com/products/index.asp.

7-Eleven home. http://www.7-eleven.com.

Tanner, D. (1992) Ito-Yokado Co., Ltd. David E Salamie (ed.) http://www.answers.com.

Toshifumi Suzuki profile. ReferenceforBusiness.com. http://www.referenceforbusiness.com/biography/S-Z/Suzuki-Toshifumi-1932.html.

Sony Playstation 3 (PS3): Phoenix from the Flames?

Vincent Agulhon

INTRODUCTION

Sony Corporation is a leading manufacturer of audio, video, communications and information technology products for both consumer and professional markets. Sony's main businesses include Sony Electronics, Sony Pictures Entertainment, Sony Computer Entertainment and Sony Music Entertainment. The company now employs 171,300 people worldwide and announced a record 98.9 billion yen loss for the fiscal year ending in March 2009, which represents the company's first reported yearly loss in 14 years. On top of that, overall sales dropped 12.9% to 7.73 trillion yen during 2008 and Sony projects an operating loss of 120 billion yen for the next fiscal year. However, there is a small ray of hope in the storm: the sales of the Playstation 3 and its games showed improvement and were up by 10% and 79% respectively.

In a new generation of video game consoles that emphasizes innovation and group interaction, Sony went again for a much more conventional approach to the video game market with the Playstation 3 that gave its competitors a good opportunity to make a breakthrough. The company's traditional strategic management based on technological innovation, competitive pricing, and brand recognition were major factors in the brand success over the last 15 years. However, Sony is now in crisis and needs to reconsider what made it successful in the past to remain competitive in today's video game market. Sony's main competitor in Japan, Nintendo, took advantage of its mistakes, and is staying one length ahead.

Often described as a complete market failure and the worst reviewed launch ever, the Playstation 3 had a close shave with death. Like a phoenix from the flames, the Playstation 3 finally seems to wake from a bad nightmare, but for the better or worse?

SONY AND THE GAME INDUSTRY

Sony's Playstation franchise was the most successful home video game console in history. The Playstation launched in 1994 had reached 125 million units sold worldwide and the Playstation 2 is about to pass 140 million worldwide[190] in its ninth year of sales. On the other hand, the Playstation 3 is still an unprofitable market and a weak competitor in Japan in its third year of sales.

THE PLAYSTATION 1

Building a brand is a tough challenge when the market is monopolized by two other brands that share 90% of it. This is exactly what Sony Computer Entertainment faced when it launched in 1994 the Playstation against Nintendo and Sega. Before Playstation, it was thought that games were only played by kids or geeks. Sony changed the gaming experience and successfully positioned its console by offering a product acceptable for teenagers and young adults. Thanks to its "Double Life" advertising campaign featuring young adults talking about the secret life they have when they play with the Playstation, Sony coined the spirit of gaming as an intense lifestyle experience. Besides, the system allowed the use of CD technology and optional memory cards that enabled players to save user data such as game progress or high scores. Through distinctive brand image and price cut from $299 to $199 in 1996, Sony gained tremendous market

---

[190] Luke Plunkett. Sony Talk Playstation Lifetime Sales, PSN Revenue, Kotaku.com.

shares and became the bestselling console in the market: in less than four years, Sony distanced itself from both Nintendo and Sega.

Sony also succeeded in building the Playstation brand, thanks to numerous exclusive games such as the Final Fantasy series (a cash cow franchise, previously a Nintendo's exclusivity) and blockbusters that became symbols of the Playstation brand (*e.g.*, *Gran Turismo*, *Metal Gear Solid*, *Resident Evil*, etc.) for their mature approach to gaming never seen before. This huge commercial success made Sony Computer Entertainment the most profitable division within Sony Corporation.

THE PLAYSTATION 2

Based on the worldwide success and the popularity of the first Playstation, Sony launched in 2000 Playstation 2 using the same market approach with its former game system. Despite manufacturing delays, the console sold more than three million units within a few months in Japan. The system allowed the use of DVD technology (making it a substitute for DVD players) and Playstation 1 emulation, which were a factor in making the machine successful in Japan. David Lynch's "Welcome to the Third World" TV commercial, was part of this success and clearly distinguished the Playstation brand from the others, making the customer feel different by buying a Playstation 2. With almost 140 million units sold worldwide by the end of 2009 (of which 21 million in Japan), the Playstation 2 became the world's bestselling video game machine to date.

SONY'S COMPETITORS

Nintendo Wii

As of January 2010, Nintendo's home video game console leads the generation over the Playstation 3 and Xbox 360 with more than nine million units sold in Japan. One of the major features of the Wii is its motion-sensing controller, a pointing device that detects movements in three dimensions and allows players to interact with items on screen via gesture recognition. Besides, the simplistic design and playability of its family-friendly games made the console very popular among young children and parents with bowling and tennis games as well as healthy lifestyle programs. Opting for a less traditional route than its competitors, The Nintendo Wii revolutionized the gaming experience and put Nintendo right back at the top of the video game console wars. Launched in Japan on 2 December, 2006 at 25,000 yen, the console itself could not compete against Sony's Playstation 3 over processing power and high-definition features, but the revolutionary nature of its controller overcame barriers to gaming accessibility and its reasonable price (cut down to 20,000 on 1 October, 2009) ensured its unexpected success.

Microsoft Xbox 360

Despite high features similar to those of the Playstation 3 and Microsoft's endeavors to hire developers from the country to create something that appeals Japanese players, the Xbox 360 is a complete failure in Japan. Such a lack of success can be explained by its heavy and unattractive design as well as the lack of engaging games which "put the brand in a sort of black-list in consumer's mind", according to Takashi Sensui, General Manager of Microsoft's Japan division. Launched in Japan on 10 December, 2005 at 39,795 yen, the Xbox 360 received a muted reception (indicating a possible nationalistic preference in game consoles) and as of January 2010, it sold only 1,200,000 units.

THE VIDEO GAME MARKET

After having shrunk by 15.3% in 2008, the Japanese game market fell 10.5% in the first half of fiscal year 2009 (15.1% in hardware sales and 7.5% in software sales), which represents the first year-to-year decline in four years. According to Enterbrain, the 2008 market value hit 582.61 billion yen, down from 687.95 billion yen as seen in 2007.[191]

   Traditionally regarded as recession-proof, the Japanese gaming industry mainly suffers from the decrease in value of the U.S. dollar and

---

[191] Enterbrain Inc — 株式会社インターブレイン .

the euro against the yen due to the global economic crisis. Knowing the fact that Nintendo and Sony respectively obtain 88.5% and 80% of their revenue from overseas sales, their revenues are decreasing significantly. This is a serious problem for Japanese companies as it eats into their profit margins and could lead to an increase in prices or cut expenses.

GROWING BEYOND "GALAPAGOSIZATION"

In the past several years, it has often been demonstrated that in some business aspects, "Japan is like the Galapagos Islands, in that Japanese companies endeavoring to meet the demands of the Japanese market are similar to the animals living in the Galapagos Islands that followed a unique evolutionary process",[192] and this peculiar phenomenon reached the Japanese video game market.

Roughly speaking, the Japanese tend to play more with mobiles and handheld console while the rest of the world prefers the comfort of the living room and high-definition graphics (i.e., home console). As Japanese predominately play on the public transportation or in family restaurants (where they usually gather to play over LAN),[193] high spec consoles like the Playstation 3 have trouble in selling machines and adapting to this recent change in players' habits. A quick glance at Sony or Nintendo's handheld console sales in Japan, in particular the PSP (Playstation Portable) and the NDS (Nintendo Dual Screen) further demonstrate this trend.

Hardware	Wii	PS3	PSP	NDS
LTD Sales (01/2010)	9,739,320	4,598,115	13,964,824	29,448,830

A possible explanation for this tendency is the absence of a real substitute product to the Playstation 2 (i.e., an affordable console with high power computing capabilities) that encouraged consumers to play videogames on handheld systems.

---

[192] Fumikazu Kitagawa. Growing Beyond Galapagosization NRI Papers No. 146, 2009.
[193] Local area network.

Otaku: A Japanese phenomenon

Otaku is a Japanese term, which is also often used outside of Japan to refer to people with obsessive interests, particularly in Japanese animation, manga and video games. They are generally believed to be very knowledgeable of their area of interest. The word *otaku* can best be equated to the English words "nerd", "geek" or "fanboy". Even if its usage in Japanese society is also understood to mean someone who has an antisocial personality, serious devotees of Japanese subculture often called themselves *otaku.*

The *Otaku*, the passionate obsessive, the information age's embodiment of the connoisseur, more concerned with the accumulation of data than of objects, seems a natural crossover figure in today's interface of British and Japanese cultures. I see it in the eyes of the Portobello dealers, and in the eyes of the Japanese collectors: a perfectly calm train-spotter frenzy, murderous and sublime. Understanding otaku-hood, I think, is one of the keys to understanding the culture of the web. There is something profoundly post-national about it, extra-geographic. We are all curators, in the post-modern world, whether we want to be or not.

William Gibson
Modern Boys and Mobile Girls, April 2001

What makes the *otaku* market so peculiar is that their consumption behavior is driven by sympathy, admiration and pursuit of "ideals" (i.e., creating fan-fictions based on their interpretations) as well as the orientation towards forming a strong community hardly approachable by ordinary people.

THE OTAKU MARKET AND THEIR INFLUENCE ON THE GAME INDUSTRY

Sony Playstation 3 buyers mainly consisted of *otaku* until recently because of the console's expensive launch price and technological features which proved hardly approachable for the mass market. Besides, the launch of the Playstation Network Video on Demand service in

Table 1. Size of the Otaku Group in the five major fields.

Field	Population* (thousand)	Market size (1 billion yen)	Major indexes
Comics	1,000	100	— Number of participants in spot sale of fanzines — Circulation of specific magazines
Animation	200	20	— DVD sales per title — Circulation of specific magazines
Idols	800	60	— Size of concert audiences — Sales of first-release CDs
Games			
Home-use	570	45	— Number of hours spent playing games
PC	140	19	— Circulation of specific magazines
Network	30	1	— Rate of game players who participate in network games
Arcade, etc.	60	13	— Number of specific parts sold
PC assembly			
Wealthy	30	30	— Sales at PC parts shops in Akihabara
Junk	20	2	— Circulation of specific magazines

*Including overlapping categories.
Source: NRI, *Survey on Enthusiastic Consumers in Japan, *August 2004.

2008, allowing Playstation 3 users to rent and own video content from a variety of Japanese animation, secured and strengthened the loyalty of Sony Playstation 3 *otaku* audience.

According to a survey (see Table 1) conducted by Nomura Research Institute targeting five fields (comics, animation, idols, game and PC assembly), the total number of *otaku* was estimated to be 2.85 million with a market size of 290 billion yen in 2005. Thus, the *otaku* group can no longer be considered as a niche market.

While repeating consumption patterns (e.g., breaking game record scores or collecting items), *Otaku* never attain their goal and keep giving themselves new tasks and fall into a cycle of endless consumption. Such a *bizarre* consumption pattern encouraged companies in Japan to create series of games using the same background, as well as creating never-ending TV animation programs to satisfy *otaku*'s extreme passion and pursuit of ideals.

THE PLAYSTATION 3: CHRONICLE OF A DISASTER FORETOLD?

Introduction to Japan

After the incredible success of its previous video game console worldwide, Sony based the Playstation 3 launch on the popularity of the Sony brand, as the firm did before with the Playstation 2 in 2000. Yet, what made it different from its predecessor is that in 2006, Sony was not only selling a new video game console, but a complete new technology capable of much more than merely playing games. The Playstation 3's powerful processor, conjugated to its high power computing capabilities and Blue-Ray drive, opened the possibility of enjoying home theater and proxy server experience (once connected to the Internet, the Playstation 3 can access a computer's files and enable PS3 system owners to watch their pictures or downloaded movies).

According to Media Create, the Playstation 3 was first released in Japan on 11 November, 2006 and only 81,639 systems were sold within 24 hours of its introduction.[194] A week later, the sales dropped 50% to 42,099 units. In comparison with its predecessor, the Playstation 2 sold over a tremendous 980,000 units in Japan by 5 March, 2000.

"If you can have an amazing experience, we believe price is not a problem", said Ken Kutaragi, former Chairman and chief executive officer of Sony Computer Entertainment (SCEI), known as "the

---

[194] Media Create Co. Ltd — 株式会社メディアクリエイト.

father of the Playstation". However, for consumers, a $600 purchase is a problem, especially when it is to buy the most expensive video game console ever made, Sony-branded or not. Some will say that a blue-ray gaming console is worth it, but-back in 2006, consumers were apparently not ready to pay for this.

"This is the Playstation 3 price. Expensive, cheap — we don't want to think of in terms of game machines, because the Playstation 3 is like nothing else. [...] With the Playstation 3, you can have next generation game experiences that could previously not be experienced. And, as with Playstation and Playstation 2, we believe people who like games will, without question, purchase it", said Ken Kutaragi, E3 Expo 2006, in a Sony Press Conference.[195]

Due to Playstation 3's lack of game blockbusters at its launch (only 15 games were available and few exclusives), Sony made the decision to advertise its new product as a computer and not a gaming system, thus targeting Playstation fanboys and video game geeks. However, in 2006, who would know that a new gaming phenomenon, the so-called "casual gaming", which was far from the computer world and geek's pixilated dreams, was about to born and surprise the entire video game marketing world? Unfortunately, for Sony, Nintendo did.

Analyzing Sony Playstation 3 Market Positioning at Launch

Sony decided to fit the Playstation 3 to its usual audience, which mainly consisted of young adult males with age that vary from 15 to 35, and prefer playing mature video games as opposed to Nintendo's childish games and brand equity. Contrary to the Playstation 2 (which was initially priced at 37,800 yen), two Playstation 3 SKUs[196] were available at launch: a basic model with a 20 GB hard drive

---

[195] Electronic Entertainment Expo, one of the biggest video game exposition in the world.
[196] Stock-keeping units.

(49,980 yen) and a premium model with a 60 GB hard drive (59,980 yen) and additional features. Clearly designed to be perceived as high-definition gaming systems, both models come with a blue-ray drive and hardware-based Playstation 2 emulation. Supposed to be the world's most powerful game console ever created, the Playstation 3 suffered mainly from a lack of original and exclusive games to compete with its main rival, the Nintendo Wii, which was launched in Japan three weeks later, on 2 December, 2006 at only 25,000 yen.

Even though Sony was selling great technology, back in 2006, were consumers ready to buy a 59,980 yen video game system that requires a costly high-definition television to use its "next generation" features? Sony thought it was the case and forgot that in the consumers' minds, console games at that time were only seen as entertainment; features like proxy servers, Wi-Fi connection or high definition pictures were not necessary. In January 2007, the Playstation 3 only sold 385,831 units while the Nintendo Wii (launched three weeks later) already sold 823,311 units, despite manufacturing delays.

Ask any Sony Playstation 2 owners why they did not buy the Playstation 3 on Christmas 2006 and they will reply the same way, arguing that the Playstation 3 was then too expensive and they could not afford a high-definition television. Ken Kutaragi was wrong and price *was* a problem. Sony positioned the Playstation 3 in the video game market as the most expensive and powerful game console. It did not detect the starting of a new casual gaming trend, pitching on a computer-like experience that strengthened the Playstation 3's *otaku* image in Japan, a console obviously way too complicated and unaffordable to enjoy. Too early to think about a brand repositioning strategy or price cuts, Sony got caught in the chains of its own game, and then continued to focus desperately on its *otaku* audience.

Until fall 2007, Nintendo Wii sales were often seven times higher than that of Sony Playstation 3 (which stabilized at around 10,000 units sold a week) while Playstation 2's weekly sales surpassed it several times. This was quite unexpected for a next generation console that was supposed to be "like nothing else" before. The Sony Playstation brand has gone from a ten years old dominant position in Japan's gaming industry to a distant second place behind Nintendo.

Between Price Cut Controversy and Dilemma

In November 2007, Sony introduced a new Playstation 3 model at 39,980 yen with a 40 GB hard drive and no Playstation 2 emulation. At the same time, the 20 GB and the 60 GB Playstation 3 price dropped to 44,980 yen and 54,980 yen respectively, representing a 5,000 yen cut, before ceasing their production one year later. Yet again, it was not the best strategy to adopt and it confused both customers and gamers even further. Three Playstation 3 models with different storage capacity, core features and prices were then on the market at the same time.

On the one hand, cutting prices by 10% never showed significant results in the long-term, particularly when it comes to buying a 60,000 yen product. Yet, on the other hand, slashing prices significantly just one year after a product launch could also have raised consumers' suspicion. As a result, Sony bargained on the success of its few exclusive games (such as Metal Gear Solid 4, one of Playstation blockbuster franchise), but this strategy turned out to be merely a flash in the pan; hardware sales were up by 64,000, reaching a total of 75,311 in the game's launch week, before dropping back down to 20,000 units the week after.

The Playstation 3 has continued its downward sales slide in Japan and the release of larger hard drive models in October 2008 (80 GB) and April 2009 (160 GB) at 39,980 yen did not change things. Until Fall 2009, the sales of Playstation 3 hardware kept fluctuating on average between 10,000 and 20,000 units a week (depending on new game releases), well below Nintendo Wii sales.

CONCLUSION

In theory, unless a value-creating strategy is implemented, no business is possible and Sony's value management remains a complete failure. The problem with the Playstation 3 mainly lied in its unaffordable price at launch as well as the company's misunderstanding of the changes in the video game market and its "galapagosization", which made the console a weak competitor in Japan. Furthermore, the lack of exclusive titles (which can be explained by the very high cost of game development on Playstation 3) and the use of the same old strategy (i.e., improving technology and marketing the console by boasting better graphics) were part of Sony's failure. Despite its great technological features, the Playstation 3 suffered from a lack of concrete innovation. Currently, the driving force in the business is Nintendo, which successfully changed its strategy and surprised its competitors with a new approach to games like Sony did 15 years ago with the Playstation 1. Sony must reorganize its core competencies and rethink its business-level strategy to be able to compete efficiently in the video game market.

QUESTIONS

1) What strategy should Sony implement/develop to change its situation in the Japanese market?
2) How is Playstation 3 positioned in the Japanese market?
3) What are the particularities of the Japanese video game market?
4) How are Japanese gamers different from other gamers?
5) Investigate the otaku phenomenon in more detail. Which role do they play in the Japanese market?

BIBLIOGRAPHY

Aoyama, Y and Izushi, H. (2003). *Hardware Gimmick or Cultural Innovation? Technological, Cultural, and Social Foundations of the Japanese Video Game Industry.* New York: Elsevier.

Enterbrain. http://www.enterbrain.co.jp/.

Famitsu Award 2009. http://www.famitsu.com/sp/awards2009/.

Fumikazu Kitagawa (2009). Growing Beyond "Galapagosization NRI Papers no. 146.

Gamekult. (*Charts Japon: la PS3 devant la Wii* 16 November, 2007). http://www.gamekult.com/finances/articles/A0000062622/.

Kohler, C. (2004). *How Japanese Video Games Gave the World an Extra Life*. Brady Games.

Media Create, Weekly Ranking. http://www.m-create.com/ranking/.

Morden, T. (2007). *Principles of Strategic Management*. Hampshire: Ashgate.

Price cuts for the 7th Generation. Wikia Gaming. http://vgsales.wikia.com/wiki/Price_cuts.

Sony Corporation (2008). Corporate Information. http://www.sony.co.jp/SonyInfo/CorporateInfo/.

White, S and Leung, K. (2004). *Handbook of Asian Management*, Boston, Kluwer Academic.

Part 2

MARKETING MANAGEMENT IN JAPAN

Rise and Fall of the Japanese Luxury Market

Ekaterina Ignatova

INTRODUCTION: THE STATE OF MASS LUXURY

Japan is known as the world's first and only mass luxury market; the luxury fashion consumption in urban Japan is much higher than in any other similarly developed city in the world, be it Milan, New York, London, or Paris. While the words "mass" and "luxury" might not be synonymous in western eyes, the Japanese have quite a different view on the subject. Davide Sesia, president of Prada Japan, said that the Japanese have a "psychological need to own something considered beautiful" and that their "attention to beauty concept is ... maniacal". Many Europeans, on the other hand, believe they are violating a "moral code" if they devote too much attention to luxury (Dominic, p. 1).

This case study will examine the Japanese luxury market and its consumers in an attempt to shed some light on the mysterious phenomenon of the Japanese obsession with luxury goods. It will also address the changing trends in consumer preferences and the consequences these shifting appetites have on the global suppliers of the luxury market.

LUXURY MARKET TODAY: JAPAN

Japanese consumers are the world's biggest spenders when it comes to luxury goods. The market for imported luxury products

163

was worth 1.2 trillion ($10.2 billion) yen in 2007, a drop of 39% since 1996 (Atsmon Salsberg and Yamanashi, 2009, p. 7). Sales to the Japanese account for over half of the global luxury goods sales: an estimated 20% of all luxury goods are sold in Japan and another 30% are sold to the Japanese traveling abroad. Some of the most famous shopping destinations include Korea and Hawaii. Out of Hawaii's seven million visitors each year, 1.5 million are Japanese (Thomas, 2007, p. 86). They stay for a few days and most of them just come to shop. More than half of Chanel's sales in Hawaii are to Japanese people. "The Japanese know what they are going to do from the time they land until they leave. They come with an agenda and know what they are going to buy in each store", said Okano of Chanel (Thomas, 2007, p. 86). According to Visa Worldwide, Japanese travelers in South Korea charged more to their credit cards than visitors from any other country in 2008. The total amount neared $450 million, which is an 18% increase over the previous year (Japanese biggest visa card users in S Korea, 2009).

Moreover, researchers claim that approximately 40% of all Japanese own a Louis Vuitton product (Thomas, 2007, p. 74). In Tokyo, an often repeated claim is that 94% of women in their 20s own at least one piece, 92% own Gucci, 57% own Prada and 51% own Chanel (Seeking Alpha, 2009). While these statistics might seem mythical, it is a fact that the proportion of the urban population in Japan that owns expensive luxury brand items is large. Louis Vuitton, the most popular brand in Asia (see Table 1), generates 88% of its

Table 1.   Favorite brands of Japanese women.

Top Ten Favorite Brands for Japanese Women	
1. Louis Vuitton	6. Cartier
2. Coach	**7. Dior**
3. Hermes	8. Chanel
4. Gucci	**9. Prada**
5. Burberry	10. Tiffany & Co

Source: Dominic Carter, September 2008.

Luxury sales by region
US$ bn

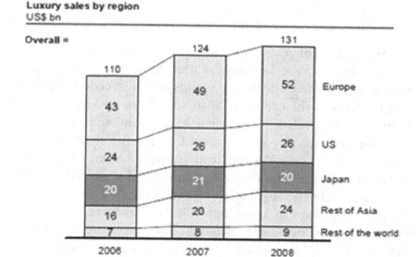

Figure 1.   Global luxury sales by region 2006–2008.
Source: Based on figure from McKinsey Asia Consumer and Retail Practice, 2009.

global sales from Japanese consumers — 38% in Japan, and 50% by Japanese tourists (Chadha and Husband, 2006, p. 2).

A McKinsey Asia Consumer and Retail (2009) study (see Fig. 1) on Japanese luxury markets confirms that between 2006 and 2008, the sales of luxury goods in Japan stayed in the 15–18% range of total global sales ($20 billion), excluding sales to the Japanese outside of Japan (Atsmon, Salsberg and Yamanashi, 2009, p. 11).

Luxury goods have become a necessity in Japan — they are a powerful tool to show one's social status and wealth. The luxury consumption has become a national phenomenon, which is stimulated by the substantial political, social, and economic changes. In Japan, you are what you wear. Luxury items are a "new social protocol where your identity and self-worth are determined by the visible brands on your body. A new luxury-brand defined social order [replaced] old ways of marking status (Chadha and Husband, 2006, p. 3)".

The happy victims

In his book, Tokyo Style, the Japanese journalist Kyoichi Tsuzuki refers to the Japanese as the "happy victims of brand marketing." Indeed, the luxury brands have succeeded in taking over the lives of the ordinary Japanese citizens and have turned them into "luxeholics." Regardless of their financial status, the Japanese flock to the luxury brand stores for their share of Gucci, Chanel, Louis Vuitton, and Hermès. Often, such indulgences in the luxury goods are way above their financial means.

Tsuzuki tells the story of an Hermès collector — a Japanese executive who lives in a tiny flat in Tokyo, and keeps all of his purchases in the original packaging. After spending half a million yen on a Hermès briefcase, he carries it with a towel over the handle, so that the briefcase is not damaged from the slightest perspiration from his own hands. And he is not alone — there is an alarming number of Japanese consumers who act in a similar manner and are willing to spend a fortune on numerous luxury items, while living in cramped rundown apartments and paying off outrageous debts.

Source: Thomas, Dana (p. 73–74).

LUXURY MARKET: THE BEGINNING

The first luxury brand names made their way to Japan in the early 1900s, when Japan started trading with Europe after the long Edo-period of isolation. British Burberry was one of the first luxury brands to set up a shop in Tokyo as early as 1920. The Second World War had devastating effects on the Japanese economy, and as a result, luxury brands went into "hibernation" for several decades (Chadha and Husband, 2006, p. 14).

During the 1960s and 1970s, the Japanese economy flourished: it grew by 3.7% annually and the post-war generation experienced a dramatic increase in disposable income (Thomas, 2007, p. 79). The newly formed middle class had strong purchasing power and their appetites for luxury escalated. This gave local designers the opportunity to get their foot in the door: Kenzo Takada, Kansai Yamamoto, Issey Miyake, Yohji Yamamoto, and Rei Kawakubo were among the few who managed to succeed (Chadha and Husband, 2006, p. 15). Others were not as fortunate in their entrepreneurial pursuits, as the Japanese seemed to show more interest in foreign-made products. The production quality in post-war Japan was quite low, and thus the majority of Japanese believed that foreign-made goods were superior in quality and durability to domestically-produced goods. This belief grew into an obsession, with strong emotional ties to brands; owning foreign-made luxury goods became a "badge of economic success and social acceptance" (Atsmon, Salsberg and Yamanashi, 2009, p. 11).

Nevertheless, the distribution of foreign luxury brands in Japan was very limited, which created a clear imbalance between supply and demand. In order to overcome this problem, the entrepreneurial Japanese merchants traveled to Europe, purchased luxury items in bulk, and sold them back in Japan for a profit by tripling the price. This created a so-called parallel market, which has proved to be very damaging to brand names (Thomas, 2007, p. 76). The aggressive shopping pattern undertaken by the Japanese merchants and tourists that left the European stores empty did not go unnoticed by the luxury brand executives. At first, in order to stimulate sales, European store assistants were trained to speak Japanese. However, as the consumption was increasing rapidly, luxury companies became alarmed, since they did not have control over their products' distribution overseas, and placed a limit on the number of products that could be purchased by the Japanese. Louis Vuitton was among the first brands to react to this phenomenal behavior by initiating a research project on the Japanese luxury consumption with the intention to expand into Japan. Kyojiro Hata, a consultant for an international accounting firm, was hired to oversee this transition. In March 1978, Louis Vuitton was represented in five different departmental stores in Tokyo and one in Osaka (Thomas, 2007, p. 77). The second most popular luxury brand in Japan at the time, Gucci, opened its first Japanese store in 1972 (Chadha and Husband, 2006, p. 16).

The unique characteristic about the Japanese luxury consumption was that, unlike in most countries, the middle class was the most interested in purchasing luxury goods. Ownership of luxury goods alone, however, did not put one in the upper-class category, but simply indicated the status and financial capabilities of the owner. Those who were on a budget were willing to sacrifice other purchases, even essentials like food, in order to be able to afford a luxury item. Fashion magazines and departmental stores were aiming their advertising at middle class consumers. As a result, the luxury market in Japan boomed in the 1980s and despite the economic ups and downs, continued to grow steadily until 2007.

FOREIGN LUXURY BRANDS AS STATUS MARKERS

In the Edo period, the Japanese had the Samurai-Farmer-Craftsman-Merchant stratification with the Shogun as ruler and the people's identity was defined by the social class they were born into. It was compulsory for a reputable female to wear a good quality kimono with a matching "obi" — a beautiful wrap worn over the waist. The fabric quality and the overall appearance of the kimono were of great importance, and reflected the social class and wealth of the wearer. This tradition might have been transposed into the modern era by substituting kimono with western luxury goods and accessories as a way to display one's social standing. Foreign luxury goods "may simply be the modern aesthetic mode of signaling social acceptability in Japan" (Carter, 2010, p. 1) Why did the Japanese choose to use foreign luxury goods as status markers? While there are some successful Japanese luxury designers, such as Yohji Yamamoto, none of them have the combination of quality, reputation and universal recognition that European luxury brands enjoy (Chadha and Husband, 2006, p. 97).

Globalization is a major factor that helped the European luxury brands to get established in Japan (Chadha and Husband, 2006, p. 97). While remaining loyal to their traditions and customs, the Japanese are eager to trade a kimono for a pair of jeans, and study foreign languages instead of calligraphy. The Japanese see luxury brand ownership as a sign of international ties, brand awareness, and overall standing. Most importantly, luxury goods are a great remedy for one's ego and sense of self-realization.

SPREAD OF LUXURY IN JAPAN

Japan went through all of the stages of the luxury spread model and is currently at the last stage, where luxury consumption is a "way of life" (see Fig. 2). During the "subjugation" stage, the Americans ruled Japan after the defeat in World War II. After the war, the economy boomed, producing a rapidly growing wealthy middle class, which put Japan into the "start of money" stage. The middle class consumers now had more buying power, and were able to afford washing machines and televisions, while the upper classes were already involved in buying western luxury goods. As the middle class consumers was getting stronger, they developed a need to show their wealth and social standing, so they started using western luxury accessories as status markers. The "fit in" stage is the key in the spread of luxury in Japan; due to the collectivist nature of Asian countries, once a proportion of the population accepted a trend, it became a necessary attribute for the population as a whole (Chadha and Husband, 2006, p. 75). Today, the luxury goods in Japan are a way of life and the majority of Japanese consumers do not hesitate to spend thousands of dollars a year on those status markers.

DISTRIBUTION CHANNELS

In the 1970–1980s, when luxury goods were entering Japan by boat, the standard procedure was to either find a local distributor, such as a departmental store, or have a licensing arrangement that

Figure 2.   The spread of the luxury model.
Source: Based on model from Husband & Chadha (p. 43).

gave the local partners the right to use the brand name. However, over time, the luxury producers sought more control over their product, and by the 1990s, most major brands cancelled their licensing agreements and took charge of their own distribution (Chadha and Husband, 2006, p. 75). The post war economic boom and urbanization in Japan led to the explosion in retail development. Currently, there are two main distribution channels for luxury goods in Japan: departmental stores and company-owned boutique stores.

The first departmental stores in Japan were Mitsukoshi, Sogo, Isetan, Seibu and Daimaru. The modern departmental stores are huge in size, generate an estimated $2–3 billion in sales, and 450 million people pass through the top 15 stores annually. Department stores have increased the abundance and marketability of luxury goods in Japan by offering an upscale retail space and appropriate atmosphere for luxury brands. Traditionally, they "played the stamp-of-authority role for luxury brands" (Chadha and Husband, 2006, p. 77). At first, Japanese consumers were not sure what to think of the expensive imported merchandise, but later, they thought that if the goods were sold in the reputable department at stores, it must because they are of good quality and worth the money. Yano Research Institute's study on the luxury import brand market in Japan shows that departmental stores generated an estimated 55–60% of total luxury goods sales in Japan, but have been on the decline since the 2000s (see Fig. 3).

Departmental stores have been experiencing severe financial problems in recent years and the number of the stores decreased by nearly 30% since 1995; (Yano Research Institute, 2008) Sogo even declared bankruptcy in 2000 (Chadha and Husband, 2006, p. 78). McKinsey's research suggests that the departmental store sales of fashion apparel and accessories were down by nearly 20% in 2009, which reflects decreases in foot traffic and reduction in transaction size (Atsmon, Salsberg and Yamanashi, 2009, p. 19).

The global financial crisis is only one of the reasons for why departmental stores are struggling. Luxury brands that were represented in the departmental stores attracted crowds of luxury-hungry

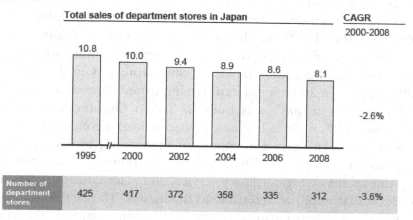

Figure 3. Total sales of departmental stores in Japan (1995–2008).
Source: Yano Research Institute, 2008.

customers. However, over the past few years, the luxury brands have changed their retailing strategies, and reduced the number of luxury goods sold in departmental stores. They felt the departmental stores took away the luxury brand's image by mixing luxury brands with cheaper brands, and not making them stand out enough. Husband & Chadha made the following comment during their visit to an upscale Mitsukoshi departmental store in Ginza: "we found prestigious imported brands presented in a homely setting, rubbing shoulders with lesser-known brands, completely lost in the sea of clothes racks" (Chadha and Husband, 2006, p. 75). This dissatisfaction of luxury brand managers with the departmental stores gave rise to the outlet shops that were brand specific, and had exclusive atmosphere and carefully selected and trained staff.

Departmental stores have been trying to bring luxury products back by upgrading store interiors, and offering value-added services. Louis Vuitton is paying as little as 15% of their sales to the departmental stores, while smaller brands are paying at least 30%. Not only are departmental stores willing to charge smaller commission to bring luxury back, they often take care of interior decoration and refurbishing costs (Chadha and Husband, 2006, p. 75).

Once the luxury brand companies got the distribution of their products under control, they started aggressive retail expansion in the form of outlet boutique shops and magnificent flagships. Louis Vuitton was the first brand to "kick off a luxury architecture war" in Japan by building a glass façade flagship store in Ginza (Thomas, 2007, p. 94). In 2002, a modern flagship store "of randomly stacked Louis Vuitton trunks" was built in Tokyo Omotesando district (Thomas, 2007, p. 94). The new store provided a concierge service, as well as a VIP salon for important customers, which could be accessed via a private lift. The privileged customers had an opportunity to experience extraordinary service, and place custom orders for products that were not accessible to the masses. The new store was a great success: 1,400 Japanese luxury lovers camped outside the store to be the first ones to shop, and first day sales amounted to over a million US dollars (Thomas, 2007, p. 94).

In 2001, La Maison Hermès built a stunning $137 million 12-story glass brick flagship store in Ginza. The new luxury tower had over 1,400 square feet of retail space, as well as an art gallery and a film-screening room. Prada followed with an $80 million six-story glass facade temple in Omotesando, designed by the Swiss firm Herzon & de Meuron. In December 2004, Chanel built a $240 million ten-story building "done up in absurdly expensive materials" in Ginza (Thomas, 2007, p. 75). According to Thomas, a year and a half after the opening of the store, there were still lines out front. Christian Dior constructed an elegant five-story glass building in Omotesando, designed by the Japanese avant-garde architects Sejima and Nishizawa. Once a quiet, tree-lined art and culture hotspot in central Tokyo, Omotesando has so turned into a luxury-lined avenue, often referred to as the Japanese Champs-Elysées. The flagship trend is the major reason for the changes in the face of retailing in Japan and the development of shopping districts (Chadha and Husband, 2006, p. 75).

There are a number of unofficial channels for the distribution of luxury goods in Japan. The rise of the unofficial channels was stimulated by the "mismatch between the demand and supply of the hot items" and the 40% markup of prices in Japan compared to Europe (Chadha and Husband, 2006, p. 78). Organized shopping tours to

Europe, Hawaii and Korea supply the unofficial multi-brand stores with the items that are either in high demand or not available to the masses. The multi-brand stores have a first-class service and trained staff that is readily available to answer any questions about products. Parallel imports are not illegal and can be very damaging to the brand names; if there are too many products available through unofficial channels, the brand stores will not be as attractive, and the increased availability of the products in the market will bring their perceived value down.

LUXURY CONSUMER PROFILES

Most luxury consumers share the following characteristics (Okonkwo, 2001, p. 68–69):

— *Smart and intelligent*: Today's luxury consumer has high brand awareness and is knowledgeable about the products' materials and sources.
— *Powerful*: The customer is the one who dictates the rules, and not vice versa.
— *Individualistic*: Although historically not a common characteristic of an Asian consumer, individualistic style is becoming more popular.
— *Highly demanding*: Especially true in Japan, where consumers have very high expectations and will not accept anything sub-standard.
— *High expectations*: Luxury consumers want to be "constantly delighted and surprised".
— *Disposable attitude*: Luxury consumers are no longer contented to staying with a single luxury item for years; they have become brand hoppers and are no longer loyal to a single brand.
— *Strong values and principles*: Luxury consumers are likely to be associated with the luxury brands that share their moral values.

According to research findings of McKinsey Asia Consumer and Retail, the typical Japanese luxury consumer is a female over the age

Table 2.   Luxury consumer categories.

Luxury Gourmands	Luxury gourmands are high net worth individuals (HNWI) who indulge in luxury from head to toe. They include individuals with over a million dollars in financial assets, their wives, mistresses, and children.
Luxury Regulars	Luxury regulars are affluent individuals with financial assets exceeding a hundred thousand U.S. dollars. Doctors, lawyers, middle and top managers, bankers and financial consultants typically fall under this category.
Luxury Nibblers	Luxury nibblers are the new "asset poor, income rich". They are usually comprised of a mix of junior executives, secretaries and teenagers. Those individuals stick to accessories and do not spend a large amount of money at the luxury stores.

Source: Based on Husband & Chadha, p. 47–51.

of 35; within that bracket, there are two large segments that reflect the demographic situation in Japan: the above 45 years old segment, and the below 45 years old segment (Atsmon, Salsberg and Yamanashi, 2009, p. 12). The luxury consumers in Japan can be classified into three categories: Luxury Gourmands, Luxury Regulars, and Luxury Nibblers (Chadha and Husband, 2006, p. 56) (see Table 2).

Although "office ladies", those holding secretarial and junior administrative positions, primarily fall into the luxury nibblers category, their consumption pattern is worth looking into. They are mostly interested in luxury accessories and bags. In Japan, it is very hard for a woman to climb up the corporate ladder and so "office ladies" are trapped in their jobs with no prospects of advancement. As a way to compensate for the lack of respect they endure at work, "office ladies" rejoice once they leave the office and eat out, take part in cultural events, entertainment and shop (Chadha and Husband, 2006, p. 56).

"Parasite singles" is a term used for young working women in their mid 20s to early 30s, who have a steady job and income, but still reside with their parents. Japanese society has traditionally been male-dominated with low status accorded to women. Once a woman got married, she becomes responsible for all the housework, while the husband is the breadwinner. In the recent years, an increasing number of women are choosing not to get married, but rather to work and spend their income on social aspects of their lives and shopping. The parental homes not only provide a place to live, but also take care of all the housework, which leaves the "parasites" with a significant amount of disposable income. "Disregarded, insignificant, with no voice and no opinion, forced to toe the line and keep their feelings bottled up — women's self-esteem is very low. The act of buying luxury goods becomes an affirmation of their existence, of momentary power (Chadha and Husband, 2006, p. 56)". Parasite singles are an important consumer segment of luxury markets in Japan. In fact, young working women account for the largest portion of luxury consumers and the 20–35 age group accounts for 75% of luxury accessory shopping. There is an estimated eight million parasite singles in Japan (Chadha and Husband, 2006, p. 56).

LUXURY BRAND MARKETING

Brand positioning and promotion in Japan have played a significant role in the success of luxury companies. There are a number of advertising channels that luxury companies use to market their products. There are various television programs devoted to fashion, as well as numerous magazines and websites, not to mention digital billboard advertising. Some of the popular fashion magazines in Japan are Elle, Vogue, Cosmopolitan, Classy, Oggi, Miss, Very, 25 Ans, and teen fashion, JJ, Can Can, and Vi Vi. Japanese luxury consumers are devoted to staying current with the newest fashion trends and they use information sources aggressively.

Luxury companies often use celebrities to market their product: they appear at social events in brand clothing and spark up discussions among Japanese fashion gurus. Traditionally, Japanese consumers are known to follow the fashion trends bluntly, without any adaptations or personal touches. "Women in Asia are known to tear out pictures from magazines, shots straight from the ramps and walk into stores seeking the entire look, head to toe (Chadha and Husband, 2006, p. 34)."

WHAT DROVE LUXURY EXPANSION IN JAPAN?

Lack of Space

The post-war era of rapid economic development provided wealth to masses of people, but it failed to provide a high standard of living. Due to the lack of space, Japanese do not have the same means of displaying their financial capabilities and success as their counterparts in the West. A typical wealthy American, for instance, would build a huge house, buy expensive cars, dig out a pool, spend a fortune on interior decoration, and enjoy himself in that setting. The Japanese do not have that privilege due to land scarcity, jammed traffic and other limitations. Most Japanese employees, regardless of social status, use public transportation to get to work and are in the public's eye most of the day. The only way Japanese can make a statement about their status to the public is through the physical symbols on their bodies. Luxury products are perfect agents for that purpose: they are small, expensive and fit into their physical requirements. This need to show one's social standing to the public explains why a vast majority of Japanese choose to spend money on outrageously priced pieces of clothing, rather than invest in home improvements (Chadha and Husband, 2006, p. 34).

Parasite Singles

Parasite singles were discussed in detail in the previous sections. Their overwhelming presence is a uniquely Japanese demographic phenomenon and their existence has greatly contributed to the spread and popularity of luxury goods in Japan.

Pressure to Conform

Since kindergarten, the Japanese are taught the importance of fitting into the social circle. The Japanese society has clear norms and strict adherence to those norms is expected. This overpowering pressure to conform extends to the ways of dressing and presenting oneself. This social need to fit in is the reason behind the rapid spread of new fashion trends in Japan. Most rapidly, the trends spread among teenagers. Chadha & Husband (2006) claim that if 5% of high school girls have a particular item, soon all the high school girls across Japan will have the same item. Unlike in western countries, lack of individuality in Japan is not seen as a bad thing. In fact, individual thinking is discouraged and the Japanese are encouraged to rely on higher authority for guidance in all aspects of their lives. When it comes to fashion, the magazines, specialized television programs and websites are used as the indicators of new fashion trends. The new fashion propositions are perceived as laws, and have to be followed without any room for doubt or adaptation. "In Japan, if it's a bag which everybody loves, maybe 90% of your friends will have that same bag", said Mukai Noiri, a marketing assistant manager at Desco Luxury (Hoel, 2008).

A combination of those three factors, lack of space, parasite singles and pressure to conform, is what created a very favorable environment for the spread of luxury in Japan.

RECENT TRENDS OF JAPANESE LUXURY MARKET — THE FALL OF THE LUXURY MARKET

The history of luxury products in Japan and their ability to take over daily lives of the Japanese made it seem as if the luxury market in Japan is inelastic, meaning it is resistant to any economic ups and downs and that the luxury lifestyle will always be valued by Japanese consumers. However, recent statistics show that there have been some major changes in the way Japanese consumers perceive luxury: sales are down and the whole luxury market is declining. Japan's market for imported luxury goods fell 10% to $11.9 billion (1.06 trillion yen) from 2007. Tokyo-based researchers forecast that market would shrink to 992.7 billion yen in 2009–2010, compared to its peak of 1.9 trillion yen in 1996 (Versace to close its Japanese stores, 2008).

LVMH has 57 clothing and merchandise stores in Japan and markets top-shelf alcohol. Total sales fell 10% in 2008. Sales of bags and merchandise suffered particularly steep declines. Louis Vuitton cancelled plans to open a 12-story flagship store in Ginza, which was supposed to be the world's largest Louis Vuitton store. The store was going to be completed in 2010 and would have rivaled the Paris main store in size. Louis Vuitton executives decided that business environment was not right for a large investment (Luxury goods slump as shoppers pinch pennies, 2009). Tiffany & Co. has 56 stores in Japan and experienced a 7% sales drop in 2008; a 13% slide occurred in the February–July period (Luxury goods slump as shoppers pinch pennies, 2009).

Swiss Compagnie Financiere Richemont, that owns Cartier, experienced a 7% sales drop from April to August 2008. Executives said the company is having the most difficult stretch in its 20-year history (Lewis, 2009). Due to decreased sales, Chanel was forced to abandon its flagship shop in central Osaka (Lewis, 2009).

Hugo Boss had to close its flagship store in Tokyo's Aoyama to deal with the crisis (Lewis, 2009). Versace was one of the hardest hit brands. It experienced a more than 50% drop in sales between 2004 and 2008, from 4.1 billion yen to 1.6 billion yen (New York Times, 2009). Versace said that it has closed the last three stores in Japan because they "no longer represented the brand image (Integral to buy Yohji Yamamoto Inc out of bankruptcy, 2009)." Bulgari's fourth quarter sales in 2008 dropped 25.4%, after having increased 2% in the January–September period (Europe's luxury brands see mixed results in Asia, 2009).

Hermès' sales declined by 12.9% in the fourth quarter of 2008, after having increased 2% between January and September (Europe's luxury brands see mixed results in Asia, 2009) and during his visit to Japan, Michael Burke, CEO of Fendi, said that Japanese consumers could no longer be won over by the cachet of luxury brands alone (Luxury brand chieftains make pilgrimage to Japan to boost sales, 2008). Japanese brands were also hit by the crisis. Yohji Yamamoto, a Japanese luxury brand, announced on 9 October, 2009 that it has filed for bankruptcy protection with the

Tokyo District Court, with total liabilities of about 6 billion yen ($67.8 million) (Integral to buy Yohji Yamamoto Inc out of bankruptcy, 2009).

WHAT HAPPENED TO JAPANESE LUXURY CONSUMERS?

Consumer confidence in Japan is currently at its lowest since 1982. This means that consumers are careful about their spending because they are unsure of their future financial standing. This ambiguity about the future has affected the economy as a whole, not excluding the luxury sector. McKinsey research revealed the following traits in luxury consumer behavior (Atsmon, Salsberg and Yamanashi, 2009, p. 21).

To some consumers, luxury is no longer as attractive as it used to be. A December 2008 survey by Nikkei Institute of Industry suggests that only 32% of respondents said they were very or somewhat interested in luxury products, compared to 54% in 2004. That means that between 2004 and 2008, over 40% of luxury consumers decreased their interest in luxury products. Even consumers with the highest confidence level reduced their luxury spending. Fashion apparel and leather goods were among the hardest hit categories of the luxury market.

While the luxury gurus remain brand loyal, they are looking to promotions and sales. Another recent trend is "trading down" within the same brand, which concerns luxury brand executives, who might have to re-evaluate their pricing strategies.

Luxury consumers are looking for better deals overseas. The number of Japanese travelers to Korea has doubled in the last year, while travel outside Japan declined nearly 10% in the same period (Korea National Tourist Organization). Japanese luxury consumers take advantage of the exchange rates to afford luxury products.

While 65% of consumers across various age groups are planning to return to their luxury spending patterns after the economic crisis, an alarming one-third of all consumers claimed that they are no longer going to spend the same amounts on luxury items.

Change in Consumer Attitudes

Researchers at McKinsey Asia Consumer and Retail concluded that, in addition to the global financial crisis and the shrinking luxury bubble, several important shifts in consumer attitudes contributed to market downturn (Atsmon, Salsberg and Yamanashi, 2009, p. 6):

In the past, luxury brands were purchased as badges of social status and membership to the new urban class; the Japanese market has moved on from that stage, and is "beginning to resemble the norms of mature brand behavior seen in the Western world" (Carter). As a result, Japanese women today are much more confident about selecting their own style. Their purchasing patterns are not as predictable as before and many mix and match various styles. There is also a new trend which consists of mixing expensive and cheap clothing.

Another relatively new trait of the Japanese luxury market is the increased popularity of luxury experiences. An increasing number of Japanese luxury lovers choose to spend their money on traveling, dining out at up-scale restaurants, spa services and entertainment, rather than on luxury clothing and accessories.

Nowadays, one does not have to spend a fortune to be trendy. There is a growing number of affordable and stylish stores such as H&M and Zara all over Japan. The range and availability of various styles reduces societal pressure to conform and customers feel at ease making their own fashion decisions. Consumers now have more product choices and the lines between luxury and casual fashion are blurred.

Once powerful fashion centers, departmental stores have been on decline for almost a decade. Japanese consumers are more attracted to the personalized services the outlet shops and luxury boutiques can offer.

FROM LUXURY TO FAST FASHION?

McKinsey and Co. principal, Brain Salsberg noted, "…for every one luxury [brand] bag, there are ten Uniqlo, Forever 21, or H&M bags" (McGinn, 2009). Indeed, while the luxury giants are suffocating, the so-called fast fashion retailers have been drawing hundreds of eager shoppers. Swedish casual-wear chain, Hennes & Mauritz (H&M), which entered Japan in September 2008, has already opened five shops and opened its first "concept store" in November 2009. With only two stores open, H&M pulled in about $94.4 million in sales in nine months through August 2009, which is equivalent to a year's worth of revenue at a regional departmental store (Fast-fashion chains thriving, 2009).

U.S. Forever 21 debuted at the end of April in Harajuku, and draws on average of 20,000 shoppers a day. Zara, run by Spain's Inditex, already has over 50 outlet shops in Japan and is a year ahead of schedule. UK's Topshop is another fast-fashion brand that is planning to fully develop its network in the coming year. Larry Myer, the CFO of Forever 21, believes the increase in business has to do with luxury not being "in vogue" (H&M and Forever 21 take on Japan, 2009).

The key of the attraction of fast-fashion is its triple balance among fashion, quality and price, according to the manager of H&M's Japanese unit, Christine Edman. The fast-fashion chains make small batches of clothing and put new garments on the shelves several times per week.

SYNOPSIS

The recent decline in the luxury industry has been hard on the major luxury goods players and they must take immediate action in order to preserve their share of the market. The issue at hand is complicated, as there are various internal and external factors affecting the industry. On one hand, the global economic recession is shifting consumers' preferences. The Japanese are changing their shopping patterns and are becoming more budget conscious, as consumers' confidence levels are very low. Fast-fashion chains, however, have managed to attract crowds of customers by offering more affordable and trendy goods. Luxury companies need to carefully analyze their core competencies and change the existing strategies to draw their customer base back. The business model that most luxury players have in Japan today still relies on brand equity and expects continued customer patronage. This approach to luxury marketing is no longer sustainable. Western luxury brands need to rethink their strategies for the worlds' only mass luxury market.

QUESTIONS

1) How does luxury consumption in Japan differ from other countries?
2) Why did the Japanese luxury retail market develop this rapidly?
3) What explanations can be found for the sudden change in luxury consumption in Japan?
4) What strategies should European luxury brand develop for the Japanese market?

BIBLIOGRAPHY

Atsmon, Y., Salsberg, B and Yamanashi, H. (2009). "Luxury goods in Japan: Momentary sigh or long sayonara? Market Research.

Carter, D. Carter Associates (2010). Marketing information and consultancy. www.carterassociates.net/aboutJapan/view_04_Luxury.html.

Chadha, R and Husband, P. (2006). *The Cult of The Luxury Brand*. London: Nicholas Brealey International.

Europe's luxury brands see mixed results in Asia (9 March 2009). *The Nikkei Weekly*.

Fast-fashion chains thriving (16 November 2009). *The Nikkei Weekly*.

Hoel, J. (2008). *Hey, Big Spender*.

Hall, ET. (1977). *Beyond Culture*. New York: Anchor Books.

H&M and Forever 21 take on Japan (12 November 2009). http://cocoperez.com/2009-11-12-hm-and-forever-21-take-on-japan#ixzz0Xajr9eUW.

Integral to buy Yohjo Yamamoto Inc out of bankruptcy (11 October 2009). *The Nikkei Weekly*.

(2009). Japanese biggest visa card users in S Korea. *Nikkei Marketing Journal*.

Korea National Tourist Organization. http://www.knto.or.kr.

Lewis, L. Japanese change view on what looks good as luxury brands struggle (8 October 2009). *The Times.*

Luxury brand chieftains make pilgrimage to Japan to boost sales (29 December 2008). *The Nikkei Weekly.*

Luxury goods slump as shoppers pinch pennies (10 September 2009). *The Nikkei Weekly.*

McGinn, D. Japan's luxury market won't recover soon (23 September 2009). *Newsweek.*

Okonkwo, U. (2007). *Luxury Fashion Branding: Trends, Tactics, Techniques.* New York: Palgrave Macmillan.

Seeking alpha. http://seekingalpha.com/dashboard/global_markets?source=headtabs.

Thomas, D. (2007). *Deluxe: How Luxury Lost Its Luster.* New York: Penguin Group.

Versace to close its Japanese stores (8 October 2009). *The New York Times.*

Toyota Lexus: Number One at Home but Struggling at Home

Nathan Michael Echols

INTRODUCTION

Toyota Motor Corporation is one of the most successful automakers in the world. Since the founding of Toyota Motor Company in 1937, Toyota automobiles have been produced and prevalent throughout Japan. Toyota has enjoyed enormous domestic success and is currently the leading automaker in Japan. Toyota's luxury brand, Lexus, has achieved extraordinary success in the United States market and is currently the most popular among America's wealthy consumers. However, Lexus remains the brainchild of then Toyota chairman Eiji Toyoda and was created solely for the purpose of entering the United States luxury automobile market as a rival to the already entrenched brands of European and domestic automakers. [8] Lexus has enjoyed enormous success in the United States market and is now the leading luxury automaker in North America, although the best-selling Lexus ES and IS sedans and the RX crossovers in the $30,000–$42,000 price range are cheaper than many European counterparts. [12]

As a result of this incredible success in the United States, Toyota attempted to introduce the Lexus luxury line domestically into the Japanese market in direct competition with already entrenched European brands such as BMW, Mercedes-Benz, and Audi. American luxury vehicles such as the Lincoln Town Car and the Cadillac pose little threat to Lexus in Japan as many Japanese view American luxury automobiles as unreliable and of low quality. [21] Ironically, the quality control positions have completely reversed over the past 20 years as the Japanese have made significant strides to improve Japanese-owned brand products. As one American columnist stated, "When I was growing up, 'made in Japan' meant cheap junk. We even were leery of a 'Made in USA' label because we'd heard there was a city called Usa in Japan, so if there were no dots between the U, S and A, the product was suspect. Today, nobody would say 'junk' about a Lexus or any of the other world-class products that boast a 'made in Japan' pedigree". [3] Modern day Lexus reflects a quite different image of Japanese engineering, boasting impeccable quality and service. Yet, despite entering the Japanese automobile market in August 2005, Lexus has faced a severe uphill battle in attempting to effectively compete with European competitors. Introducing Lexus to the Japanese market turned out to be one of Toyota's greatest challenges.

TOYOTA—THE COMPANY

The company, now known as Toyota Motor Corporation, was created in September 1933 as a division of the parent company, Toyoda Automatic Loom, founded by Sakichi Toyoda. Sakichi Toyoda is well known in Japan as the inventor of the then revolutionary Type-G Toyoda automatic loom that allowed for non-stop shuttle change motion. The result of this invention allowed Toyoda to greatly increase the income of Toyoda Automatic Loom, and these funds were later used by his son, Kiichiro Toyoda, to create the first Toyota automobile engines.

Toyota Motor Corporation became an independent company in 1937 and was strongly encouraged by the Japanese government to produce automobiles for military use. Although the company was founded by Kiichiro Toyoda, the name was changed to Toyota because it was easier to pronounce, represented a separation of personal and business life, and for superstitious reasons. The Japanese word "Toyota" is written in the katakana script and the number of strokes is equal to eight — a lucky number in Japan.

Although Toyota Motor Corporation initially produced military trucks for the war effort during World War II, the company now focuses largely on the commercial, small car market where it holds enormous market shares in Japan, the United States and Europe. Recent years have been marked with enormous success for Toyota in the United States market as the company has overtaken all other industry leaders but General Motors in sales. [17]

TOYOTA CORE COMPETENCIES — PRODUCTION MANAGEMENT AND INNOVATION

Yet, Toyota Motor Corporation does have one advantage over the competition. Much of the success of Toyota Motor Corporation's profit margins can be attributed to the world-acclaimed Toyota Production System that has proven extremely successful in maximizing profits and efficiency. This system has been emulated, albeit less successfully, by multinational companies across the globe and has allowed Toyota to maintain significant profits and savings without resulting to the mass layoffs that many foreign automakers often implement. The Toyota Production System also gives Lexus an advantage in any market as the efficiency of this system is often unrivaled. [11] The Toyota Production System has been heralded in recent years as a major contributing factor to the success of the Toyota and Lexus brand vehicles. While many American automakers believe the most efficient way to cut expenses is to engage in mass layoff of employees, Toyota cuts costs through improving efficiency. This system even allowed Toyota to almost overtake DaimlerChrysler to become the third-largest producer of automobiles in the North American market. "Toyota has repeatedly outperformed its competitors in quality, reliability, productivity, cost reduction, sales, and market share growth, and market capitalization". [11]

Essentially, Toyota Motor Corporation devised a method of standardization that informs employees of what is expected before work begins and observes work being carried out to ensure that delays and inefficient hindrances are eliminated. Rather than executives depending on their own experience in making exclusive management decisions, Toyota encourages management to work closely with subordinate employees to create solutions cooperatively. This management style is often quite effective in eliminating the barriers between practical workplace knowledge and management theory or strategy.

Specifically, there are four fundamental principles that Toyota Motor Corporation attempts to communicate to all new management employees. First, Toyota believes that there is no substitute for direct managerial observation when setbacks occur. Rather than attempt to correct a problem abstractly, managers observe and address problems firsthand so that they are sure to understand the circumstances surrounding a given decision. Second, managerial decisions that are designed to correct a given problem should always be tested and checked to ensure that the problem has been efficiently and effectively resolved. Simply making decisions on observation without any testing or follow-up observation can result in wasted time and effort with little gains in efficiency and profit. Third, Toyota encourages managers to work closely with subordinate employees in order to identify gaps in efficiency and to engage in rapid fixes to improve the workplace. While foreign firms often spend a lengthy period of time on major problem-solving endeavors, Toyota Motor Corporation realized that solving many small problems quickly can add up to significant increases in overall efficiency. Finally, Toyota encourages management to guide subordinate workers rather than make all executive decisions. Only by encouraging and guiding employees can managers ensure that the individuals who know the most about their work environment make the most effective improvements. [11]

The Toyota Production System has created a workforce within the company that is versed on a variety of aspects of the necessary components of the company and individuals; thus, employees are able to work together effectively and efficiency to solve problems that arise. It is this fostering of problem-solving capabilities that largely accounts for Toyota's steady increase in profits since the 1950s and a steady increase in a competitive advantage over the foreign and domestic automakers. [11]

LEXUS IN THE UNITED STATES — TOYOTA'S FIRST LUXURY CAR

In order to increase sales in the United States, Toyota introduced the Lexus brand to the American market in 1989. Initially, Lexus management pondered emulating the existing 12 cylinder six-figure luxury flagship models of BMW, Mercedes and Audi, but soon realized that simple emulation would not be sufficient to appease discerning consumers. Hence, Toyota engineers and managers collaborated and engaged in direct consumer research to create a truly innovative luxury vehicle that implement hybrid technology while not sacrificing performance. The result was that Lexus was able to deliver a trendy and environmentally-friendly vehicle with the horsepower of the best European luxury vehicles. Other innovations include a greater soundproof cabin to assist in blocking irritating noise pollution as well as a more spacious interior. On high-end models such as the LS600hL, Lexus even introduced the latest safety technology including cameras to monitor the driver's facial motions to ensure that he is awake as well as sensors to warn of any nearby objects. This system can even initiate braking procedures and deviate the vehicle's course if a collision seems imminent. As one Toyota engineer stated, "The car could drive itself if all of the components were put together in the right combination". [1]

Toyota has spent an enormous amount of financial and marketing resources to create a luxury brand image of the Lexus and is now ranked as the leading manufacturer of luxury vehicles in the United States. [8] The success of Lexus has been largely credited to the Japanese's extremely high level of quality and service that often trumps domestic and European brands.

BRINGING LEXUS TO JAPAN

As late as the 1980s, virtually 80% of citizens in Japan fell into the middle class income segment. Despite a booming capitalist mentality in countries such as the United States, which allowed for vast disparities in income, the Japanese economy supported a strong middle class. Little disparity existed in the income ratios of average employees and a conservative mentality prevailed over many of that generation. However, this trend has begun to shift dramatically since the Japanese economic bubble burst in the late 1980s and in conjunction with demographic change.

Recent decades have resulted in a Japanese citizenry with increasing disparities in income with the dismantling of the lifetime employment system and an increasing promotion of young and promising managers. While these younger and wealthier Japanese will be prime targets for luxury automakers, the society of Japan is aging with a birthrate well below what is necessary to sustain population growth.

This shift in the economic structure of Japanese society is also coupled with an expected increase in wealthy retirees willing to spend money in the luxury automobile market. The major luxury automakers in Japan predict that the baby boomer generation will start retiring in increasing numbers from 2007, resulting in a spike in the sale of luxury cars. Although Toyota Motor Corporation has a strong hold on the domestic automobile market in Japan, European automakers such as Mercedes-Benz, Audi, and BMW still maintain an overwhelming presence in the luxury market. As the luxury market has an overwhelmingly larger profit potential per vehicle sold than the minicar market, Lexus has the potential to take in significant profits for Toyota if successful. [19]

With the wealth distribution continuing to diminish the middle class, much of the dispensable wealth will be in the hands of the upper class. This will likely create an expansion in the luxury automobile market that the domestic Japanese automakers do not intend to leave solely to be exploited by BMW, Mercedes-Benz, and Audi. As Commerz International Capital Management (Japan) Ltd. President Hitoshi Yamamoto stated, "There's increasing diversity in consumer demand. Automakers have to respond". [6]

Therefore, some analysts are predicting that wealthy, retired consumers will join the wealthy, youthful consumers in purchasing luxury vehicles, which will greatly expand the market in Japan by 2010. Although the luxury market has been relatively stable with an average of 500,000 luxury vehicles sold each year in Japan, many analysts at

Lexus, BMW, Mercedes-Benz, and Audi are expecting to see a significant increase in sales over the coming years. The stagnation of the Japanese luxury automobile market to date can largely be attributed to the state of the distribution of wealth among the Japanese people until recent decades.

One journalist has even produced evidence from the Researchers Global Insight group, which indicates that the surge in consumer demand will reach upwards by 90% within five years since the initial introduction of Lexus to the Japanese market. [19] At the same time, the introduction of the Lexus brand has helped to affirm in the minds of many older, conservative Japanese that it is socially acceptable to flaunt wealth and enjoy retirement in luxury. [6]

TOYOTA'S BIGGEST CHALLENGE

Lexus was introduced to Japan in August 2005 in the hopes of emulating the success the brand enjoys in the United States and stealing a significant portion of market share from European competitors. However, the success of the car was not as expected. Despite the inherent advantage of the Toyota Production System, Toyota has not achieved the amount of success through implementing the Lexus brand in Japan as the management had initially hoped.

Toyota Motor Corporation faced an uphill battle in entering the luxury market in Japan, however, as they no longer had the benefit of exceptionally high customer service that had propelled the Lexus brand to the top in the United States. Furthermore, the three Lexus brands that were initially introduced to the Japanese market (the GS sports sedan, the SC convertible, and the IS sedan) all resembled high-end Toyota brand models previously available in the Japanese market. The only significant and noticeable difference to the average Japanese consumer was the 20% price hike and a change in the nameplate from "Toyota" to "Lexus". [9]

In order to further the image of Lexus as a luxury brand that rivaled the European competitors in Japan, Toyota Motor Corporation poured millions of dollars into advertising campaigns. However, reports from BMW, Mercedes-Benz, and Audi indicated that purchases of foreign luxury vehicles actually spiked during the aggressive Lexus campaign period. Apparently, the introduction of the Lexus brand to Japan prompted curious Japanese consumers to visit European luxury automobile dealerships to make comparisons.

Toyota is facing severe setbacks in legitimizing the Lexus brand as a luxury vehicle that rivals European models in Japan. Chris Richter, an automobile analyst, stated, "Getting Lexus accepted as a bona fide luxury brand seems to be a lot harder in Japan than in the U.S. It is one of the rare times Toyota has stumbled". [9] Another analyst commented that Lexus has only significantly affected the Toyota consumer market rather than steal a significant market share from BMW, Mercedes-Benz, and Audi. At the initial introduction of Lexus to the Japanese market, 80% of early buyers were Toyota owners, while only 5% defected from the German luxury automobile dealerships. [9]

In order to convince Japanese consumers that Lexus is in fact as luxurious and exotic as German vehicles, Toyota allocated approximately $1.6 billion for the creation of 160 extremely luxurious showrooms across Japan. [9] Despite this enormous investment in the Japanese market, Toyota did not make significant headway into the luxury market share of European competitors. Hans Tempel, the CEO of DaimlerChrysler at this time, stated, "I think [Lexus] will expand the market". [20] In other words, Lexus will not convert many avid European luxury automobile enthusiasts, but will create a new consumer group that will purchase Lexus models and enter the luxury market.

These indicators were further supported, however, by actions taken by Lexus prior to the release of the brand into the Japanese market in August 2005 as only previous Toyota owners were invited to preview the Lexus models to be introduced to Japan. [14] Toyota spares virtually no expense at these advertising venues as well. For example, in order to promote the new gasoline-electric hybrid Lexus models that debuted in 2006, Lexus constructed a 2,000 square meter pavilion at the National Yoyogi Stadium in Shibuya, Tokyo. According to Toyota President Katsuaki Watanabe, he believed that such extravagant expenditures were necessary to illustrate that Lexus is truly on par with the European competitors. [18]

By several indications following the debut of Lexus in Japan, Toyota initially had doubts about the success of initially making a significant dent in the market. For example, the strong Toyota media and advertising campaigns to promote the Lexus brand prompted many potential Japanese consumers to inquire at the luxurious Lexus showrooms as to the differences between the domestic and imported luxury vehicles. However, the usually well-trained sales staff in the Lexus showrooms were inadequately prepared to answer questions related to European models, prompting Japanese consumers to then visit BMW, Mercedes-Benz, and Audi showrooms to find the answer to their questions. Ironically, Lexus prides itself on providing customers with the "highest quality of service", which prompted many analysts to infer the unpreparedness of Lexus staff to be an indicator that Toyota was targeting its own consumer base rather than the competition. [15] The President of Toyota Motor Corporation at the time, Katsuaki Watanabe, quickly made a statement to the media that Toyota was fully confident in the viability of the Lexus brand and that the training deficiencies of the sales staff would be quickly addressed. [20]

CONSUMER REACTIONS

The Japanese business culture of an extremely high level of quality and customer service is largely what propelled Lexus to the pinnacle of the United States luxury automobile market, but that strategy is useless in Japan where quality and service are taken for granted. Moreover, the Japanese view European automobile brands with an image of individuality and exotic appeal — a view that Lexus will — be hard-pressed to compete with as a domestic automaker. On top of these already difficult challenges, Toyota's extremely expensive and aggressive advertising campaigns have had the negative effect of driving an increasing number of Japanese luxury automobile customers to visit European automobile dealerships in order to compare the foreign models with Lexus. It is likely that Lexus' introduction to Japan has resulted in greater sales for foreign automakers. [9]

Yet, despite this predicted increase in the Japanese consumer market for luxury vehicles, Lexus faces stiff cultural challenges that are a part of the Japanese mindset. The high level of service that accounted for success in the United States has always been a part of the Toyota Motor Corporation, however, and Japanese consumers did not associate this service exclusively with luxury. Thus, Lexus faces the threat of losing its competitive advantage when engaging in business in the Japanese domestic market. [7] For many Japanese consumers, domestic brands simply are not exotic enough to be luxurious. For example, BMW owner, Masayoshi Haku, stated, "Lexus makes excellent cars. But if you ask me whether I'd buy one, the answer is no. Foreign brands have more individuality". [9] In a culture that depends largely on social interactions and group orientation, owning a foreign vehicle that allows the owner a small sense of individuality appears to be quite important to many wealthy Japanese.

Lexus did not seem to realize that Japanese consumers wanted distinction from other brands when it initially debuted in Japan. Many consumers were familiar with the high-end Toyota brands that were previously available in the Japanese market and considered Toyota Motor Corporation to simply be changing the nameplate to Lexus and increasing the price. While this inference was largely accurate, the brand image alone was not strong enough in Japan to justify the increase in prices. [9]

Shotaro Noguchi of Mitsubishi Securities Company recently stated, "I think Toyota knows what Japanese consumers want". [21] Yet, Lexus still has not conformed and reached the individuality and exotic nature for which the foreign brands maintain a certain appeal. Rather, Toyota has reacted contrary to expectations by branding Lexus vehicles as traditional Japanese luxury automobiles. For example, the new Lexus IS sedan was especially constructed from scratch to give Lexus a unique but Japanese feel in an attempt to satisfy customers. This new model does not attempt to be exotic by becoming European; rather, it is designed to be stereotypically luxurious from a Japanese cultural perspective. The interior doors are designed to imitate images of Japanese calligraphy and Japanese swordsmanship. There are also extra comfort features added such as outside noise reduction and airbag safety measures. [13]

Although Lexus received satisfactory sales following the initial introduction of the brand to the domestic Japanese market in August 2005, the automaker is currently at a disadvantage to European competitors and must create a corporate strategy that will allow the luxury brand name to become entrenched the minds of Japanese consumers. [16]

COMPETITOR'S REACTIONS

Due to the additional features by Lexus, European automakers have also begun to initiate intensive competition campaigns designed to limit the proliferation of the Lexus brand in Japan. BMW, Mercedes-Benz, and Audi have all released plans to introduce several new and improved vehicle models into the Japanese market and plan to intensify research and development in an attempt to maintain a competitive advantage over Toyota Motor Corporation. [4]

BMW has especially increased efforts in the Japanese market by introducing four new BMW 3 Series sedans in recent years while continually making efforts to improve upon existing model types currently available. BMW President Jesus Cordoba understands that Toyota Motor Corporation poses a serious threat to European automakers in the Japanese luxury market and believes it is vital that BMW responds aggressively. Audi has also recently introduced a new version of the A4 premium vehicle and Mercedes-Benz has also implemented significant improvements. [2]

In response to European efforts to prevent the success of the Lexus brand in Japan, Toyota Motor Corporation has also implemented an aggressive campaign to improve the vehicle models. Not only has an advanced computer system been implemented to assist the growing elderly population in Japan by giving the vehicle the capability to perform tasks such as automatic parking, Lexus also believes that it can appeal to the wealthy through producing environmentally-friendly vehicles. [10]

Lexus has an advantage over the European competition in the field of hybrid technology. Toyota Motor Corporation believes that many wealthy Japanese are also environmentally conscious and would appreciate vehicles that are low on harmful emissions. As European automakers have lagged behind Toyota Motor Corporation in the field of hybrid technology, many luxury automakers have little recourse and made the argument that their vehicles are also available with diesel engines that save on emissions. However, diesel has not been popular in Japan and hybrid technology is seen as more innovative. [5] Moreover, the Lexus brands have continued to implement the latest comforts and technologies including seat heating and cooling, massage chairs, and safety sensors. [1] [7]

THE FUTURE OF LEXUS

Toyota Motor Corporation has faced problems ranging from a lack of exoticness to poor marketing strategies to stiff competition from European automakers since introducing Lexus into the Japanese luxury market. Lexus had hoped to steal a significant portion of market share from the competition as the luxury automobile market provides a greater profit margin than the standard automobile market.

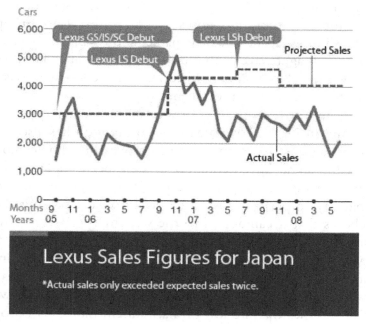

Figure 1.   Lexus sales in Japan (2005–2008).

Source: Toyokeizai Online http://www.toyokeizai.net.

However, Lexus has so far not managed to reach the level of success that many had initially hoped.

Although Lexus achieved respectable sales figures shortly after the initial introduction of the brand in 2005 (see Fig. 1), Lexus has failed to improve significantly in a market dominated by BMW, Mercedes-Benz, and Audi. Furthermore, many analysts wonder if Lexus will gradually begin to lose momentum in the coming years if the brand name does not achieve a greater appeal among Japanese consumers. Many new business ventures in Japan see moderate success as Japanese consumers tend to be curious and flock to the latest business trend. However, as the years pass and the newness of Lexus fades, it is possible that sales figures will deteriorate in the face of increasing European competition (see Fig. 2). [16]

How can Lexus continue to maintain a hold on the luxury automobile market in Japan while also ensuring a steady increase in sales

Brand	Standard	Small	Total	Brand	Standard	Small	Total
Alfa Romeo	52,631	4,518	57,149	Land Rover	13,520		13,520
Aston Martin	1,265		1,265	Lotus	3,444	3,556	7,000
Audi	136,677	5,159	141,836	Maserati	4,274		4,274
Autobianchi		823	823	Maybach	132		132
Bentley	3,123		3,123	Mercedes-Benz	624,898	5,590	630,488
BMW	448,149	49,946	498,095	MG	156	2,349	2,505
BMW Alpina	2,547		2,547	Mini		12,173	12,173
BMW MINI		88,253	88,253	Mitsubishi	4,473	3,107	7,580
Buick	3,465		3,465	Morgan	219	494	713
Cadillac	21,012		21,012	Nissan	32,943	3,250	36,193
Chevrolet	43,683	68	43,751	Opel	37,735	38,809	76,544
Chrysler	89,040		89,040	Peugeot	49,859	60,593	110,452
Citroen	14,491	9,298	23,789	Pontiac	3,195		3,195
DAEWOO		746	746	Porsche	50,546	1,280	51,826
Ferrari	9,387		9,387	Renault	10,583	19,123	29,706
Fiat	2,236	25,377	27,613	Rolls Royce	1,908		1,908
Ford	73,609	4,757	78,366	Rover	22,892	53,826	76,718
GMC	1,598		1,598	Saab	13,348	1,838	15,186
GMDAT		294	294	Saturn	941	1,075	2,016
Honda	109,372	46,978	156,350	smart		11,811	11,811
Hummer	2,650		2,650	Ssangyong	189		189
Hyundai	7,809	2,970	10,779	Subaru	10,825		10,825
Isuzu	8,734		8,734	Suzuki		3,191	3,191
Jaguar	49,380		49,380	Toyota	104,035	17	104,052
Kia	56	2	58	Volvo	209,670	401	210,071
Lamborghini	1,563		1,563	VW	404,124	221,998	626,122
Lancia	3,511	1,532	5,043	Others	1,392	3,178	4,570
				Total	2,691,287	688,380	3,379,667

Figure 2. Imported cars in operation in Japan (2009).

Source: Automobile Inspection & Registration Information Association. http://www.jaia-jp.org.

Note: As of the end of March, 2009.

and market share? Toyota has been pouring money into advertising and developing luxurious showrooms only to fuel interest in comparisons with foreign brands among Japanese consumers. Furthermore, European competitors are quickly implementing counterstrategies in an attempt to keep Lexus from making any significant gains within the market. As the Japanese population continues to age and an increasing number of wealthy citizens begin to retire, the luxury automobile market will likely see growth and expansion. It remains to be seen if Lexus will succeed in this market in the upcoming decades.

QUESTIONS

1) Why is Lexus positioned differently in Japan and the United States?
2) How is luxury perceived in Japan and the United States?
3) How can Toyota reposition its products in Japan?

BIBLIOGRAPHY

1. Aukofer, F. Lexus aims at rarified customer base with LS600hL (11 May 2007). *The Washington Times (DC)*.
2. BMW Japan unveils 4 new BMW 3 series models (12 April 2005). *Kyodo News International (Japan)*.
3. Dzwonkowski, R. Detroit Free Press Ron Dzwonkowski column (18 November 2007). *Detroit Free Press (MI)*.
4. FY 2005 new imported vehicle sales up 0.4% in Japan (6 April 2006). *Kyodo News International (Japan)*
5. Hutton, R. Toyota's green drive to the top (2 September 2007). *The Sunday Times*.
6. Inoue, K. Japan's market, for richer or poorer (7 January 2006). *Toronto Star (Canada)*.
7. Karube, T. Lexus hybrid flagship sedans launched in Japan ahead of overseas (17 May 2007). *Kyodo News International (Japan)*.
8. Lexus official website. http://www.lexus.com.
9. Rowley, I. and Tashiro, H. Lexus: Too Japanese for the Japanese (31 March 2008). *Business Week*, 72.

10. Smart innovations need more school (31 March 2007). *Toronto Star (Canada)*.

11. Spear, S. (2004). Learning to lead at Toyota. *Harvard Business Review*.

12. Teahen Jr., John, K. Mercedes again is true-luxury king (17 March 2008). *Automotive News*.

13. Toyota adds IS luxury sedan to Lexus lineup in Japan (28 September 2005). *Kyodo News International (Japan)*.

14. Toyota holds Lexus preview for Toyota customers (19 August 2005). *Kyodo News International (Japan)*.

15. Toyota launches luxury Lexus brand in Japan (30 August 2005). *Kyodo News International (Japan)*.

16. Toyota Lexus orders prove nearly 4 times monthly sales goal (30 September 2005). *Kyodo News International (Japan)*.

17. Toyota Motor Corporation official website. http://www.toyota.com.

18. Toyota unveils 3 series of Lexus brand for Japan (26 July 2005). *Kyodo News International (Japan)*.

19. Treece, JB. In Japan, suddenly it is OK to drive rich (12 June 2006). *Automotive News Europe*, 10.

20. Treece, JB. Lexus meets '05 launch goal in Japan (30 January 2006). *Automotive News*, 22.

21. Yamaguchi, Y. Cadillac to bring STS to Japan next month (25 October 2004). *Automotive News*, 6.

Part 3

DEALING WITH CRISIS

Schindler Elevators and the Challenges of the Japanese Market

Pascal Kalbermatten

> *"Crisis is a productive condition. One has to remove only the smack of the catastrophe".*
>
> *Max Frisch*

INTRODUCTION

Schindler Elevator is in serious trouble in Japan; it has a bad reputation and a weak market position. This is due to its unsuccessful growth strategy, and its internal difficulties, as well as the challenging market conditions in Japan. The situation worsened after a fatal accident involving a Schindler elevator in the year 2006. Due to inadequate crisis management, the public reputation of Schindler became seriously damaged and the company thus inherited the image of an arrogant company which produces unsafe and low quality products. In 2007 a new president for Schindler Japan was employed and the company now struggles to improve growth. In this case study, an overview about Schindler in Japan and the escalator/elevator market will be given. The events surrounding the fatal accident are then described as well as the public perception in Japan and abroad.

SCHINDLER GROUP AND THE JAPANESE ELEVATOR MARKET

Historical Development

Schindler was founded 1874 in Switzerland by Robert Schindler and Eduard Villiger and was called at that time Schindler & Villiger. In a mechanical engineering workshop on the river Reuss Island in Lucerne, Switzerland, the company produced lifting equipment and machines of all types. The company internationalized early, entering the German market in 1906 and the French market in 1909. Year after year, Schindler established subsidiaries in more countries, mostly in Europe and America. It later pushed into Africa, the Middle East and British India. In 1980, Schindler established the first industrial joint venture between the People's Republic of China and a western company: the China Schindler Elevator Co., in Beijing; in 1981, it entered in the Australian market. In 1985, Schindler entered the Japanese market through a 30% stake of shares in the Japanese Nippon Elevator Industry Co. Ltd. and two years later took a majority stake in the company. Schindler was always growing internally as well as through acquisitions and has regularly presented the world with novelties. In the course of time, the company developed from an engineering to a service providing company.

In 2006, Schindler employs around 44,000 people worldwide and is active in two areas of business: elevators and escalators, which contributed 70% of sales in 2006, and ALSO, an IT distributor in Europe. Schindler is listed on the Swiss Exchange (SWX). The company is a leading global manufacturer and service provider for elevators and escalators with subsidiaries in around 130 countries and more than 1000 branches on all five continents. Schindler Group is today the largest supplier of escalators and the second largest manufacturer of elevators worldwide. The company designs, installs, services and modernizes transport systems. Schindler equipment moves more than 700 million people per day.

Schindler runs production plants and R&D centers in America, Europe, and as well as in China, while its headquarters as well as some of its production and R&D facilities are located in Ebikon,

Switzerland. The operating revenue in 2006 was 11.106 billion Swiss francs. Revenues in the escalator/elevator business accounted for 7.83 billion francs (revenues from Asia, Australia and Africa represent 16% of this figure). The operating profit EBIT (escalator/elevator only) was 726 million Swiss francs (Schindler, 2007). The fight for market share, especially between Schindler and Thyssen-Krupp, which is globally ranked third, is going on mainly in Asia today (Chalupny, 2006).

THE GLOBAL ELEVATOR MARKET

The worldwide market for elevator and escalator products and services is forecasted to expand 5.4% annually through 2011, surpassing $57 billion. The global market for moving walkways is still growing stronger, 8.3% annually to $2.5 billion in 2011 (Bharat Book Bureau, 2006). The strongest growth can be expected in India and China.

Worldwide, there were 8,300,000 elevators (11% of them in Japan and Korea) in operation in the year 2006. 405,000 new elevators (11% in Japan and Korea) were sold. There are also 400,000 escalators in operation (23% of them in Japan and Korea) and in 2006, 35,000 new escalators were sold (11% in Japan and Korea). The maintenance business is more stable than the new equipment business and offers higher profits. Manufacturers try to attract customers to long-term service contracts. The maintenance segment benefits from stable recurring revenues and predictable cash flows as the majority of the costs consist of labor in local currency (Kone, 2007).

SCHINDLER IN JAPAN

In 1985, Schindler entered the Japanese market and acquired about 40% of a relatively small Japanese manufacturer, Nippon Elevator Industry Co. Ltd. Six years later, the firm was renamed Schindler Elevator and Schindler increased its stake to 96.7% over the following 4 years (Nikkei, 2006). In the past, the company had manufactured in Japan, but in 2005, it closed its Japanese manufacturing plant in

Fukuroi due to cost reasons. Today, Schindler sells its standardized escalators in Japan which are produced in a large scale plant in Shanghai. However, standardized products have to be adapted to the special Japanese legal requirements, for example, unique control units for the Japanese market have to be developed (Management, 2007). Schindler Elevator K.K. management stated that it was so far impossible to establish the global Schindler culture in the Japanese subsidiary. The culture of the "old" Nippon Elevator Industry Co. Ltd. is still strong and inside Schindler and Japan has always been treated as a special case. In recent years, Schindler Elevator K.K. had numerous changes in its management. The main strategies continuously fluctuated between strong growth and cost cutting. These market entry processes led to a number of problems when Schindler tried to expand on the market.

Today, Schindler has a market share of approximately 1% in Japan in the escalator market, in terms of units sold (Nikkei, 2006). Every year, Schindler Elevator K.K. sold a few hundred escalators and elevators. As a consequence of the accident and insufficient crisis management, which will be described later, Schindler Elevators now only sells escalators in Japan. The low number of products sold is a big disadvantage for Schindler. In contrast with larger companies, Schindler is not able to benefit from economies of scales of products which are especially adapted to Japanese market requirements (Management, 2007).

In 2007, Schindler had maintenance contracts for several thousand devices all over Japan. Strong competition exists in this industry and local companies which have good knowledge of the market and good business partnerships are snatching service contracts from Schindler. As a measure to insure success in the service business, Schindler took over an independent Japanese maintenance firm, Mercury Ascensore Co. in 2005, which has around 170 employees. Mercury Ascensore only offers maintenance services for third party products, and has several thousand service contracts. Mercury Ascensore has yet to be integrated to Schindler (Management, 2007).

As of 2007, the company has around 360 employees in 12 branches and 18 service stations all over Japan. Schindler has had some trouble finding enough high-skilled employees in Japan, not unlike other foreign companies in the country. In November 2007, there were a fair number of open positions at the company (Schindler Elevator K.K., 2007). A former chairman of Schindler Japan mentioned in an interview that "Japan is the only country where Schindler is little known. For this reason, Schindler in Japan is not perceived as a company which is able to handle large projects. Due to that fact, a lot of Schindler's business is with government offices, which determine the suppliers through an open bidding. Only in such instances will a "junior player" like Schindler [in Japan] has chances to get orders (Graf *et al.*, 2006).

Most of the profits in the elevator industry are created by service contracts. Schindler makes a vast majority of its revenues in Japan with service contracts and a minority stake in sales of escalators (and elevators). On average, elevator companies derive about 50–55% of their revenues from maintenance — contracts, as such revenues in the industry are relatively safe from cycles in construction activity (Global Industry Analysts Inc., 2007).

THE CHALLENGES OF THE JAPANESE ELEVATOR MARKET

The demand for new elevators follows the general economy and developments in construction activity with about a one-year lag. There are several inter-related factors supporting growth, including demographic and socio-economic development, desire for efficient use of space, increasing movement of people and goods through airports and metros and safety requirements. The escalator market shares many characteristics with the market for elevators. Services are the more lucrative segment and consolidation is steadily progressing and growth is the highest in Asia, except for Japan, where the infrastructure is already well developed. In Japan, there are more than 650,000 escalators and elevators in use. Every year, 25,000–28,000 pieces are sold (for new buildings and replacements). The industry is linked very strongly to the construction economy (Management, 2007). The price differences between the companies are marginal

(Schuette and Ciarlante, 1998) and the prices for elevator and escalators as well as for services are similar to other markets (Management, 2007). Furthermore, the products of the Japanese competitors are very similar to each other, somewhat a confirmation of the concept of *yokonarabi*, which enounces that it is a tradition in Japan to do something the way everybody (others) does (Haghirian, Markteintritt in Japan, 2007).

In the Japanese market, Schindler faces a very particular competitive situation. The three main players, Mitsubishi Elevator, Hitachi Elevator and Toshiba/Kone Elevator have strong market power and are all divisions of large Japanese conglomerates.

The largest player in the Japanese market is Mitsubishi (28% market share). Mitsubishi is present in five continents and is number one in Asia (Schindler, 2007). Mitsubishi Elevators is a division of Mitsubishi Electric Corporation Energy and Electric System division (Mitsubishi Electric, 2007). In April 2001, Mitsubishi Electric signed a cooperation agreement with Schindler, covering the reciprocal supply of key components for elevators and escalators and the delivery of Aramid to Mitsubishi; the cooperation agreement has since expired (Schindler, 2007).

Hitachi has 24% market share in Japan and is one of the world's leading electronic companies. Hitachi Smooth Movers is a company of the Hitachi public/urban/transportation division. Hitachi and Mitsubishi Electric agreed upon a joint venture in home elevator operations in October 2000 in order to effectively respond to the development of the Japanese elevator market. Both of the top manufactures enjoy high customer praise for product development abilities, high product reliability and extensive nationwide service networks. The alliance cooperates in the development, sales, production and installation of home elevators in order to achieve a combination of respective technologies, quicker time to market for new products, integration of product lineups, condensation of product facilities and more efficient manufacturing (Hitachi Corporation, 2007). "Alliances are very important in order to accelerate product development and to strengthen one's competitive position in the Japanese market. In the elevator industry, new plants are often sold below costs. That's why one has to have an adequate portfolio and number of orders to sell new plants. Without a strong partner, this is almost impossible. That explains why a minority stake or joint venture often serves as a stepping stone toward acquiring a majority interest and then fully integrating the company in the corporate group in Japan", emphasized a former top executive (Graf *et al.*, 2002).

Toshiba Elevator has a 16% market share in Japan and 20% of the company is owned by Kone since 1998. Toshiba has a strategic alliance with Kone, the fourth largest elevator and escalator company in the world, which is based in Finland. The other 80% of the shares of Toshiba Elevator and Building Systems are held by Toshiba Social Infrastructure Systems, a Domain of Toshiba Corporation (Toshiba Corporation, 2007). Toshiba had an increase in sales and maintenance contracts in Japan in 2006. Furthermore, the company accomplished market readiness to innovations in the field of earthquake recognition.

Nippon Otis is fully owned by Otis. Otis is the world's elevator market leader and owned by U.S. United Technologies. Since its market entrance in Japan in 1896, Otis has been successful and has a market share of 12%. The products are called Nippon Otis and most consumers perceive it as a Japanese brand (Management, 2007). Otis Elevator Co., a wholly-owned subsidiary of United Technologies Corporation (UTC), is the world's largest manufacturer, installer, and service company of elevators, escalators, moving walkways and other horizontal transportation systems. Besides Schindler, Otis is the only other significant foreign company in the Japanese market. Sharing strengths with UTC allows Otis to draw on remarkable resources in engineering, product testing, purchasing, marketing and information systems (Graf *et al.*, 2002).

With a market share of 8%, Fujitec is the only independent elevator and escalator company in Japan, which has a considerable market share. Fujitec is still managed by the founder family. The company is active in America, Europe, South Asia, East Asia, and China (Fujitec Corporation, 2007). An important proportion of shares, but less than 50%, was recently bought by a financial investment firm which plans to sell the stakes to United Technologies, the holding company of Otis Elevator Co. As of now, Fujitec has been defending against a hostile takeover bid by United Technologies Holding (Management, 2007).

Thyssen Krupp Elevator is the elevator division of the Thyssen Krupp group. The company is the third biggest escalator/elevator business in the world and is not yet active in the Japanese market. In 2006, it established a subsidiary in Tokyo. Officials of the company mentioned that they would be interested in a large scale merger with a Japanese competitor (aktiencheck.de, 2006). On top of these competitors, there are 200 little companies in addition to Schindler which are active in the elevator and escalator business, or in related industries (Management, 2007).

THE JAPANESE CONSTRUCTION ECONOMY

After a decade of deflation and losses, the Japanese economy was back on a path of growth. Between 2003 and the 2008 crisis repercussions, the GDP had been growing stronger every year. This is low in comparison with other Asian neighbors, but one also has to consider the absolute size of the GDP. Long term forecasts estimate a decrease in public spending on housing (20–40% till 2020 based on reference year 2003) as well as a decrease of the public spending on maintenance of buildings (around 5% till 2020). Housing expenses of the private sector were to increase by around 5% until 2010 and then most probably slowly decrease (around 10%). This is most probably related to the decreasing population. Private sector spending for maintenance is increasing between 20% and 40% until 2020 (Research Institute of Construction and Economy, 2007).

Increasing migration into the cities (Schoettli, 2007) leads to a more dense settlement, which means that the number of multi-story buildings will increase. This and the increasing share of older people in Japan's demographics pyramid are deemed for have a positive effect on the demand for elevators and escalators. Standard products have to be adapted for the Japanese market due to the very strong regulations regarding fire and earthquake safety (Graf *et al.*, 2002).

A strong maintenance network for an outstanding service and close relations with large contractors are essential to winning orders. Basically, profits for companies in Japan are higher than in other countries, which still makes it a very interesting market (Roland Berger, 2003).

THE JAPANESE MARKET AS A CHALLENGING BUSINESS ENVIRONMENT

The business environment in Japan is rather complex and protective. A good example of this is the elevator business in which, in contrast to other countries, only the world leader Otis could reach a strong market position. The quality of Japanese companies' products is high as well as the expectations of the customers. Japanese customers do not accept interferences and they remember quality problems from a particular company many years after (Haghirian, Markteintritt in Japan, 2007). Japanese buyers often prefer Japanese products due to patriotic reasons (Graf *et al.*, 2002). The special Japanese specifications and regulations make local innovation extremely costly, especially for companies with lower market shares (Management). Moreover, product life cycles in Japan are shorter due to the continuous demand from Japanese customers for new and better products.

One of the former presidents of Schindler Elevator K.K. was convinced that foreign companies have to struggle with many prejudices, such that they are not able to fulfill Japanese customers' expectations and their products are of lower quality (Graf *et al.*, 2002). In contrast, a study with German companies shows that they believe that this handicap is slowly changing in favor of a *gaijin* premium (foreigner premium). The bonus is based on the higher flexibility of foreign companies, the positive image of certain countries in popular culture (e.g., Switzerland or Germany), and their strong global networks, which many foreigners characteristically have (Berger, 2003).

Students and young people want to work for large companies, even if some of these find themselves in precarious conditions. People believe that job security is inherently higher in large companies. Hence, it can be hard for smaller companies like Schindler, which are unknown or even have a negative image to retain sufficient numbers of highly qualified employees. Furthermore, the language barriers are still pretty strong and there are relatively few people who can work in an English-speaking environment (Berger, 2003). In Japan, there is robust relationship and emotional connection between a company and its employees. Hence, a company crisis and public attacks are very serious issues for the employees of that organization (Haghirian, Social concepts in Japan and their relevance for Japanese management, 2007). Another factor is that many Japanese students apply only at companies which gave a clear commitment to stay in the Japanese market and not leave as soon as crisis occurs (Haghirian, Markteintritt in Japan, 2007).

The quality requirements of Japanese customers are very high. This leads to serious trouble if the quality level is not perfect. Based on the product liability law, the producer can be punished for defects. The law is similar to the EU law but does not include paragraphs which can lead to extremely high penalties (Berger, 2003). As the former chairman of Schindler Japan once mentioned, in Japan, customers see the responsibility of product and service quality as lying solely with the manufacturer (Graf *et al.*, 2002), which is in contrast with customers in western markets.

In Japan, *keiretsu* still exists to a certain degree. Companies that are in a *keiretsu* are linked through cross-shareholdings and collaborate together to protect against market forces and foreign competitors. *Keiretsu* are often involved in large construction projects, but the proportion of *keiretsu* is decreasing (Berger, 2003).

It is difficult to do business without a relationship with the customer. It takes time for relations to be established and the foreign company must show commitment to stay in the Japanese market, but as soon as relations are established, it becomes much easier to do business. A foreign executive described Japan as a Jumbo-Jet: an entity which takes a lot of energy to take off, but as soon it is flying, it keeps flying for a long time (Haghirian, Markteintritt in Japan, 2007). Long-term relations are sometimes even more important than price. It is essential not to push too hard for consensus, as it will come when the company is ready. Urging a company to come to a decision before they are ready is in fact a sign of mistrust that must be avoided. The slow business process results in strong loyalty to vendors, but carries the cost of high levels of support and quality of deliverables.

From a cultural standpoint, Japanese take a much more formal view of personal interactions. Follow-up and social graces, like thank you notes and invitations to social events after meetings, generate more than just expense account line items, but rather indicate a willingness to understand and work within a different culture which the Japanese expect. Most Japanese companies have a step-by-step business development process that can take a very long time by U.S. standards — up to a year for major purchases. The general practice of obtaining consensus within the company before deciding upon any changes means that you must meet with all of the various constituents and managers.

Due to the long-term horizons that exist within Japanese companies, frequent changes in strategy and business conditions are considered unstable and make the company unworthy of consideration for any significant purchases. The good reputation of a company within society is key. The local media and press have different focus and content requirements than those of U.S.-based media, so securing direct access to media is important (Maniwa, 2007).

In case of quality problems or a corporate crisis, there are special requirements on the Japanese market. It is not enough to merely apologize for the failure and potential damage dealt. Japanese customers and society react extremely emotionally — sometimes irrationally — and expect an immediate apology. Furthermore, they want a detailed description of the problem and the reasons for them as well as information about the measures taken to prevent further incidents (Haghirian, Markteintritt in Japan, 2007). A company should try to maintain a harmonious relation with society as a whole, for example, after a crisis, strong efforts must be shown to re-establish the relationship. Cooperation and compromise towards problem-solving are a virtue. Through trust, goodwill and reaching mutual positions through fine adjustments, a good relationship can be reached (March, 1988). There are ritualized and formal behavior patterns which tend to reduce or even eliminate open conflict or embarrassment (Haghirian, Social concepts in Japan and their relevance for Japanese management, 2007). The most famous strategy is *naniwabushi*. It means to first emphasize on one's outstanding track record in Japan, for example, the market success and the high quality of the products and then describe what happened and express with sorrow for what had happened. A *naniwabushi* plea can or should even be tragic and dramatic, which makes it easier for Japanese listeners to forgive (March, 1988).

THE FATAL ACCIDENT AND THE REACTION OF SCHINDLER

On 3 June 2006, 16-year-old high school student Hirosuke Ichikawa was getting his bicycle off a Schindler elevator in a 23-story building of Minato Ward, Tokyo. Suddenly, the elevator started to move upwards, with the doors still open. The boy was pinned between the raising elevator and the door frame and died from impact. Before the accident, occupants had already reported interferences to the building manager, but no action was taken. Furthermore, the service contract was passed over to an independent maintenance service company in 2004 and one year later to SEC Elevator Co. by the building management company for cost reasons (Nakamura, 2006).

Just one day after the accident, Schindler organized a press conference and put a press release on the website. In the press release, Schindler expressed its sympathy to the family of the victim. Nevertheless, the president of Schindler Elevator K.K. gave no comments about the accident and reverted to the ongoing inquiry process. Internally, the Tokyo subsidiary asked for support from the headquarters, but due to a long weekend in Europe, most employees had been out of office and nobody there perceived the urgency. A second press conference was scheduled on the seventh of June. Due to the preliminary investigation by police, the press conference had to be cancelled and only a few statements were given to journalists in front of the office. Schindler Elevator K.K. informed that such fatal accidents happen mostly due to inappropriate service or dangerous utilization, as an error in the technical design would be implausible

(Mijiuk, 2006). In a subsequent press release, Schindler emphasized having no design-related user fatalities on record. Furthermore, Schindler stated that "the elevator involved in the accident is a state-of-art product fully certified by various international authorities and in use in many markets around the world" and that "Schindler is moving safely over 700 million people per day or the equivalent of Japan's population every four hours. The risk of having a fatal accident with an elevator is lower than with any other means of transportation. "Safety is Schindler's most important value" was also stressed (Kyodo News, 2006). Schindler communicated to the public immediately after the crisis, but did not apologize for the accident or meet the victim's family (see Fig. 1).

One week after the crisis, there was a "take-over" of the Tokyo office by staff from the Swiss headquarters and four consultancies were engaged. It was not very motivating for the local staff to be patronized. Furthermore, the headquarters in Switzerland published press releases regarding the accident without prior contact and coordination

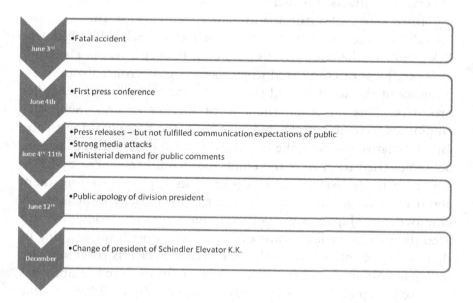

Figure 1. Course of action of the crisis in 2006.

with the Japanese subsidiary (Management, 2007). After nine days of keeping away from the media, Roland Hess, president of Schindler Holding's escalator and elevator division, flew to Tokyo and offered a Japanese-style bow of apology to a packed news conference, broadcasted live on some networks. Furthermore, Schindler announced that they wanted to meet the family of the boy and reiterated that they are not producing deadly elevators and that Schindler products are very safe and only few accidents have ever occurred (XFN-Asia, 2006). In the press release on 12th June, Schindler apologized for the insufficient information, but there was still no written apology for the accident.

In the weeks after the accident, around 100 Schindler experts from all over the world flew in to support the local staff and check all the Schindler elevators. This was ordered by the Ministry of Land Infrastructure and Transport (Suzuki, 2006). Nine elevators with control unit program glitches were found, but these elevators had different control units from the elevator in Minato Ward (Kyodo News). The accident caused a sales collapse as well as a loss of service contracts. Furthermore, Schindler decided to stop offering third party elevator maintenance (except for the Mercury subsidiary) due to further reputational risks (Schindler Elevator K.K., 2007). The company also suffered financial losses. The front office staff was often stressed when they were confronted with questions about the accident and the quality and reliability of Schindler products. This increased the risk of further failures. Schindler employees were also under pressure from their families due to the rather negative image of the company. During events with the press, Schindler tried to protect the employees from harassment by keeping them in the background as journalists kept confronting them about the fatal accident (Management, 2007). Many of Schindler's employees in Japan were very ashamed of their company and according to journalists, some even threatened with suicide, due to their strong identification with the company which is commonplace in Japan. Schindler also had trouble in finding new employees because its reputation was seriously damaged (Mijiuk, 2006). Public sensitivity towards incidents with Schindler products was getting (and is still) very high. If somebody gets trapped in a Schindler elevator in Japan, it is published in the media all over the country and journalists will refer to the fatal accident in 2006. Schindler claims that if such incidents happen with products from other companies, nobody gets informed about it. Therefore, Schindler prepared communication strategies to parry the effects of any eventual incidents and changed its information policy. Today, Schindler responds to every request by journalists immediately and shares as much information as possible (Management, 2007). Furthermore, an independent advisory committee was set in place, which consists of two Japanese engineering professors as well as two lawyers (Schindler Elevator K.K., 2007).

In December 2006, Ken Smith, president of Schindler Japan, resigned and was replaced by Gerhard Schlosser, who has extensive managerial experience in Japan. The resignation was announced by Mr Hess, the head of Schindler's elevator and escalator division. Ken Smith was not present at the press conference. Journalists tried to interview him at his house but he did not respond.

In March 2007, there was another scandal with inspectors who cheated in order to obtain a required inspection license. In Japan, elevator inspectors need official licenses. Applicants must have work experience of between two and 11 years, depending on their academic background. Between 1987 and 2003, 53 inspectors at Schindler obtained their licenses by inflating their number of years in the field. Schindler had to re-examine 1,300 elevators, which were checked by those inspectors and deeply apologized for the mistake (Asahi Shimbun, 2007). After this incident, Schindler reacted immediately and the potential damage to their image was contained through their improved communication policy.

As a consequence of the accident, Schindler Elevator K.K. only sold escalators in the Japanese market for 2007. After the fatal accident of 2006, Schindler decided to adapt its service portfolio due to reputational risks. As long as the investigations on the Tokyo accident kept continuing, Schindler wants to keep Mercury Ascensore autonomous. Another measure which was taken was the adoption of an open communication and media-relations policy.

PUBLIC PERCEPTION AND MEDIA ECHO

In Japan

News articles published on the fourth of June talked mainly about the accident itself and gradually covered other incidents on Schindler installments. The name Schindler was not mentioned and only the word "maker of the accident-prone elevator" was used in most of the newspapers while Schindler's name appeared only in the last paragraphs of few newspapers, such as Sankei Shimbun. At that time, the name "Schindler" was totally unknown to the Japanese public, as well as to Japanese journalists. On the seventh of June, almost all newspapers started putting "Schindler" on the headlines and/or in the first paragraph and mainly covered other incidents happening on Schindler installments in Japan other than the Tokyo Takeshiba accident (Management, 2007). The (apparent) silence on Schindler's part was not appreciated by the Japanese media and society. Immediately after the accident, the media's interest in Schindler was low and as the report shows, Schindler's information did not reach all Japanese media. One reason could be that the company was unknown at that time. Even if Schindler set up a press conference and distributed press releases just one day after the accident, most media treated Schindler's behavior as silence. Ken Smith, the president of Schindler Japan, was not answering questions which are directly related to the accident and kept a straight face when reporters asked him questions about it. Japanese television stations showed these pictures and labeled Schindler as a company which is arrogantly ignoring the Japanese culture (Veigl, 2006). Public discussion was shifting from the question of guilt to the refusal by Schindler to apologize in public (Fuster, 2006). The minister for land, transport and infrastructure held a press conference in which he publicly asked Schindler to comment on the accident (Mijiuk, 2006).

Some journalists attacked Schindler very heavily. A reason for that could be that the accident happened in a publicly-owned and managed building. The maintenance contract was handed over to independent maintenance service companies twice in two years before the accident happened at the hands of the public building managers.

Reports of the events by Japanese media were extremely negative. There was a review of past accidents, some of which had occurred years before, with Schindler products all over Japan, and there were claims that Schindler products were more dangerous than others and that the service and quality level of Schindler products is lower than that of its competitors. For example, there was an article in Mainichi Daily News with the title "Schindler elevators trapped users in 320 incidents in 2004" or another article in the Japan Times with the topic "Schindler lists six other elevator malfunctions". Schindler's image was very seriously damaged and the company was seen as arrogant, untrustworthy and greedy (Bossart, 2006). Journalists claimed that a company which is very insensitive to cultural aspects and not interested in the public's requests to not qualified for the people transportation business. Some reporters even found very creative reasons for the late reaction of Schindler. One reporter implied that the executives apologized on the day of the World Cup match between Japan and Australia to reduce coverage of the news conference (Asahi Shimbun, 2006).

The accident and the company's crisis management created negative media attention for Schindler. In March 2007, when the inspection license scandal leaked out, the Ministry of Transport suspected Schindler to have instructed the applicants to lie (Asahi Shimbun, 2007).

Today, the public opinion of Schindler is still somewhat tarnished. The company is sometimes viewed as unsocial, arrogant, and ignorant of the Japanese culture. In Japan, a discussion on elevator safety was started due to the accident. There was criticism due to a missing recall system for elevators as there is for automobiles. Furthermore, it was seen as a danger that elevator makers do not have to report problems to the ministry (The Daily Yomiuri, 2006). A Japan Elevator Association official argued that independent firms do not possess the expertise to make proper repairs. "If they make maintenance contracts with building owners, they should have the ability to deal with any problems the elevators under their care encounter", the official said. In the same interview, he also stated as that independent firms would not contact the manufacturers for manuals if they do not know how to fix malfunctions because that would only reveal their lack of expertise". Following the accident, an advisory panel at the Land, Infrastructure and Transport Ministry began discussing ways to prevent elevator accidents (Nakamura, 2006).

Schindler has recognized its shortcomings, as the following statements from its head of information shows: "We had, here in Ebikon (Switzerland), insufficient knowledge about Japanese customs after an accident" and the company expects lots of work to re-establish the company in Japan (Veigl, 2006).

In Switzerland/Other Parts of the World

The focus of the reports outside Japan was on the insufficient crisis management by Schindler and its weak position in Japan. The media described what happened, the slow reaction, and the actions taken by Schindler, as well as the subsequent reaction of the Japanese media and public. Therefore, the media coverage outside Japan began a week after the accident and in every article, journalists mentioned the company name "Schindler". There were no reports abroad which claimed that Schindler products would be less safe and reliable than products from its competitors. The foreign media also did not start reporting about other harmless incidents with Schindler products abroad, to the contrary of what the Japanese media did. The media coverage abroad was much more objective, fact-based, and less emotional than in Japan. Foreign media never accused Schindler of bad will. The international media were able to comprehend the behavior of Schindler, even though it was perceived as wrong in the Japanese market. There were articles with titles like "The mistakes of Schindler in Japan" (Mijiuk, 2006) or "A behavior full of mistakes and blame" (Veigl, 2006) or "Schindler stumbles over *sumimasen*" (Fuster, 2006). Furthermore, there was no general discussion about elevator safety and government control going on, like it was the case in Japan. In Japanese as well as in foreign media, the political dimension of the accident was never mentioned. The case led many newspapers to publish articles about intercultural management, pitfalls of foreign markets, and the culture of apologizing which exists in Japan. The license scandal in March 2007 was hardly mentioned in foreign media. The image damage for Schindler was smaller outside of Japan. Basically, the main criticism was on the lack of sensitivity for intercultural management and the publication of the weak market position of Schindler in Japan. In other markets, Schindler shows no difficulty in finding enough people to occupy open positions; the incident in Japan had no effect on the number of applications. Furthermore, no other government than the Japanese have attacked Schindler and in no other country has the incident had an influence on sales figures or led to the cancelation of service contracts.

FUTURE OUTLOOK

In 2008, Schindler has kept its brand alive in Japan and strives to act behind the scenes and foster smooth stakeholder relations. The image and reputation of the company are damaged very seriously and the company has trouble retaining high-skilled employees. Furthermore, Schindler did not manage to sell a single elevator in Japan for the last year and a half. Many customers lost their trust in Schindler products due to safety and quality reasons and because the company is seen as arrogant and careless, boasting lower skills than its competitors. Incidentally, the employees need care and support to regain pride in their company and be convinced about a new vision for growth. Finally, a global Schindler culture has yet to be implemented. The headquarters have given strong financial commitments for the future of Schindler Elevator K.K. For Schindler, the Japanese market is very important, even if Schindler is only a minor player. "If you want to be someone in Asia, you cannot afford not to be in Japan and China. Schindler would never even think of leaving the market", (Graf *et al.*, 2002). Even for Mr Schlosser, the current president of Schindler Elevator K.K., a retreat from the Japanese market is not a viable option, as this would damage Schindler globally and affect the trust shown by customers. Therefore, the Japanese market is strategically important for the global company. Japan is a key market in Asia. Established products in Japan have an influence on customers in other Asian countries while it often acts as a trendsetter for other Asian markets. Most importantly, though, Japan is the second largest economy in the world (Berger, 2003).

As soon as the investigation case is closed, Schindler has prepared strategies which will be implemented to improve growth and to improve its image in Japan. Schindler believes in future opportunities in the Japanese market due to its strength in design and product features, as well as its expectation to benefit from the intended adoption of the EU regulations for elevators and escalators for the Japanese market (Management, 2007).

Besides its growth strategy, Schindler has to continuously care about its image and reputation. This includes fostering good relationships with journalists and government officials, in addition to collaborating with universities to get in touch with students as well as to be prepared to act accordance with the Japanese culture. The establishment of a strong "Schindler culture" would have a positive influence on employee motivation and could also improve Schindler's attractiveness as an employer. The faulty crisis management led to an essential crisis within the company. With plenty of time and money as well as the right strategy, a return to growth appears to be possible. Incidents will still happen in the future, even with the highest quality and safety standards, but further crisis management issues should be prevented at all costs. One of the most important tasks for Schindler is to establish a state of the art crisis management framework and a structure which allows reacting immediately and appropriately.

QUESTIONS

1) Why is culture so important when dealing with crisis in international management?
2) How did the "correct" solutions for dealing with the crisis look like in Japan and in Switzerland?
3) What should Schindler Elevator have done to avoid such a PR disaster?
4) How can the company improve its image in Japan?

APPENDIX 1: LONG TERM FORECAST FOR JAPANESE CONSTRUCTION ECONOMY

(Units trillion yen)

	(Reference) FY 2003		Case 1		Case 2		Case 3		Case 4	
			FY2006–2010 GDP; +1.5% FY2010	FY2011–2020 GDP; +2.5% FY2020	FY2006–2010 GDP; +1.5% FY2010	FY2011–2020 GDP; +2.0% FY2020	FY2006–2010 GDP; +1.5% FY2010	FY2011–2020 GDP; +1.5% FY2020	FY2006–2010 GDP; +1.5% FY2010	FY2011–2020 GDP; +1.0% FY2010
Construction	55.2	53.9	48.4–51.5	48.2–51.4	47.6–50.8	45.1–48.3	47.3–50.5	42.7–45.8	46.9–50.1	39.9–43.1
Investment										
Government	23.5	23.0	15.3–18.5	15.3–18.5	15.3–18.5	15.3–18.5	15.3–18.5	15.3–18.5	15.3–18.5	15.3–18.5
Private sector	31.7	30.9	33.0	32.8	32.3	29.8	32.0	27.3	31.5	24.6
Housing	18.4	17.9	17.9	14.4	17.9	14.0	17.9	13.7	17.9	13.3
Non-housing (building)	8.0	7.8	9.5	12.7	9.1	10.6	8.9	9.0	8.6	7.2
Non-housing (civil engineering)	5.3	5.2	5.5	5.7	5.3	5.1	5.2	4.7	5.0	4.0
(Four Highway Corporations)	—	—	1.1	1.1	1.1	1.1	1.1	1.1	1.1	1.1

(*Continued*)

(*Continued*)

	(Reference)	Case 1		Case 2		Case 3		Case 4	
	FY 2003	2006–2010 年度 GDP;+1.5% FY2010	FY2011–2020 GDP;+2.5% FY2020	FY2006–2010 GDP;+1.5% FY2010	FY2011–2020 GDP;+2.0% FY2020	FY2006–2010 GDP;+1.5% FY2010	FY2011–2020 GDP;+1.5% FY2020	FY2006–2010 GDP;+1.5% FY2010	FY2011–2020 GDP;+1.0% FY2010
Maintenance & Repair	22.4	24.2–24.4	28.1–28.5	24.1–24.3	27.8–28.0	24.1–24.2	27.4–27.6	24.0–24.2	27.0–27.1
Government	6.3	5.8–6.0	5.7–6.0	5.8–6.0	5.9–6.0	5.8–6.0	5.9–6.0	5.8–6.0	5.9–6.0
Civil engineering	5.4	5.1–5.2	4.9–5.1	5.1–5.2	4.9–5.1	5.1–5.2	4.9–5.1	5.1–5.2	4.9–5.1
Housing	0.3	0.2–0.2	0.2–0.3	0.2–0.2	0.4–0.3	0.2–0.2	0.4–0.3	0.2–0.2	0.4–0.3
Non-housing	0.6	0.5–0.6	0.6–0.7	0.5–0.6	0.6–0.7	0.5–0.6	0.6–0.7	0.5–0.6	0.6–0.7
Private sector	16.2	18.4	22.4	18.3	21.9	18.2	21.6	18.2	21.1
Housing	7.2	8.1	9.5	8.1	9.5	8.1	9.5	8.1	9.5
Non-housing (building)	6.9	7.6	9.0	7.6	9.0	7.6	8.9	7.6	8.9
Non-housing (civil engineering)	2.1	2.7	*3.9	2.6	3.4	2.5	3.2	2.5	2.7
(Four Highway Corporations)	—	0.3	0.3	0.3	0.3	0.3	0.3	0.3	0.3

Notes:

1. Figures are all real based on FY1995 prices, unless otherwise stated.
2. GDP growth rates for FY2004 and FY2005 are based on the forecast made by RICE in "Forecast of construction investment based on the construction economy model".
3. Construction investment for FY2003 in form "FY2004 construction investment outlook (June 2004)" by the Ministry of Land, Infrastructure and Transport.
4. The forecast of the size of government construction investment based on demand is not necessarily accurate as it is finally determined by the policy makers. Several different rates, therefore, were used in the forecast.
5. Figures for maintenance and repairs, including the figure in FY2003, are based on estimates by RICE.
6. Due to a conventional method of classification, the maintenance and repairs of the government civil engineering sector is included both in "Construction investment" and "maintenance & repairs" in the forecast.
7. Figures have been rounded off, and the totals may not match.
8. Four highway corporation are removed from the government and included in the private sector from 2006 (the year when they are scheduled to be privatized).

APPENDIX 2: SCHINDLER PRESS RELEASE ON 8 JUNE 2006, EBIKON/SWITZERLAND

On Saturday night, 3 June, 2006, a 16-year-old boy died in a tragic accident involving an elevator manufactured by Schindler and maintained by a third party maintenance company in Tokyo, Japan. The boy was deadly injured when the elevator abruptly moved upwards with open doors while he was leaving the elevator. The Schindler Group deeply regretted this accident and offered its condolences to the family of the boy. Schindler fully supported the local authorities and welcomed the investigation to establish the root cause of the accident.

The tragic accident happened in a Tokyo government housing development that had six Schindler elevators installed in 1998. For more than a year, the elevators are no longer serviced by Schindler, but by two different local third party maintenance companies.

Schindler has no design-related user fatalities on record. Fatal accidents in the elevator industry are mainly due to inappropriate maintenance or dangerous user behavior in the context of entrapment. The elevator involved in the accident is a state-of-art product fully certified by various international authorities and in use in many markets around the world.

Schindler is moving safely over 700 million people per day or the equivalent of the Japanese population every four hours. The risk of having a fatal accident with an elevator is lower than with any other means of transportation. Safety is Schindler's most important value.

APPENDIX 3: SCHINDLER PRESS RELEASE ON 12 JUNE 2006, TOKYO

First, our thoughts are with the victim and his family. We pray for him and extend our condolences to the family involved in this tragic accident at Minato-ward.

(Continued)

(Continued)

We apologize that we didn't provide sufficient information up to now. Our focus was to get all the facts together before making any comments. We also apologize that this has caused distress to the family, the residents, the users, and the general public including people who have to use stairs due to elevators under inspection.

The Schindler Group is 130 years old, our primary value is to provide safe and high quality products and services.

All Schindler components and products are certified through Public Authorities before being sold. However it is possible that there may be the need for intervention on any installation. For the most part the issues are minor, such as defective buttons, and in no way present any safety hazard. Elevators usually remain in operation for 30 or more years. Because of this long life-time, proper maintenance is very important to assure the correct and safe operation of the equipment.

We have been doing everything to support the authority's investigation into the accident. The on-going investigation by the authorities has not been completed and thus the root cause of the accident has not been identified yet. While the investigation is proceeding, we are inspecting our elevators. So that we can respond as quickly as possible, the Schindler Group is providing additional resources. We will be regularly informing the public through the media of the inspection status and results. Schindler is giving full support to the authorities and their investigations, while all possible root causes are being considered.

Roland W. Hess,
President Schindler
  Escalator and Elevator
  Division
Ebikon, Switzerland

Ken Smith
President Schindler Elevator K.K.
Tokyo, Japan

APPENDIX 4: SCHINDLER PRESS RELEASE ON 28 MARCH 2007 (THIS IS A TRANSLATION OF THE OFFICIAL JAPANESE VERSION)

The Misrepresentation of Working Experiences of Inspectors for Elevators

It has been revealed after Schindler Elevator K.K.'s (SEKK) internal investigation that 44 people among all 159 licensed inspectors are, as of 16 March, SEKK's employees who have obtained their licenses with incorrect work records. The Ministry of Land, Infrastructure, and Transport (MLIT) announced its investigation result and further actions yesterday, and officially informed SEKK of the actions today. We will promptly take the actions guided by the MLIT and strictly manage and control procedures to prevent a recurrence. We sincerely apologize for distress and inconvenience caused to all the affected people.

SEKK'S ACTIONS

SEKK have taken this past behavior so seriously that the company will take the action items mentioned below by incorporating the further actions officially guided by the MLIT today.

1. Severely continue to give caution to the departments involved and return the licenses of the identified inspectors to the Japan Building Equipment and Elevator Center Foundation (BEEC).
2. Develop a plan of re-inspection by licensed inspectors for the installments inspected by the identified inspectors for the past year, submit the plan to the MLIT by 10 April, carry out all inspections as planned, and report the inspection results to the local authorities.
3. Send letters to the owners of the installments inspected by the identified inspectors for the past year to give our apology for the inconvenience caused and to ask for their cooperation for the re-inspections.
4. Submit a plan of improvement measures by 10 April, which will be developed based on the actions which SEKK has already taken to prevent a recurrence, and report the performance of the

measures. We again would like to apologize that the past behavior has caused distress and inconvenience to all the affected people: the MLIT, BEEC, the passengers, the customers, the suppliers, and others in the public. We will put in our best possible efforts in taking the above-mentioned actions.

BIBLIOGRAPHY

Asahi, S. (2007). Fifty-three elevator inspectors with Schindler. *International Herald Tribune*.

Berger, R. (2003). *Making Money in Japan: Eine Studie zur Gewinnsituation Deutscher Unternehmen in Japan*. Tokyo: Deutsche Industrie und Handelskammer Japan.

Bossart, R. (2006). Schindler massiv unter Druck. *Basler Zeitung*.

Chalupny, A. Aufzugsindustrie (2006). *Handelszeitung*.

Fujitec Corporation (2007). Corporate Website. http://www.fujitec.co.jp/english/company/file01.htm.

Fuster, T. (2006). Schindler stolpert über Sumimasen. *Neue Zürcher Zeitung*.

Global Industry Analysts Inc. Elevators and escalators: A global strategic business report.

Govt to tighten lift safety system (2006). *The Daily Yomiuri*.

Graf, M., *et al.* (2002). Case Study: Schindler Elevator K.K. [To be published]. Tokyo.

Haghirian, P. (2007). *Markteintritt in Japan*. Wien: Lexis Nexis.

Hitachi Corporation corporate website. http://www.hitachi.co.jp/Prod/elv/en/network/sales/index.html.

Kaufmann, M. Wer sich in Japan nicht verneigt, der hat verloren (2006). *Tages Anzeiger*.

Kobayashi, K. (2006). Troubled Swiss elevator maker overlooks Japan's 'apology' culture. *Kyodo news*.

Kone. http://www.kone.com/en/main/0,,content=48409,00.html.

Management, Schindler Elevator. Interview. Pascal Kalbermatten. 14 November 2007.

Maniwa, T. Gabe on EDA blog (20 January). http://www.gabeoneda.com/node/37.

March, R.M. (1988). *The Japanese Negotiator*. Tokyo: Kodansha.

Mijiuk, G. Die Fehler von Schindler in Japan (2006). *Aargauer Zeitung.*

Mitsubishi Electric. Annual Report 2007.

Nakamura, A. Elevator death bares systemic ills (2006). *The Japan Times.*

Report: Schindler defends record after deadly elevator accident in Japan (12 June 2006). *XFN–Asia.*

Research Institute of Construction and Economy. Quarterly outlook on construction and macro-economy (2007).

Schindler Elevator K.K. Company presentation. Tokyo, 2007.

Schindler fixes 9 elevators with program glitches (2006). *Kyodo News.*

Schindler Group — about us. http://www.schindler.com/group_index/ group_kg_about.htm.

Schindler in crisis over elevator death (2006). *Nikkei weekly.*

Schindler. Annual Report 2000.

Schindler. Annual report 2006.

Schindler. Welcome to Schindler Group and Schindler Elevator, 2007.

Schoettli, U. Ein rascher demografischer Wandel prägt Japan. *Neue Zürcher Zeitung.*

Schuette, H and Ciarlante, D. (1998). *Consumer Behavior in Asia.* New York: New York University Press.

Social concepts in Japan and their relevance for Japanese management. Lecture Sophia University, Tokyo.

Suzuki, H. (2006). Japan orders nationwide inspection of Schindler-made. *Bloomberg.*

The bowing by Schindler executives came too late for many (2006). *International Herald Tribune.*

Thyssen Krupp will Aufzugbauer in Japan übernehmen (24 May 2006). aktiencheck.de. http://www.wiso-net.de.

Toshiba Corporation. Annual report 2007.

Veigl, S. (2006). Ein Verhalten voller Fehl und Tadel. *FACTS.*

World Elevator forecast 2011 & 2016. *Bharat Book Bureau.* http://www. bharatbook.com/bookdetail.asp?bookid=9576&publisher.

Lost in Translation? Toyota and the Recall Scandal

Elena Neufeld

SUCH STUFF AS DREAMS ARE MADE ON

The history of the Toyota corporation begins with the invention of the Toyoda Model G automatic loom by Sakichi Toyoda in 1924. With the funds from the sale of the patent, he turned to work on gasoline engines, and soon the Toyoda Automatic Loom Works Ltd had a thriving vehicles department. In 1937, the Toyota Motor Company Ltd was launched, and within seven years, it had made a successful entry into the U.S. market. Once they had adjusted their vehicles to match American requirements, Toyota's cars became a great success. [23]

Toyota's first overseas factory was opened in Brazil in 1959. By 1967, the company was well-known in the U.S., and was producing approximately 600,000 cars per year. Seven years later, Toyota merged with General Motors and opened a factory in California. 62 years after the company had been launched, its shares became listed on the New York Stock Exchange under the name "TM". Further factories were established, in China and then in France. [24]

Customer satisfaction surveys from 2005 ranked the company in first place; in fact, it had been at the top for years. Toyota built the most popular vehicles in the world, followed by Ford and Volkswagen. [3] In early 2008, posting vehicle sales worth $4.818 million, Toyota overtook

General Motors ($4.540 million) to become the world's biggest producer of automobiles. Volkswagen AG stood in the third place with sales worth $3.266 million, followed by Ford ($3.217 million), and Hyundai ($2.187 million). [18]

However, some thought that Toyota had become too big too fast. In becoming the biggest carmaker on the planet, it was said that something had been lost. The events of 2009 — during which Toyota stumbled from crisis to catastrophe — seemed to confirm these doubts. But was there really any substance behind Toyota's recall troubles? Or was this nothing but a case of cross-cultural miscommunication — spiced with corporate jealousy — writ large across the world stage?

OUR REVELS NOW ARE ENDED

Toyota's share price had risen rapidly, especially in America, having buoyed by its excellent reputation for quality and reliability. In 2004, the company sold 2.27 million units in North America alone. However, dark clouds were gathering on the otherwise bright horizon. Early in 2005, engine problems compelled Toyota to recall 790,000 vehicles in the U.S. and 880,000 units worldwide. Later that year, problems with the Prius model were reported. However, as no accidents occurred, there was no recall of the vehicles. [5] Nevertheless, more recalls were to follow: 1.23 million cars were recalled in Japan in October and a few weeks later, 246,592 more cars were recalled across the world.

Toyota had once been considered as the safest car-maker in the world. Now its reputation is under threat. Trying to turn things around, the company launched a campaign called, "Back to Basics", which aimed to re-instill traditional Toyota construction values in its new factories and among its new staff. For some time already, the heads of Toyota have been concerned about the possibility that speeding up production would affect quality. Shinichi Sasaki, the president and Chief Executive of Toyota in Europe, later expressed the opinion that putting up of factories hastily and rapid recruitment in Japan had damaged production values. The rapid expansion meant a decreasing proportion of experienced staff among the workforce, and insufficient time for new recruits to acclimatize themselves to the company culture. The rapid pace of production also put the designers under pressure, meaning that the decline in quality went to the core. The company now admits that by accelerating the process, both production and designs may have become defective. In the race to be first among car-makers, the company's reputation took a dive: customer surveys showed that Hyundai now stood in the first place. [7]

The following year brought Toyota no relief. Worse, failings began to emerge in both its internal and external communications. The company received a report indicating possibly grave problems with some vehicles, but failed to take action. The authorities advised the company to improve its recall procedures. In July, the company was forced to recall 380,000 Lexus and Toyota Highlander models worldwide for failing engines. Altogether, 1.2 million vehicles had to be improved and repaired in 2006.

2007 brought yet more complaints and recalls, and once again, the authorities had to put the company under pressure before the necessary recalls were made. First, after a report citing 11 accidents, Toyota finally recalled 500,000 vehicles in order to fix problems with the steering. By the end of the year, a further 470,000 cars had been called back for the same problem as well as engine troubles. In 2008, faulty seatbelts were reported, which led to the recall of a further 90,000 SUVs in the U.S. alone. [4]

The river of recalls then expanded to a flood. In January 2009, a total of 1.3 million cars were recalled worldwide, reporting problems with the exhaust system and seatbelts. Toyota had to fight these "worst results in its history" against the background of the economic crisis. The reputation of the company continued to slide, customers were disappearing, and communication with the public failed on several occasions. In August, a further 690,000 vehicles produced in China had to go back because of problems with window switches.

TOTAL RECALL

A month later, "the biggest recall in Toyota's history" was launched: 4.2 million cars were recalled in the U.S. These vehicles had problems with their floor mats, and several models had to be taken off the market. [11] At almost the same time, the company received reports of problems concerning the accelerator and brakes [4]; but Toyota would only comment that it was looking into the matter alongside the NHTSA (National Highway Traffic Safety Administration) in the U.S. [12] Toyota posted a loss of $7.7 billion.

The peak rate of recalls had passed, but the problems still continued. In January 2010, Toyota announced a recall of approximately 2.3 million vehicles in the United States, and an additional 1.1 million shortly. [2] To prevent further mistakes and possible defects in its cars, the company slowed the production of eight models in the U.S. and also delayed sales. The company was finally starting to react to the problems and trying to regain the trust of its customers.

The financial losses due to the recalls amounted to around $2 billion. Sales in the U.S. went down by 20% and the share price fell by 16%. [27] In the same year, a further 8,500 vehicles were recalled in the UK, and 1.8 million cars across Europe. A further 3,800 Lexus vehicles were recalled in May, adding to the number of defective cars. [25] In July, in the U.S., the company took a further 17,000 vehicles back to the repair shop for failing their crash test. [21]

THE GLITCH AND THE REACTION

Since 2001, many complaints had reached the authorities about acceleration problems on the Lexus and other Toyota models. The speeding problems were not the only cause of minor accidents: some deaths had also been reported. Some of these accidents were investigated; other cases were closed on grounds of insufficient evidence. The NHTSA itself closed down some of its investigations, explaining that there were not enough problems reported to mount an investigation. However, federal regulators reported that Toyota had a larger number of such accidents than any other car producer.

In the year 2003, with owners of the Lexus reporting difficulties with their cars, the NHTSA had begun investigations, but had rejected 36 out of 37 complaints; the one remaining investigation was also stopped on the grounds that they "found no data indicating the existence of a defect trend". The accidents, however, continued to occur. After a *Financial Times* investigation, it became known that the NHTSA had recorded 15 deaths linked to acceleration problems with Toyota cars, and 1,000 complaints of the same problem. The *FT* uncovered thousands of complaints and investigation reports, some by independent safety authorities and police agencies, as well as lawsuits against Toyota. [14] When asked to comment on its past actions, NHTSA gave no explanation other than that they had continued to observe Toyota vehicles and that many of the complaints they had received did not include the acceleration and brake faults.

Toyota's announcement regarding this case was that since the NHTSA had investigated the complaints over the years 2003–2009 and found no faults, the reports were closed. The company rejected any complaints regarding the acceleration, stating that the "fail-safe in its throttle system makes it impossible to cause the [anomalous] acceleration". In 2008, Toyota brushed off the accusations, saying that they were reactions from "media and Internet exposure". [14]

But January 2009 brought even more rumors about defects in Toyota cars — especially regarding the accelerator. In the middle of the month, Toyota recalled 2.3 million vehicles. Only a few weeks later, it was reported in the press that the company was continuing to install the defective accelerator parts in its cars. The day after this report emerged, Toyota finally stopped the sales of eight models. Cars in the U.S. and Europe had to be examined and the producer was unsure of exactly which cars had the defective parts installed.

The authorities, media, and the public were all puzzled: after the recall of four million vehicles the previous year, the company should have been able to handle the PR better this time around. However, with Toyota remaining silent, while doubts and criticisms were growing ever larger. [9]

Toyota at first denied having flawed vehicles, showing, in effect, that it did not trust its customers. To make things worse, in July 2010, an internal memo emerged in which it was said that millions of dollars had been saved by avoiding the safety regulations. The company also refused to comment on the number of complaints received in 2005, at which time it had recalled 900,000 cars with accelerator problems. [12] Toyota also confirmed that it had long known about the defects on their vehicles, but that rather than revealing them, it had kept silent and tried to fix the problems privately. [10]

Experts on Japanese management explained this behavior through reference to the complicated decision-making structures in Japanese firms. One person alone is not supposed to make a decision: rather, even the smallest decision has to be discussed with the whole team. This takes time — often valuable time — and leads to opportunities being missed. Fast reaction to crisis is therefore a major challenge for Japanese firms. Another characteristic of Japanese firms is to hide failure and to try to solve the problem in-house before communicating it to the world. From a western perspective, this seems like a lack of transparency; the Japanese company, however, usually focuses on solving the problem first, and only then apologizes to its customers for its failures.

THE ISSUE OF THE BLACK BOX

The authorities were continuing to try to find out what exactly had gone wrong with Toyota's vehicles. Information on this matter could have been obtained from a device called the "black box" (or "event data recorder") installed in the cars. This box records the speed of the vehicle and the positions of other devices in the car, such as the brake and accelerator. The data could have helped to determine the reason for the accidents. The authorities, however, had difficulties in getting the data: only Toyota could decode the output from the black boxes and the company denied the authorities access, allowing it only for the purpose of law enforcement. Toyota argued that the information from the black box was still in an experimental phase and had faults, and that it might be inaccurate and misleading in reconstructing the accidents. However, other carmakers — such as GM, Ford Motors, or Chrysler group LLC — have made their black boxes available for crash analysis without casting doubt on the data thereby retrieved. [26]

The Toyota vehicle recalls concerned problems with the brakes, gas pedals, steering, and oil leaks. However, after the biggest recall, the company made no comment for two weeks, during which the mistrust grew ever larger, and retailers and investors became anxious about what might happen next.

In February 2010, Toyota President Akio Toyoda finally made a statement and apologized officially to customers for the breakdowns. In his speech, he emphasized that the cases would be investigated, and he asked the public to believe him. The company had accepted its responsibility, he said, and they finally understood how important it is to communicate with customers. Toyoda also confessed that the company had not only lost its way with respect for the customer, but it also had not been paying attention to management abroad. [10] He announced that they would be decentralizing management and streamlining decision-making processes.

During the hearing, the Toyota boss, though not speaking English very well, gave the impression of being overwhelmed by the events. In fact, in view of the Japanese company structure, he — even though he was the president — was probably not making any of these decisions alone. The American media, however, portrayed him as the man responsible for the public relations disaster.

As a result of the breakdown of the Toyota vehicles and the delayed recalls, the NHTSA fined Toyota 12.2 million euros. It argued that Toyota knew beforehand about the problems with the acceleration but had failed to react. The Japanese government did not comment on this record penalty. Toyota pointed out that it had already taken action in order to improve its collaboration with the authorities. After a rapid decrease in sales, Toyota addressed the crisis in the U.S. by offering steep discounts on its vehicles; the tactic was successful, despite the earlier safety concerns. [16] Toyota then tried desperately to make their cars safe again. The company introduced a new special function in its new cars such that it would brake even if the driver pushed the brake and the gas pedal at the same time. With this decision, Toyota finally reacted to the problem with the gas pedal. Furthermore, the company created a new multinational team, which is responsible for quality control and customer complaints. The team is intended to react faster to complaints from across the world, and so organize faster and more effective recalls where necessary. [15] However, by this time, 9.5 million vehicles had been recalled by what had previously been the world's biggest car-maker. [20]

BY THE PRICKING IN MY THUMBS ...

This biggest crisis that the company had ever faced made the world question not only the safety of Toyota, but also the value of Japanese management. Toyota's crisis management was discussed all over the world, and comment was passed on its slow reaction times and muddled, ineffective attempts to gloss over the problem.

However, it is worth noting that Toyota is not the only car company to have ever recalled its products. Other car-makers before Toyota have also made huge recalls. Ford, for example, had to take back 9.6 million vehicles in 2008, and GM recalled 3.6 million cars in 2004 (see Appendix 1). In the worldwide ranking of recalls, Toyota takes the sixth position with the first five positions being occupied by American giants such as Ford and GM — both companies have recalled more than 40 million cars in past decades. The recalls by these companies, however, did not create such a sensation. They would hardly have made it to the cover of *Time* magazine as Toyota did.

The U.S. Department of Transportation accused Toyota of only making the recalls under pressure from the media and the authorities. At the height of the crisis, the attacks on Toyota grew after every week, and almost every newspaper ran sensational stories on the failure of the company. [4] U.S. Transportation Secretary Ray LaHood made a comment that dealt incredible damage to the company's reputation, saying: "My advice is, if anybody owns one of these vehicles, is to stop driving it and take it to a Toyota dealer because they believe they have the fix for it". Only hours later, he took this comment back, saying he had only meant to suggest that the cars be inspected — but in those few hours, Toyota's market value fell by $4.6 billion. [17]

Illinois congressman Bobby Rush commented that the citizens driving Toyota cars "had no idea that their trusted vehicles had the potential to become, literally, killing machines". The state of Illinois, coincidentally, contains mainly American plants and cars, which may partly explain the strength of the congressman's concerns. States with Toyota plants defended the company rather strongly.

Japan, meanwhile, was puzzled by the aggressiveness of the politicians towards Toyota and was of the opinion that this was extremely unfair — after all, Japan had spent large amounts to help American companies which were in a similar situation. Suspicions arose that these attacks might be intended to help the U.S. national car producers. Concurrent events such as the "receivership" of GM and Chrysler and the political challenges facing U.S. President Barack Obama were cited in support of these speculations. [4] Another suggestion was that the U.S. media and public were trying to find someone to blame for the country's economic problems; foreign companies are always convenient scapegoats in such circumstances, as they can be safely blamed for such problems as "the devastation of auto industry workers' jobs, pay, and conditions". [27] The damage to Toyota's reputation was good fortune for American car producers who immediately launched a propaganda campaign about "safe American cars".

The low point in this witch-hunt against Toyota was a bigoted attack on the company by the UAW (United Auto Workers) and Teamsters unions. They held a two-day protest before the Japanese embassy and declared that "Toyota's defective vehicles make the company a 'danger to America'". Citizens, they said, should refuse to buy Toyota's vehicles, and they called for "government trade war measures against Asian auto makers". UAW Vice President Bob King and Teamsters boss James Hoffa blamed the company for "turning its back on American workers and American taxpayers by closing the plant in the state where they sell the most cars in the U.S., shipping these jobs to Japan, and then importing the cars back to the United States for sale". No one mentioned the loss of jobs for Japanese workers, or the Japanese government's support for American car producers who were also in dire straits. Ford had recalled 14.3 million vehicles over four years (see Appendix 1), the largest recall in U.S. history without provoking the media or the government to pursue them for losses. The cars used to "burst into flames" even when not in use because of the "cruise control switch problem". It took years for the company to launch a recall for those vehicles. [27]

Even Japanese politicians started to voice critical comments about Toyota. Particularly surprising was the criticism by Seiji Maehara, the Minister of Transport, who launched an investigation and reprimanded Toyota in public "for being insufficiently sensitive to customers' concerns" and poor "in dealing with defects and safety regulators". [10]

FULL OF SOUND AND FURY, SIGNIFYING NOTHING?

In the aftermath of the crisis, some of the stories about unwanted acceleration and problems with brakes could not be confirmed at all. After several emergency calls about sudden problems with the car, inspection revealed no faults at all. It was suggested that these may have been instances of attention-seeking people who had no concern about how damaging this might be to Toyota's reputation. [4]

As the investigations proceeded regarding the safety of Toyota vehicles, interesting facts have emerged. After three months of intensive investigations, the U.S. experts could not find any electronic problem in the vehicles. The assumption had been that the brake problem in Toyota's cars was due to a failure of electronics. Ray LaHood, in particular, alleged that the company had hidden the true cause for the acceleration of the cars. However, as the Bureau of Transport Safety later commented, they could not in the end find any evidence of a defect in the electronic accelerator control system. As Toyota had confirmed earlier, the only reasons for unwanted acceleration were the sticking gas pedal and sliding floor mats. [22]

The losses to Toyota did not only concern sales and reputation. As a result of the recalls and the slowdown in production, the company faced a "headcount surplus". In other words, many jobs were at risk. 6,000 jobs were cut in Japan, and thousands more jobs in the car parts sector were lost as a result in the slowdown of production. [27]

Even with these losses, however, Toyota remains as one of the biggest car producers in the world. The recalls damaged its reputation, sales went down, and many customers lost their trust in the company. Nevertheless, Toyota still exists, and is growing — in 2010, the company finally returned to profit.[1]

QUESTIONS

1) Toyota's recall was not the biggest in history, but it was the most widely covered. What do you think were the reasons for this?
2) How should Toyota have reacted? Were their reactions based on cross-cultural misunderstandings?
3) What strategy should Toyota apply in the future to guarantee safety and service for their customers?
4) Why were American and Japanese reactions to the incidents so different? Discuss in class.

REFERENCES

1. Allen, K and J Sturcke. Timeline: Toyota's recall woes (23 February 2010). *Guardian.*
2. ARD. Toyota trotzt Pannenserie. http://www.boerse.ard.de/content.jsp?key=dokument_434966, accessed 26.07.2010.
3. Aubé, V. Ten biggest auto recalls. *MSN.*
4. Berger, A. Toyotas ungebremste Pannenfahrt (27 January 2010). *Financial Times.*
5. Crawley, J. Transport secretary comment shakes Toyota (3 February 2010). *Reuters.*
6. Erneute Schlappe für Toyota (19 May 2010). *Tagesschau.*
7. Hays, J. Toyota recalls and problems (2009). *Facts and Details.*
8. Husko, M, M Kölling and M Ruch. Nichts ist unmöglich (1 February 2010). *Stem.*
9. Ibison, D. Toyota Motors suffers double blow in US (18 May 2010). *Financial Times.*
10. Kim, C. FACTBOX: Ranking of world's top 10 auto groups by sales (1 September 2008). *Reuters.*

11. Kingston, J. Toyota's Fall from Grace, Japan's Moment of Truth (March 2010). *Globalasia*.
12. Linebaugh, K and D Searcey. Toyota woes put focus on black box (14 February 2010). *Wall Street Journal*.
13. Mackintosh, J. Toyota strives to steer back towards quality (13 July 2006). *Financial Times*.
14. Messenger, A. Toyota recall highlights crisis in global auto industry (12 February 2010). *WSWS*.
15. Nakamoto, M. Hitachi may face turbine damage claims (2 August 2006). *Financial Times*.
16. Nakamoto, M. Toyota falls short of its high expectations (21 November 2005). *Financial Times*.
17. Reaktion auf Gaspedal-Skandal — Toyota startet Qualitätsoffensive (30 March 2010). *News Deutschland*.
18. Reuters, Sales. http://www.reuters.com/sectors/industries/rankings?industryCode=72&view=sales, accessed on 29.05.2010.
19. Schrader, M. Toyota überholt General Motors (24 April 2005). *DW-WORLD*.
20. Toyoland. Toyota history: Corporate and automotive. http://www.toyoland.com/history.html, accessed on 25.05.2010.
21. Toyota prüft Rückruf von 270.000 Autos (1 July 2010). *Tagesschau*.
22. Toyota recalls 3.8 million vehicles.
23. Toyota. History of Toyota. http://www2.toyota.co.jp/en/history/index.html, accessed on 25.05.2010.
24. Toyota. Toyota to expand product quality field offices across United States and Canada (8 July 2010). http://pressroom.toyota.com/pr/tms/toyota/toyota-consumer-safety-advisory-102572.aspx, accessed on 20.07.2010.
25. Toyotas Reaktion auf die Rekordstrafe in den USA (6 April 2010). *Podcast*.
26. Valdes-Dapena, P. Toyota recalls top 5.3 million vehicles (28 January 2010). *CNN Money*.
27. Vartabedian, R and K Bensinger. Runaway Toyota cases ignored (8 November 2009). *LA Times*.

APPENDIX 1: WORLD HISTORY RECALLS

1) Ford, 2008–09 (14.1 million)
   2008: Recall of 9.6 million vehicles due to an electrical fire exposure caused by faulty cruise control switches;
   October 2009: Recall of additional 4.5 million
2) Ford, 1996 (7.9 million)
   1988–1993: Recall of 7.9 million vehicles due to defects in the ignition system
3) GM, 1971 (6.7 million)
   1971: Recall of 6.7 million due to the engine falling back on the throttle cable, producing full-throttle acceleration
4) GM, 1981 (5.8 million)
   1981: Recall of 5.8 million due to loose suspension bolts while driving
5) Ford, 1972 (4.1 million)
   1972: Recall of 4.1 million due to seatbelt problems
6) Toyota, 2009 (3.8 million)
   2009: Recall of 3.8 million due to loose floor mats
7) GM, 1973 (3.7 million)
   1973: Recall of 3.7 million due to problems with steering while driving
8) Honda, 1995 (3.7 million)
   1995: Recall of 3.7 million due to problems with seatbelts
9) Volkswagen, 1972 (3.7 million)
   1972: Recall of 3.7 million due to problems with windshield wipers
10) GM, 2004 (3.6 million)
    2004: Recall of 3.6 million due to problems with support cables for the tailgate

Source: http://autos.ca.msn.com/photos/gallery.aspx?cp-documen-tid=22338216.

APPENDIX 2: SALES OF TOP AUTOMOBILE COMPANIES

1–20 of 37 companies.   **Data as of 24 Jun 2010**

Ticker	Name	TTM Sales $	3Yr. Sales Growth Rate %	5 Yr. Sales Growth Rate %
	MktCap Weighted Average	3,526,995.598	7.53	8.71
7203.T	TOYOTA MOTOR CORPORATION	18,950,970.000	−7.50	0.43
7267.T	HONDA MOTOR CO., LTD.	8,579,174.000	−8.19	−0.16
TAMO. BO	Tata Motors Limited	943,123.688	42.61	36.83
HROH. BO	Hero Honda Motors Ltd	160,961.406	16.85	16.32
F.N	Ford Motor Company	123,459.000	−10.10	−7.56
BAJA. BO	Bajaj Auto Limited	89,367.102	6.13	–
ASOK. BO	Ashok Leyland Limited	73,151.562	0.68	11.83
MAHM. BO	Mahindra & Mahindra Limited	49.899.020	28.63	30.78

Source: http://www.reuters.com/sectors/industries/rankings?industryCode=72&view=sales.

APPENDIX 3: TOYOTA SHARE PRICES 2001–2010

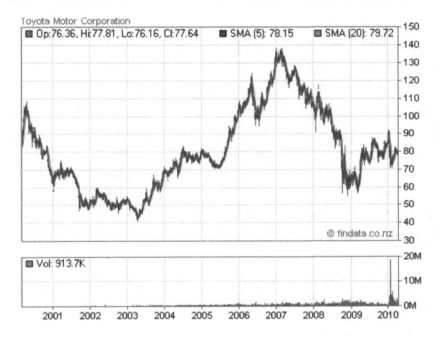

Part 4

CROSS-CULTURAL ENCOUNTERS

Japanese Perfectionism Meets American "Easygoing-ism"

Christina Wright

Miss Ryoko Moto writes for numerous Japanese women's fashion magazines. She works with the publishing company, Kobunsha, located in Gokokuji, Japan. Miss Moto is 27 years old and has been working as a writer since her graduation from Meiji University five years ago. She loves her job — but she only loves doing it in Japan. This is due to a critical incident that occurred to her after about two years with the company.

Miss Moto is a very typical Japanese fashion writer: she has model-like good looks and is both a fountain of knowledge on fashion and an extremely hard worker. However, being a writer for a Japanese magazine is by no means easy. Miss Moto explained that for every shoot she does (about four a week), she has to come up with concepts, locations, staff, permits, transportation, setting/props, and writing/editing. The amount of work she puts into each and every aspect of the shoot is unbelievable. It is amazing how utterly smoothly every shoot with her goes. Nothing ever runs late; everyone knows exactly what they are supposed to be doing; there is rarely if ever a hitch; and she has everything timed down to the minute. The woman really is a perfectionist with a capital "P".

This is not to say that all the writers I have met in Japan are like this; but it is fair to say that the perfectionism I saw in Miss Moto is not unusual. It amazes me how meticulous people can be in

249

Japan — but this, Miss Moto explains to me, is just how it works here. When she was an intern, they taught her to plan everything down to the last detail. She was trained to leave nothing out — bathroom breaks included. There is never any confusion as to where the shoot is, or incidents such as people getting lost or being caught without a permit. Nobody is ever off for being sick; and even if a staff member is ill, he or she comes to work as usual. Miss Moto had assumed that this was how everyone worked in the fashion industry. She never thought that it was possible to do a fashion shoot without having everything planned out meticulously — until, that is, a critical incident happened, and she learned a very discomforting lesson.

After being a writer for two years, Miss Moto was allowed to go on her first foreign photo shoot. She was extremely excited — and her excitement doubled when she learned she was going to be shooting in L.A. Four months before the shoot, she began planning. She tried to get in touch with the coordinators in L.A., but was not able to contact them until one month before the trip. This was unnerving for her, but in all the excitement, she just went right on planning. The coordinator she eventually got hold of, Mrs Rie Miller, was of Japanese descent and spoke fluent English and Japanese. Her job was to translate, and to help the Japanese staff find locations and permits in a foreign country. It turned out, in the end, that Mrs Miller discharged her duties effectively and nearly gave Miss Moto a heart attack in the process.

The moment Miss Moto got through customs and out of the airport, she knew she was in trouble: Mrs Miller was nowhere to be found and it took four calls to get her on her cell phone. She explained she was stuck in heavy traffic, but Miss Moto was stunned when she eventually turned up over 30 minutes late. However, in her excitement at being in America, she did not say anything; she was angry, but her Japanese training told her to *gaman* (endure the situation) and not to make a bad first impression. It was not until later, as it neared dinner time, that Miss Moto really started to worry. Mrs Miller had made no restaurant reservation, and as for the schedule sheet that Miss Moto had faxed over a month ago, she "had not really looked at it". Now, Miss Moto was panicking.

That night, after a last-minute meal at "In 'n' Out Burger", they all went back to the hotel. Miss Moto was planning on having a meeting about the next day's work schedule, but was told "to get a good night's rest". She passed a restless night.

The next morning, Mrs Miller came to pick them up, and showed them a stack of Polaroids from which Miss Moto was supposed to pick places to shoot. Miss Moto was stunned at how everything was done at the last minute. Hiding how uncomfortable she felt, she picked ten spots and they started their day's work.

At first, things seemed to be going fine. Mrs Miller knew where she was going and helped with the translation the whole way. However, when they began shooting at the beach, they were suddenly stopped by the police. Mrs Miller quickly told the staff to hide their cameras and went to talk to the cops. "I felt my heart stop", Miss Moto explained to me.

Not only was Miss Moto scared, she was embarrassed. The rest of the staff looked to her to find out what was going on, but for the first time in her professional life, she had no idea what to do. Why were the cops here? Why did Mrs Miller tell them to hide the cameras? Finally, Mrs Miller came back with the answers: the beach they were shooting on was private, and since they had no permit, a resident had called the cops. Miss Moto was now angry. They had wasted time and she had bruised her pride, and it all happened because Mrs Miller had not done her planning properly. This would never have happened in Japan! Miss Moto would never try to shoot somewhere without a permit! Was this how Americans worked? If so, how did they ever get anything done? Silently and furiously, Miss Moto asked herself these questions, but she could not present these questions to Mrs Miller.

However, Mrs Miller soon showed her the answer: she walked straight up to one of the houses and asked if they could shoot on the beach. The woman who lived there replied "of course", and the problem was solved. They returned to the beach and started shooting again. For the second time in that hour, Miss Moto was stunned. Although it was not how she would do things, she was impressed by how Mrs Miller was able to go up to a complete stranger's house and disobey the police. All this was unfathomable to Miss Moto.

However, she admired how Mrs Miller quickly handled the situation. "I would have been too shy", Miss Moto told me.

She explained to me that the trip continued much as it had started — not planned and very stressful, but at least there were no more interruptions by the cops. All in all, though, the mission was accomplished: the pictures that emerged from all these chaos were beautiful, and Miss Moto's chief editor was impressed.

Since that fateful trip, Miss Moto had been on numerous foreign photo shoots, but that trip with Mrs Miller in L.A. will always be the one that she remembers most.

Miss Moto said she learned an interesting lesson on that trip. She explained to me that she learned to loosen up and "be more American". She admired the way Mrs Miller took care of the cops and handled the beach situation. She still wishes she could be "strong" like that, but told me that this is hard to do in Japan. Although at no point on that first trip to L.A. did she felt relaxed, that critical incident showed her that although Mrs Miller had a different working style as compared to her, it did not mean she could not get the job done. That lesson has helped Miss Moto on many later foreign photo shoots, and has also helped her to work with many foreign people. She explained that Western people in particular have a more spontaneous and laid back way of working. Instead of having everything planned in every detail, they often tend to go with the moment. This is still hard for Miss Moto to do herself, but she admires the beautiful pictures that come from the spontaneity of Western photographers and staff.

One of the biggest lessons that she learned and appreciates is the way that fashion shoots work in Japan. She likes shooting in foreign places, but only occasionally. It is too stressful for her to not have everything planned out. That is not how she likes to do things. Although she learned a lesson, she said she will continue to plan her photo shoots, just like she had done before. She admires the Western work ethic, but embraces the Eastern work ethic. Her heart lies in Japan, and her experience overseas had shown her that.

QUESTIONS

1) What aspects are most important in Japanese and American working styles?

2) Identify five cultural differences in the story and discuss them in class.

3) How might these differences lead to cross-cultural misunderstandings and conflicts?

4) How can Miss Moto and Mrs Miller avoid stress and misunderstanding the next time they work together?

Being Polite in Japan

Chenming Bi

I was born in China and lived there until I was 13; after that, I moved to Tokyo, and have lived there ever since. As a result, my way of thinking and my behavior often switches back and forth between the Chinese and Japanese culture. When I was in elementary school in China, I was a member of the chess club. In the club, the smartest students won the respect of the others. There was no *sempai–kôhai (senior–junior)* relation in my club, and I did not have such a concept until I came to Japan.

I first encountered the *sempai–kôhai* relation in my Japanese high school. To be honest, it really freaked me out. One day, after school, I was looking for a friend who belonged to the baseball club. I found him in the locker room talking to a guy, but in a really servile manner, making extremely respectful bows. I was taken aback when I saw this scene because I had never imagined that my friend could talk in this way. He usually adopted a very tough tone, even when talking to the teachers, but here he was, showing great respect for his club *sempai* (senior).

Since I was not a member of the club, the *sempai* asked me who I was and why I was there. I briefly introduced myself, but not with *keigo* (polite language used when talking to superiors). My friend screamed and punched me on the shoulder, saying: "To whom do you think you are talking? He is your *sempai*! He is older than you! You definitely have to use *keigo*! Now you have to apologize to him! Right now!" My friend was very serious about this, and I was very embarrassed. The atmosphere was horrible. I apologized, since I did not want to cause trouble, but on the inside, I was really upset. My friend also apologized, since it had been one of his friends who had been so impolite. It seemed that even my friend's friends were supposed to address their *sempai* with *keigo*. Somehow, we continued to talk, while I started articulating each sentence with *masu* and *desu* (polite expressions in Japanese) and speaking very carefully. During the "scary" conversation, the *sempai* asked my age, and it turned out that we were the same age as each other! This is because schools in China start in a different month, so I was one year older than my classmates, and the *sempai* and I, though in different years in school, were of the same age.

In China, what had happened to me would be impossible and unbelievable. The Chinese characters *sempai* and *kôhai* refer only to elderly and young people respectively. In China, there is no *sempai–kôhai* relationship in schools, clubs, and companies; we only respect people who do show leadership, or who have higher abilities and skills. This has nothing to do with a person's age. In Japan, though, as long as someone is older, he/she will in most cases be the decision maker and the leader.

I did not join any sports clubs in high school, so I had no more encounters with this system, and I got through school barely having to use *keigo*. However, after having had such a terrible experience, I was very careful whenever I spoke to people who were older than me. I did not want to offend them for not using *keigo*. When I entered the third year, though, I joined the English debating club, and many *kôhai* used *keigo* when they spoke to *me*! This made me feel very uncomfortable and unnatural. In my point of view, *keigo* is a barrier: I cannot have a heartfelt conversation with someone if I use *keigo*, and vice versa. However, when I asked my *kôhai* not to use *keigo*, I was surprised when one of them replied: "You are my *sempai*, I would feel strange if I didn't use *keigo*". I came to realize that the *sempai–kôhai* conception is deeply rooted in Japanese culture. It is a part of Japanese society and can never be changed. As a foreigner, I had to adapt to this culture, and as long as I live in Japan, there is no way I can escape the *sempai–kôhai* logic. There is an old saying: "When in

Rome, do as the Romans do". However, when I left high school, there was no more *keigo*! What a relief!

One thing that I noticed is that it is very hard for me to feel being respected when someone speaks to me in *keigo*. It is very common on trains, for example, to see employees talking in *keigo* to their *sempai*. To me, their conversation seems artificial: can anyone truly have a real and meaningful conversation when they are using *keigo*? Although I do think that every country has some style of speaking which is basically *keigo*, the point is that in Japan, *keigo* is a whole system in itself. The language used can be very different — that is to say, it is not just words or sentences but the whole mode of speaking changes. In Japanese companies, the language used among employees is totally different to that used between employees and superiors; it almost seems that two separate languages are being used.

Sometimes, it is hard to accept that no matter how great or adept I may be, as long as I am new, I will have to speak in *keigo* with other members of a company, simply because they set foot in that company earlier than me. This makes me start to feel that this is unjust: Why do you still have to respect people who are actually *inferior* to you?

However, using *keigo* is inevitable in Japan because the Japanese really do care about it. Needless to say, between companies and customers, *keigo* is important because the relative positions are very clear and obvious. No matter what the company does, customers always have to be treated like kings. However, I do not think you will find a similar situation in many of the clubs in Japanese schools; thus for foreigners, it is crucial to understand the *sempai–kôhai* relation and the use of *keigo*.

It is easy to see that the way the Japanese are educated has a strong influence on the style of Japanese companies. For the Japanese, the *sempai–kôhai* relationship and the use of *keigo* are thought to be logical and rational because these are what they have learned when they were young. However, people from outside Japan will face difficulties in adapting to this environment and accepting this concept. I only managed to use *keigo,* but I still hesitate. I find that it is really stressful for me to use *keigo* when I speak with someone I know. In other words, I just cannot make friends with people with whom I need to use *keigo*. I can only converse at a very polite level.

In conclusion, hierarchy in Japanese society is much more defined than in Western society. As a result, positions of power within groups are often well-defined and strictly implemented. In school clubs, these hierarchical relationships are divided into two separate categories: *sempai* and *kôhai*. Whether be it the school's *karate* club, art club, or tennis club, the *sempai–kôhai* relationship plays a significant role, just as it does in the Japanese education system. *Sempai* are seen as the leaders of the club and are expected to teach, guide, punish, and praise the *kôhai* in accordance with club rules and expectations. *Sempai* are not expected to do any of the club's dirty work, such as setting and cleaning up, since these tasks are reserved for the lower-ranking *kôhai*. *Kôhai* are not only expected to do the dirty work and follow the advice given by their *sempai*, they are also expected to use *keigo* when addressing their *sempai*, both in and out of club hours. Within school clubs, members learn how to give and take orders, to follow and to lead; they also learn to use *keigo*, as well as how to be a successful member of a group — both of which are essential tools for being a successful member of the Japanese workforce. Therefore, the *sempai–kôhai* relationship is an educational tool in itself: it teaches children to be successful members of a group, and thus be productive members of Japanese society.

QUESTIONS

1) Explain how important hierarchies are in Japan and how an outsider can recognize them.
2) Identify the differences in politeness of speech between Japan and your country.
3) *Sempai–kôhai* relationships are typical for Japanese culture. What do you think about it? How would you behave if you were in Chenming's situation?

Getting More Than I Aimed For: Cultural Challenges in the Archery Club

Roy Martinez

One of my primary objectives in attending Sophia University as an exchange student for the 2009 spring semester was to have a fully-engaged cultural experience, and not just the normal tourist stuff, like visiting the famous shines and temples, or wearing a *yukata* (cotton kimono) at a *matsuri* (Japanese street festival). Although visiting Japanese cultural sites is very enjoyable and helpful for an understanding of Japan's history and culture, it only scratches the surface of Japanese society. What these activities lack is the direct social interaction that would be considered "normal" or "everyday" for most Japanese. They do not give you a feel of the social structure or the deeper intricacies of the society. I wanted to experience what an "average" Japanese college student would experience, so I decided to join a local club. I selected the Sophia *kyudo* (archery) club which gave me the social structure and deeper meaning I was looking for. However, I soon found that I had volunteered for one of the most challenging experiences of my life so far. The world of Japanese clubs, and by extension, traditional Japanese social structure, is far more different and difficult than I could have imagined. Only when my last days at the club had finished did I realize just how challenging it had been: my views of both my home culture, and the culture of my host country, Japan, had changed.

I would be lying if I said I had not been warned. I had been given extensive lectures during orientation, which covered everything from culture shock to transportation, and cultural differences. During orientation, we were given a lecture by Dr Slater, an anthropology professor from the Faculty of Liberal Arts at Sophia University, in which he talked about the difficulties of Japanese clubs and specifically, the difficulty of being a foreigner in one. He warned us about what he called "serious clubs" — primarily sports teams — saying that even though we were entering Sophia from various years and stages in our college education, this would not matter at all when we stepped into the club. In every "serious" club, we would become first year "rookies", and be placed at the bottom of the club's totem pole. In some sports clubs, that could mean that you have to do chores the entire time and never actually get to participate in the activity. I did listen to his advice and even acknowledged that some of it must be true. However, I thought it was focused on the sports teams, like baseball and football, where players are limited in the roles they can play.

So, armed with this knowledge, I set out to choose a club for myself. The decision process was actually fairly short. I flipped through the club book provided to each of us, and though there were many interesting clubs, I homed in on martial arts. In addition to getting to know Japanese social structures better, I also wanted to participate in something that I would not be able to experience in the United States. The *Kyudo* Club announcement caught my eye: it was something I had seen only once before. During my last visit to Japan, the cousin of my host family had shown me his bow and uniform. *Kyudo*, a traditional sport, is extremely rare outside Japan. I decided to learn more and set about joining. By a strange twist of fate, I met one of the three foreign students in the club at the train station in Shinjuku while buying my commuter pass. We communicated via email. I visited the *dojo* and was able to ask questions. Everything I was told was fairly reasonable: yes, it was a serious club, but everyone gets to participate; the time commitment is reasonable and should be compatible with my classes. It all seemed good and reasonable. In hindsight, although one hesitates to use the word "lies", I would think it is fair to say that a tiny bit of stretching of the truth was going on.

The following was my estimation of the *Kyudo* schedule before I officially joined, based on the official flyer and conversations with current foreign exchange students in the club:

Official practice:

Practice time 5:15 pm–7:15 pm, Monday and Wednesday.
Practice time 9:15 am–11:15 am or 1:15 pm–3:15 pm, Saturday.
Personal practice: At least 1–2 hours a week outside of normal practice.
Competitions: Normally on Saturdays or Sundays, semi-frequent.

So I joined the club. The first week went fairly well. There was a lot of information to take in, and given that I have very limited Japanese, it was difficult at times. I was lucky that there were four other foreign exchange students from the same program in the club, all of whom were better at comprehending Japanese, and were able to help me with some of the more difficult translations. During the first week, the hours were long, which I expected. There was also a lot of stuff to learn and they needed to take the extra time to train us in all the different steps.

However, it quickly became apparent that I might possibly have bitten off a much larger mouthful than I expected. With each passing week, there seem to be additional time requirements that were fitted into my schedule, so much so that by the end of the third or fourth week, my schedule looked something like this:

Real practice time

Practice time: 4:45 pm–8:15 pm, Monday and Wednesday.
Practice time: 8:30 am–11:30 am or 12:30 pm–3:45 pm, Saturday.
Personal practice: At least 3–4 hours a week outside of normal practice.
Competitions: Both Saturday and Sunday competitions, on three out of four weekends (competitions generally ran from 8:30 am to about 4:30 pm).
Dojo cleaning: Once a week at 8:30 am on Wednesday.
Lunchtime instruction: Everyday during our lunch period (during the first three weeks).

The practice time was higher due to me being a first year. As a first year, I was expected to attend every practice, attend every competition, practice outside of the normal scheduled practice for a couple of hours a week (preferably everyday), and perform the first year's work. The work turned out to be fairly extensive. Adding up all of this, my time commitment increased quickly and unexpectedly, placing a strain on my free time and studying time. I had expected that I would still have some free time to explore and to study, but in reality, I was putting in almost double the hours. I also thought I would be participating in normal student life at the beginning of the semester. In fact, over the course of my time in the club, exhaustion was a common companion as my sleep schedule diminished and I fought to make the most of my hours awake.

Freshman *shigoto* — or work — is very extensive. As first year students, at the lowest level of the *kyudo* social structure, we were expected to do all the menial chores for the *dojo*, our *sempai* (seniors, upperclassmen), and ourselves. The work varied: we were required to show up at least 30 minutes before practice to clean the *dojo* in the manner specifically described by our *sempai*. We were also in charge of breaking down everything and cleaning the *dojo* after practice, a process that, for a while, took us 30–45 minutes. During practice, we were responsible for keeping scores, recording all strikes, moving arrows and bins at the proper moment, arrow retrieval and cleaning, and target setup and breakdown. Each one of these tasks had to be done in a specific way that was to be followed in an exacting manner. Making a mistake, or failing to perform any task, would result in a fairly extensive admonishment, depending on the severity of the mistake. There was no leniency for any of us, foreigners or Japanese students alike. If we made a series of mistakes, they would publicly call out the first years and we would have to do whatever was done wrong again till it was done right. I remember that one time, we "repapered" the targets so poorly that we were required to come back the next day during our lunch period to redo them. After a while, this became grating; even if you spotted the mistake immediately after you had made it, and knew what you had done wrong, they never failed to make sure that you *knew* you had made a mistake.

Even after weeks of doing our assigned tasks in the proper way, we were told that it was still not good enough and that we should have known better. This admonishment would then lead to more remedial instruction.

I shared earlier that one of my main objectives in joining this club was to get a good grasp of Japanese social structure. Here, it is safe to say that I got more than I ever expected. The *Kyudo* Club was set up according to a social hierarchy that confirmed everything I had heard from professors, my host family, and other students, both Japanese and foreign. Your place in the club was determined by seniority and time spent in the club. It did not matter if you were a third year college student like me, or if you had practiced *Kyudo* for the past three years at your high school: we were all grouped as first years. In American clubs, this does occasionally happen — you may be grouped into ranks of years or experience, but this generally is for setting up tasks or other organizational matters. In a U.S. club, everyone involved has an equal say: they can talk to the head of the club to discuss an issue or concern, or to any other member. Nothing stops you. However, in the *Kyudo* Club, we were instructed that, as first years, we were assigned to the "care" of the second years. If we had any complaints, we were supposed to speak to them, and not to the third or fourth years. We were not supposed to bug the higher year members with our concerns or questions, as they were much higher than us socially. Additionally, if any of the upperclassmen asked us to do something, there was no room for questioning; you just did it. You also had to use the proper and respectful language (*keigo*) when addressing the *sempai*. Some might be in the same year at school as me, but they were still higher up, and I still had to address them in very polite Japanese: no plain forms or truncated statements.

It was right around the middle of the semester that I had a complete crisis of confidence within the club, with the Japanese social structure, and with myself in general. After weeks of an extremely grueling practice schedule that seemed never-ending, I was finally hitting burnout. This burnout stemmed in part from the fact that I had to study for my midterms — and it turned out that this was not an acceptable excuse for my *sempai*. I was told specifically that I existed to work around *kyudo*, not the other way around. Never mind the fact that they had scheduled double days of competitions the weekend before the midterms, which meant that I would be at the *dojo* from about 8:30 am to about 5 pm, leaving absolutely no time to do any meaningful studying. The perceived lack of empathy was really what made me upset. I had attended almost every event and required meeting time without fail, and I had given up large chunks of my free time to participate. And when I needed just a single day to take care of my grades, I was basically told that they were not important. What was more, it was getting frustrating to be told everyday that something was still wrong with our work and that we kept making mistakes; I felt that I was doing the jobs well enough and that I should not be called out as much as I was. Lastly, I felt that the whole social structure was way too rigid and inflexible. It seemed to lead to some very high-strung, and what I perceived as arrogant individuals. Many of the upper *sempai* enforced the rule of us not talking to them unless they had something to say to us, telling us not to bother them with trivial questions and to go ask our assigned second year "caretakers", I got extremely frustrated with the whole situation, and considered dropping the club to regain what time and sanity I had left. I was in a dark mood for a few days as I thought over my situation.

I thought about it for a while, and talked to my parents, my friends, and even a few professors. In doing so, I reminded myself that this was, after all, not entirely unexpected and that maybe I was being overly critical and inflexible. I was trying to force on the club my own expectations from my prior experiences of activities in the States. In the U.S., clubs are very different. They always come second to schoolwork, whereas here, my club was expecting me to put it not just before homework, but before class work as well. Talking with some Japanese students did help clarify the matter: in Japan, grades are not overly important. Many students just go to class, do decently on the tests, and receive passing grades. There is no "A mentality". In the States, and at my home university, everyone strives to get an "A", and a high Grade Point Average because of their importance for scholarships and even general attendance status. This was further reinforced when one of my professors reminded the class that a D was, apparently, still a passing grade at Sophia. At my university, it stands for "Disaster". Now, this is not to say that students do not try hard or want good grades. It is just that they are not at the forefront of everyone's mind in the way that I am used to and demand from myself. What the Club expected of me was a little different from how I saw grades, so I could not really blame them too much for that. Eventually, I had to skip a few competitions to study. While this did not make my *sempai* happy (by any stretch of the imagination), it allowed me to strike a better balance between their desires and mine. Additionally, I started to make sure I planned my private practice schedule in advance so I could give myself additional study time when I needed it and more *kyudo* time when I did not.

As for both the perceived arrogance and overzealous correction by the *sempai*, it turns out that it was more my mood and cultural expectation that was driving my view of this. In the U.S., there is very much an "everybody is a winner" mentality: it does not matter whether you are perfect, what is important is that you "tried your best". Over here, this does not apply. There was no such thing as "good enough" when it came to our chores: they needed to be as perfect as humanly possible. However, their constant corrections and extremely high expectations did help us: by the end of our semester here, we were able to do our jobs almost without thinking, knowing all the little nuances that were expected of us. The arrogance I perceived was more a reflection of my frustration than an actual feeling of superiority. My *sempai* were my *sempai* for a reason, and this part of the structure of the club was designed to help us. We had to go to the second years because it was their assigned duty to help us. It was a two-way street: not only were they responsible for us, we were responsible for them as well. If we messed up, they also got punished alongside us for failing in their assigned tasks. It was all for our benefit. There was also the matter of learning the proper time and place to approach the older *sempai* in conversation, especially when outside normal practice.

After coming to these conclusions, and deciding to remain in the club, I felt a sense of satisfaction in what I had accomplished. Having come to terms with the social differences, I was able to enjoy the club much more for the second half of the semester. Things were not perfect; nothing is. However, I do feel that I have made it through the hardest part of the process of cultural understanding. When I entered the club, I expected to face difficulties, but I did not expect the level of commitment that would be demanded, nor the demands of the social system. I guess I can say that I "survived" *kyudo* — but really, I would like to think that I did more than that. I found new strength in myself on many levels, and gained a greater understanding and appreciation of the Japanese club system and its hierarchy. A graduate student has told me that if you can survive *kyudo*, you can survive in a Japanese company, since everything you encounter in the club is almost exactly mirrored in a full company. If I choose to work for a Japanese company in the future, I feel I am now well prepared for the challenge. Likewise, if I work for an American company that deals with Japan, my knowledge and experiences will be assets for that company. My experiences were truly stressful and frustrating; yet, at the same time, being a participant was an invigorating and enriching experience. I feel that I "lived" the cultural event. I was not just a visitor. It was a *real* learning experience.

QUESTIONS

1) Explain the differences in American and Japanese perceptions of a University sports club.
2) How would you react in Roy's place? Explain your reactions.
3) Japanese believe that a membership in a university sports club is a good qualification for a graduate to have. It therefore helps a graduate to secure a job in a famous company. What do you think about this system?

Part 5

FUTURE TECHNOLOGIES

Japanese Car Wars — Who Will Win the Race for the Future Technology?

Nathan Michael Echols

> *"A century ago, the automobile industry looked a lot like the one shaping up today...there were gasoline powered cars, steam-powered cars, and electric-powered cars all jostling for influence in a process of natural selection before the gasoline car claimed victory. History seems to be repeating itself right at the outset of another automotive century."*
>
> — *Yozo Hasegawa*

INTRODUCTION

Hybrid technology and green automobiles of the future have become an increasingly popular sector of the automotive market in recent years. Spearheaded by Japanese automakers such as Toyota and Honda, these gas-electric hybrids mark the first stage in a transition from gas-guzzling, inefficient combustion engines to a totally clean burning fuel source. Although there are many reasons for this shift in philosophy amongst automakers, it is interesting to note that the potential for hybrid or even electric vehicles has existed since the birth of the internal combustion engine. Ironically, however, environmentally-friendly automobile engines took a backseat to the less efficient but far cheaper internal combustion engines (Frank, 2004).

Early automobiles developed in the United States had to be cranked by hand, which was both troublesome and potentially dangerous. Early hybrid technology evolved as a means to resolve this burdensome method of starting the engine as well as eliminate a problem that has plagued the electric engine for over a century — the limited lifespan and capacity of the electric battery. These electric and hybrid engines briefly existed as the most popular form of automobile engine during the fledgling years of the automobile industry, but these forms of propulsion quickly gave way to the inefficient internal combustion engine — an engine that was extremely cheap to operate at that time due to an enormous supply of cheap gasoline. The result was an automobile design that is still widespread today, but damaging to the environment and wastes an enormous amount of fuel. As it is inconvenient to shut off the engine when vehicles stopped, it has been common practice to keep these vehicles running at all times. The result is that modern day combustion engines waste fuel while essentially performing no other task but idling at traffic signals or stop signs. Furthermore, these engines waste fuel both during acceleration and deceleration due to throttling up and down, which restricts airflow to the engine (Frank, 2004).

Yet, because consumers demand high performance vehicles and oil prices have generally remained low, there has been little market influence to demand greater research, development and implementation of green technologies until recent years. Americans, in particular, have almost always been willing to purchase enormous amounts of gasoline from the Middle East, but this trend gradually began to experience a shift in consumer philosophy since the 1970s (Frank, 2004). This case will explore the factors that led to this shift in automobile engine design, and examine the emerging green technologies and various Japanese automobile manufacturers in an attempt to discern which green technology holds the greatest prospects of success for the future of the industry.

THE HISTORY OF THE JAPANESE AUTOMOBILE MARKET

The emergence of the Japanese automobile market as it exists today can largely be attributed to the entrepreneurship and ingenuity of

Toyota Motor Corporation founder Kiichiro Toyoda. His contributions to the creation of a domestic automobile production facility were so vital to the development of the Japanese automobile industry that it is necessary to delve deeper into his personal history as well as the factors that led to the establishment of Toyota Motor Corporation.

Kiichiro Toyoda, born in Shizuoka prefecture in 1894, was the son of automatic weaving loom inventor Sakichi Toyoda. Kiichiro led a modest lifestyle in his grade school years, living within a family of traditionally peasant farmers who managed to earn a sustainable living by performing various carpentry jobs on the side. His first home was a tiny, four-room building constructed of straw and wood with a dirt floor. However, by sheer chance, a large shipyard began to be constructed in a nearby village when Kiichiro was in grade school, and his father would often visit this shipyard to learn about propulsion technologies and industrial factory production methods. Eventually, this interest in the industrial revolution led to practical knowledge and application when Sakichi Toyoda began to research methods to create an automated loom to improve upon the inefficient system of weaving that he witnessed growing up among peasant farmers. The result of his ingenuity was the Toyoda automatic loom, which eventually led to the creation of the Toyoda Automatic Weaving factory in Nagoya, Japan, and the Toyota Automatic Loom Works Corporation (Hasegawa, 2008).

Kiichiro Toyoda followed his father's footsteps by joining the automatic loom business and further developing upon the technology. Eventually, Kiichiro managed to create a loom so advanced that the largest textile manufacturer in the world, Platt Brothers of England, purchased the patent rights to Toyoda's loom technology for slightly less than 100,000 euros in 1934. This period in history was marked by a sharp decline in the loom industry and the Toyoda family feared for the future of their company. However, Kiichiro Toyoda had a clear vision of the future of his company; using his newfound capital from the sale of his loom patent rights, he attempted to create Japan's first domestic automobile corporation.

Kiichiro Toyoda was not alone in this goal, however, as American automakers had imported vehicles into Japan for years and spurred great enthusiasm among the Japanese to purchase such automobiles on a massive scale. Local government officials as well as the national government began promoting the production of domestic automobiles and Kiichiro began to feel the pressure of competition. It was also at this time that the Jidosha Seizo Company and Nihon Sangyo Company merged to create the Nissan Motor Corporation, Toyota Motor Corporation's largest competitor. Both Toyota and Nissan began to develop prototypes of vehicles for family and individual use, but the risk involved in being the first movers led to virtually every other competitor vanishing from the market. Finally, with the demand for trucks and buses skyrocketing during World War II, both Toyota and Nissan increased production by ten-fold and became extremely profitable domestic automobile manufacturers (Hasegawa, 2008).

Honda Motor Corporation, which will also be discussed in this chapter, came much later on 24 September, 1948, as the result of a side business venture of motor-attached bicycle manufacturer Soichiro Honda. Soichiro Honda, like Kiichiro Toyoda, remained fascinated with the foreign automobiles that he witnessed in Japan during his childhood, thus prompting him to seek employment at an automobile repair shop prior to World War II. The expertise and on-the-job training that Soichiro Honda acquired during his years as an automobile repairman allowed him to eventually invest in his own corporation known as Tokai Precision Machinery, which was later destroyed during World War II. Yet, Honda remained undeterred and decided to rebuild his financial future in the form of Honda Motor Corporation following the end of the war. As a result of these historical factors, the three automobile manufacturers of Toyota, Honda and Nissan remain the major players in the contemporary domestic market (Hasegawa, 2008).

CURRENT SITUATION

As previously mentioned, these major Japanese automakers as well as automakers across the globe all pursued the internal combustion engine as their primary engine design due to the high degree of energy output and the relatively low costs. However, the current situation within the automobile market has begun to change due to several factors.

First, previously affordable oil prices suddenly spiked as a result of the oil crisis of 1973 when the Organization of Petroleum Exporting Countries (OPEC), unhappy with the West for supporting Israel in the Yom Kippur War, restricted the supply of oil for automobiles. This marked the first time in history in which both American and Japanese consumers significantly realized the extent to which they depended on the Middle East for this vital source of energy, and citizens of nations throughout the West became increasingly interested in alternative energy sources (Frank, 2007; Hasegawa, 2008). A second factor that further spurred development in the realm of alternative energy was that of an increasingly environmentally-conscious populace and new, more restrictive regulations on energy emissions. The early 1970s marked the introduction of the first regulatory legislation in both the United States and Japan that limited the extent to which automobiles could produce harmful emissions. This left automakers in both nations in a state of confusion and uncertainty because none of the prominent automakers of the time were quite sure of how to modify their current automobile models to meet the stringent environmental requirements. Automakers of both nations began to experiment with hybrid and electric technologies, but the available computers and energy storage devices of the time, as in Sakichi Toyoda's era, were incapable of storing the necessary energy required to power an automobile. The only batteries with potential at the time were lead-acid, nickel-cadmium or iron-nickel Edison cells, which were both bulky and unable to store enough energy to propel a vehicle. Furthermore, the computers of the 1970s were not sufficiently sophisticated to effectively manage both gasoline and battery energy sources, requiring the driver to constantly regulate the two devices — a task that would be undoubtedly dangerous while driving. American automakers made several attempts to develop new battery technologies capable of storing the required energy to power a vehicle of the time, but every attempt was met with several drawbacks and the internal combustion engine remained the choice of the major automakers (Frank, 2007). Furthermore, although primitive hybrid technology had existed for decades, hybrid engines of the era were incapable of competing with the speed and power of traditional engines, and efforts to deploy hybrid vehicles quickly lost steam with declines in oil prices. While United States automakers seemed to pursue a bare minimum strategy in order to simply comply with the new 1970s legislation, Toyota endeavored to go beyond the minimum regulations and create a truly green engine technology. Perhaps this persistence can be further explained by the bursting of the economic bubble in Japan in the early 1990s, which left Toyota in danger of losing profits during that time period. Times of uncertainty such as the early 1990s are largely responsible for pushing Toyota beyond its American counterparts to pursue truly innovative technologies as a means to ensure the survival of the company (Hasegawa, 2008).

Although hybrid and electric automobile technology had been around for over a century, the technological capacity to develop environmentally-friendly engines that were practical for modern automobiles finally reached fruition in the mid-1990s. Fearing that a corporate crisis was inevitable given external factors of the time, Toyota went to extraordinary lengths to create a technology so innovative as to ensure the survival of the company — the modern hybrid engine. Although initially met with skepticism by many automakers in the United States, the release of the hybrid automobiles created a ripple effect throughout the entire industry, provided Toyota with a marketable green image, and left American and European automakers scrambling to develop their own green technologies in an attempt to remain competitive against Toyota's ever growing market share (Hasegawa, 2008).

COMPETING STRATEGIES

While there are numerous green technology strategies that are available for each automobile manufacturer to choose, the leading technology of the moment is the hybrid engine. Popularized by Toyota, this engine design demonstrates highest efficiency at lowest costs for contemporary consumers, and virtually every major automaker has invested in comparable designs. However, this technology is extremely complex and has several subcategories and variations with each corporation banking on a different aspect of hybrid designs. Hence, it is important to delve more thoroughly into the hybrid engine to discern which technology each corporation is pursuing.

HYBRID HISTORY

The earliest hybrid automobile technology can be found in implementation in the late 1890s when engineers in the West experimented with various energy sources to create prototype automobile engines. The problem of an inability to store sufficient energy that plagues electric cars today was a major obstacle for automakers of that era, and the early hybrids were born out of this dilemma.

Over a century ago, Ferdinand Porsche grappled with the difficulties of providing a long-term energy supply to an electric vehicle in order to increase the distance covered before requiring a recharge. Even before the turn of the 20th century, Porsche's solution to this problem was to blend a gasoline engine with existing electric engine technologies, thus creating one of the first true hybrid vehicles. These hybrids models eventually took a backseat to the internal combustion engine due to the low oil prices of that era. Besides, the endorsement of that engine by the Ford Motor Company greatly assisted in establishing gasoline engines as the energy source of cars throughout the following century (Carr-Ruffino, 2007).

Despite Ford Motor Company's endorsement of the internal combustion engine, the early engines of the day lacked power and required the owner to physically turn a crank to start the vehicle. These drawbacks to the Ford engines encouraged engineers of the era to continue to develop upon existing hybrid technology because the hybrid motors allowed for faster acceleration than did the gasoline-powered counterparts. However, with advancements in technology, performance, and the introduction of the electric starter to the gasoline models, enthusiasm and interest in pursuing hybrid technology was virtually non-existent after the late 1920s (Hasegawa, 2008). It is important to note, however, that despite the affordability of vehicles powered by the internal combustion engine, the hybrids of that era are still more than four times as efficient than modern gasoline powered automobiles (Carr-Ruffino, 2007).

Historically, the popularity of green technology for automobiles appears to be proportional to the price of gasoline in international markets. Despite a virtual lack of investment in alternative energy sources since the 1920s, the oil crisis of the 1970s prompted many consumers to begin considering green automobiles as a means to defer these new costs. However, as with the value of gasoline, interest in alternative energy sources rapidly subsided following the crisis and most automakers shifted focus back to traditional gasoline powered engine development. However, the truly revolutionary moment that marked the beginning of the transition to energy efficiency occurred in the early 1990s under the Clinton administration in the United States.

The early 1990s once again marked a period of increasing oil prices and increasing concern and awareness over environmental issues such as carbon emissions and global warming. The coalescence of a milieu of factors at this point in history prompted then President Clinton to enact a research program titled "Partnership for a New Generation of Vehicles (PNGV)", which aimed to encourage American automakers to invest heavily in research and development of environmentally-friendly vehicles that could surpass the ambitious target benchmark of 80 miles per gallon. While the program succeeded somewhat and automakers such as General Motors and Ford Motor Company invested in diesel-hybrid technology, the new engine models resonated primarily with wealthy environmentalists who could afford the hefty price tag (Hasegawa, 2008).

HYBRID DESIGNS

Full Hybrids

Full hybrids are the most efficient and common type of green technology vehicles presently on the market. The Toyota Prius falls into this category and is capable of operating for several miles at low speeds on electric power alone. Benefits of this ability to run on electricity are a decrease in both noise and pollution. Energy is generated through a special braking system that converts and reuses power necessary to supply the engine. The computer systems required to process information and utilize both electric and gasoline energy sources are by far the most expensive of any hybrid model. However, this technology is so innovative and efficient that Toyota has managed to offset some costs by licensing the technology to both Ford and Nissan, which also currently produce full hybrid vehicles (Carr-Ruffino, 2007).

Mild Hybrids

Mild hybrids are quite similar to traditional automobile designs that utilize the internal combustion engine. However, these hybrid models provide slightly increased efficiency over traditional automobile engine designs by utilizing a small electric motor that assists in propulsion of the vehicle. These hybrid models are incapable of utilizing electric power alone to operate the vehicle and are less efficient than full hybrids; however, mild hybrids are cheaper to manufacture and allow consumers with tighter budgets the opportunity to experience a hybrid vehicle. Honda, Saturn and Hyundai currently utilize mild hybrid engines as an alternative to the more expensive full hybrid technology of Toyota.

Light Hybrids

Unlike full hybrids, light hybrids do not possess the ability to recycle or reuse energy in order to improve efficiency. Rather, light hybrid models utilize computer technology to stop and start the engine when needed in order to reduce the amount of fuel that would otherwise be burned while idling. General Motors is the leader in the light hybrid field, specifically with businesses that utilize the oversized electric generator in Silverado and Sierra truck lines to conveniently power construction-related power tools.

Plug-in Hybrids

Plug-in hybrid vehicles represent the next step in creating a more efficient engine design. These hybrids are capable of operating solely on electric power and boast more than 100 miles per gallon. Due to limitations in the amount of power currently capable of being stored in contemporary battery units, it is expected to be several years before viable automobiles of this type will begin to be displayed in showrooms. Toyota has already released adapter kits that are capable of converting existing Prius models into plug-in hybrid vehicles with plans to introduce a plug-in hybrid Prius in the future. However, despite the fact that Toyota has been the clear frontrunner in hybrid technology, General Motors beat Toyota to the punch with the announcement of the world's first plug-in hybrid vehicle for mass production — the Chevrolet Volt (Carr-Ruffino, 2007).

TOYOTA MOTOR CORPORATION

The original founder of Toyota Industries Corporation (which would later become Toyota Motor Corporation) and inventor of the automatic power loom, Sakichi Toyoda, recognized decades ago that the future of Japanese vehicles was not in gasoline but in renewable energy sources. In the words of Toyoda:

> You can build the best automobile or airplane ever made, yet you still need petroleum for its propulsion. Ours is a nation that must rely completely on imports for that resource. But where we are helplessly poor in petroleum, we are rich in hydropower. If we can turn that abundant resource into electricity, we can reduce our dependence on outside sources. We can power automobiles and airplanes. To accomplish this, however, we need to develop a battery that can generate high voltage, be durable, and quickly rechargeable: a battery that loses very little of its charge naturally, and meets with minimal internal resistance. It must also be simple and compact in design and construction (Hasegawa, 2008).

Although Toyoda's motives were spurred by a lack of petroleum amongst the islands of Japan rather than environmental concerns, his passion for innovation was a precursor to the success that the Toyota

Motor Corporation would have in the future in the realm of hybrid technology. As a result of this passion, Sakichi Toyoda was a great proponent of developing an efficient and powerful energy storage device or battery that could be used as a substitute for the internal combustion engine, relying on expertise both domestic and from abroad, and often offering substantial monetary awards for innovative ideas and technologies to further this goal. This endeavor and his collaboration with foreign experts in the field of alternative energy thrived from 1925 until the years prior to the start of World War II when communication with the West began to breakdown.

Toyota Motor Corporation as it is known today was founded by Sakichi Toyoda's son, Kiichiro Toyoda. Kiichiro Toyoda continued the research of his father for a renewable, electric energy source in the face of a diminishing oil supply that resulted from World War II. With demand for a new source of energy becoming increasingly desperate in lieu of the inevitable defeat of Japan, Toyota Motor Corporation's research division invested heavily in research and development of renewable energy technologies; however, much like his father, Kiichiro Toyoda was unsuccessful in developing this revolutionary energy storage device and the internal combustion energy remained as the unchallenged automobile propulsion device until the 1970s (Hasegawa, 2008).

However, by the mid-1990s following failed responses to oil shocks to again create a viable green energy vehicle, it appeared as if automakers would once again abandon plans to develop more efficient engines, but Toyota viewed the complacency of American and European automakers as an opportunity to leapfrog ahead in an area that Toyota's upper management perceived as a growing niche market (Hasegawa, 2008).

By the winter of 1994, Toyota's upper management had already created a hybrid technology design team and applied enormous pressure for rapid results on a truly revolutionary hybrid, compact car design that would provide such fuel efficiency that it would leave competitors in the dust. The design team responsible for implementing this new technology faced several challenges including a lack of expertise in hybrid technology, a lack of manufacturing infrastructure to create hybrid technology, the necessity to completely redesign the internal components of existing compact cars to allow added space for hybrid components, and constant computer glitches when attempting to regulate the flow of energy between the gasoline and electric systems. In essence, Toyota's upper management wanted this revolutionary car design operational within a year of the formation of the engineering team so that it could be displayed ahead of the competition at the 1995 Tokyo Motor Show.

Although the extremely limited time frame did not allow the new model, labeled the "Prius", to be developed completely for mass production by the time of the Tokyo Motor Show, the vehicle was presented and Toyota shocked visitors at the event by claiming that the Prius would be capable of achieving a fuel efficiency of more than 70 miles per gallon. The overwhelming support and enthusiasm for such a fuel efficient vehicle greatly impressed the newly promoted Toyota president Hiroshi Okuda who viewed the Prius and hybrid development as the innovative technology that would ensure the survival of the company. As a result, Okuda redirected an impressive 60% of the company's development resources to assist in the design of the Prius and applied enormous pressure to ensure that the automobile would be marketable by November of 1997.

Despite the pressures of designing and perfecting a completely revolutionary automobile design in such a limited time frame, the enormous resources available to the design team allowed them to virtually build from scratch the software and hardware needed to meet the specifications of Toyota's upper management. In particular, the battery technology of the time was far too large and impractical for a compact car design, and Toyota partnered with Matsushita and invested heavily to invent a battery design that was both compact and capable of the same levels of energy storage as the standard, larger batteries. As a result of their efforts, the Prius design team met the release date of November 2007, and initial sales were more than double the original estimates (Hasegawa, 2008). Clearly, Toyota had started a revolution in automobile design and views hybrid technology as the green technology of the future.

HONDA MOTOR CORPORATION

Ironically, Honda had held the title of the most environmentally-friendly automaker in the eyes of the public until the Toyota Prius debuted in 1997. As early as 1971, Honda had developed the revolutionary Compound Vortex Controlled Combustion (CVCC) technology that allowed for both low emissions and high gas mileage, which trumped much of the competition at the time. Furthermore, Honda distributed this technology to automakers across the globe and gained widespread recognition for its environmental efforts in the industry. Similarly to Toyota, the development of the CVCC technology was largely a response to increased restrictions on pollution and tighter emissions standards both in Japan and the United States. Honda heralded the development of this technology as revolutionary because it innovatively modified existing engine technology to significantly increase performance and efficiency. This allowed Honda or others who would utilize the technology to produce CVCC vehicles with existing manufacturing plants and factories (Hasegawa, 2008).

This new engine design put Honda at the forefront of green technology in the minds of consumers across the globe. At that time, in preparation for the expected stringent emissions regulations that would go into effect in the 1970s, Honda was the only automaker to design an automobile capable of meeting government standards. Toyota, specifically, came across as indifferent to the environment after the president at the time told media sources that it would be impossible to meet the standards of clean air emissions expected by government officials. Yet, behind the scenes, Toyota had also invested heavily in attempts to catch up with Honda in green technology and eventually decided on a hybrid design.

After the success of the CVCC engine, Honda achieved acclaim across the globe as a leader in environmentally-friendly vehicles. This notoriety propelled Honda's status in the United States to new heights, ultimately prompting Honda to establish dealerships throughout the world's largest automobile market. With this new-found brand image, Honda immediately began to invest in research and development to improve upon the CVCC design while also attempting to take the next step towards a zero emissions vehicle. Despite competition from Toyota and other automakers, the CVCC vehicles produced by Honda maintained the status of the most energy efficient for four years after their initial release into the market; however, amidst fears that Toyota and other rivals would attempt to surpass Honda as the green technology leader, Honda executives began to direct funds toward a completely electric vehicle as early as the 1980s (Hasegawa, 2008).

Although Honda was able to design a somewhat unreliable electric vehicle by the early 1990s, Honda engineers were reluctant to stand behind this vehicle or recommend it for mass production as it resembled a golf cart more than an actual car. Honda continued experimenting with battery technology from the mid-1990s and ultimately determined that the lead-acid batteries of that time were simply too large and unreliable to power a device the size of an automobile. Vehicles powered by these batteries had severely limited driving ranges, long charging time requirements, and were extremely susceptible to temperature and weather conditions. Undeterred, Honda began investing in the development of more reliable NiMH batteries that could better withstand extreme summer and winter weather conditions. However, despite advances in battery technology, NiMH batteries were extremely large and heavy, expensive, and still only provided limited driving distances in an era when gasoline prices were still far too affordable to justify electric automobiles.

By the late 1990s, Honda had experienced one setback after another in its attempts to create a completely electric vehicle while also witnessing Toyota take the lead as the world's leader in green technology through the implementation of hybrid engines. As a result, Honda also began to invest in the hybrid market in an attempt to retake ground lost to Toyota. While Toyota designs involved passenger cars, Honda did research specific to the United States' market and found that "many of the passenger cars running on highways were carrying only one or two people" (Hasegawa, 2008). As a result of this research, Honda determined that they could achieve an advantage over Toyota in fuel efficiency by creating two-seater hybrid vehicles with less weight. Honda viewed this technology as a necessary step in the development of a truly zero emissions vehicle because Honda engineers had learned from experience that the technology for a fully comparable electric vehicle simply did not yet exist (Hasegawa, 2008).

The result of Honda's efforts in hybrid technology was the release of the Honda Insight, which boasted a staggering 99 miles per gallon (35 kilometers per liter). Honda rushed this vehicle onto the American and European markets as soon as it was released in Japan in order to preempt the introduction of the Prius by Toyota into those markets. However, Honda's strategy to reclaim its status as the world leader in green technology backfired because Toyota had already invested heavily in overseas marketing campaigns, which had succeeded in convincing consumers that the Prius was the ultimate hybrid vehicle. Honda campaigns, however, did not mention green technology; Honda chose to emphasize that the Insight had high gasoline mileage, which somehow did not automatically connect with notions of environmental friendliness in the minds of many consumers. According to statements of former Honda executives at that time, many stated that Honda was focused more on viability than on maintaining an environmentally-friendly image due to challenges that ensued after the collapse of the economic bubble in Japan. As a result, Honda spend several years promoting traditional vehicles that were relatively safe bets and would likely ensure profits, while leaving innovative green technology and enthusiastic green marketing campaigns on the backburner. As then president of Honda Takeo Fukui stated, "Honda was not lagging behind Toyota in developing hybrid technology...we simply failed to match Toyota in its enthusiasm for hybrid technology" (Hasegawa, 2008). Honda had effectively allowed Toyota to steal its image as the leader in green technology by simply neglecting effective marketing campaigns.

Recent years have shown an aggressive comeback of Honda in the realm of hybrid technology, however, as Honda executives are investing heavily to find ways to reduce the high price tag of Honda's hybrid models. The main problem that exists with both Toyota and Honda hybrid vehicles is that hybrid technology is simply too expensive to justify the savings on gasoline. Honda feels that the demand for hybrids will skyrocket if engineers can find ways to reduce costs and create hybrid vehicles that are similarly priced as gasoline models. At the same time, Honda views this hybrid battle as a mere stepping stone to a future battle over zero emissions technologies, specifically the hydrogen fuel cell.

Honda executives have already begun investing heavily in research and development of fuel cell technology, and this energy source is viewed as the only true green vehicle technology because the only emission is water. Although these vehicles are extremely efficient, and the new Honda FCX fuel cell vehicle boasts performance capabilities on par with traditional gasoline-powered vehicles, the enormous price tag and lack of a refueling infrastructure makes this technology an impossibility for the near future. While these vehicles are available for purchase, most fuel cell vehicles cost more than $800,000 and require the purchase of special kits that allow the vehicle to be refueled at homes. However, Honda engineers predict that the development stage of fuel cell vehicles could come to an end as early as 2010 with efforts to reduce costs ending as early as 2015, thus leaving Honda with the potential upper hand in promoting a truly innovative green technology that would be far superior to Toyota hybrids (Hasegawa, 2008).

NISSAN MOTOR CORPORATION

Despite heavy investment in electric vehicle technology by both Toyota and Honda, neither company was able to successfully develop a battery-powered vehicle capable of traveling long distances, charging quickly, and withstanding harsh weather conditions. As a result, both companies have largely given up on electric vehicle designs in favor of more promising technologies such as hybrid or hydrogen fuel cell engines. Nissan, however, remains undeterred by the technological shortcomings of current battery technologies and is currently aggressively pursuing a research and development campaign to engineer the first electric car that can truly compete with Toyota and Honda in performance and efficiency.

Despite claiming to release an electric vehicle by 2010, Nissan is already testing the green technology waters with the release of the Altima, which utilizes hybrid technology licensed from Toyota. Currently, Nissan only sells this hybrid vehicle in the United States in areas that have specifically stringent regulations on harmful gas emissions: California, Connecticut, Maine, Massachusetts, New Jersey, New York, Rhode Island, and Vermont. However, by offering the Altima in these states, Nissan is still able to reach approximately 25% of the United States population and, thus get a feel of the green technology market. Nissan is currently getting pummeled by Toyota and Honda in the hybrid market; however, executives claim that they cannot justify aggressive marketing campaigns when the automobile is only available in a selected number of states (Healey, 2007). Furthermore, despite releasing the Altima into the United States market, Nissan executives are not convinced that hybrids are a mass-market product that will continue to be profitable well into the future. The major reasons why Nissan has been slow to enter the hybrid market can be explained by the fact that Nissan was on the verge of bankruptcy by the late 1990s, rapidly losing market share to Toyota and operating in the red. Things only began to turn around for Nissan after it approached Renault for assistance and fell under the management of current CEO Carlos Ghosn (Hasegawa, 2008). However, it appears that Nissan will attempt to release future hybrid models through its Infiniti luxury brand in order to stay in the market and also develop its own hybrid engine capabilities (Greimel, 2009). Nissan CEO Carlos Ghosn has stated that the company will need to conduct further research into hybrid technology to determine if this "promising" technology has the future profit potential to justify current investments in its development, but that he ultimately envisions Nissan pursuing other alternative energy sources in the future (Treece, 2006).

The current focus of Nissan's green technology efforts is in the realm of electric vehicles. Although both Toyota and Honda failed to engineer a purely electric vehicle that met both performance and comfort levels of comparable hybrid and gasoline automobiles, recent developments in battery technology may have opened the possibility to future vehicle innovations. Specifically, the old nickel-metal-hydride (NiMH) batteries utilized by automakers have become outdated due to the development of lithium-ion battery technology. These new lithium-ion batteries generate energy as lithium ions travel from one electrode to the next and electrons travel from anode to cathode. During charging, the opposite occurs and the batteries are able to retain energy (Schneider, 2007).

Although the Toyota Prius still utilizes the older NiMH batteries, the benefits of a lithium ion battery are twice the power, energy density, and lifecycle of older batteries. Furthermore, lithium ion batteries are cheaper to produce and much smaller in size. Automakers across the globe are following Nissan's lead and investigating this new energy source. Toyota has already formed a partnership with Matsushita in response to Nissan's partnership with NEC. General Motors has also joined the race by partnering with Compact Power in an attempt to be the first to develop the first promising lithium ion battery pack for automobiles (Cervi, 2008).

Serious potential dangers and setbacks exist with lithium ion technology, however. The cobalt required for various components of the battery is quite expensive, and oxygen released from these batteries could pose fire and explosion hazards within automobiles. Lithium ion batteries are used in small scales in many notebook computers, and these batteries have been known to catch fire occasionally. As this is a problem with small-scale computer batteries, automakers are reluctant to risk the consequences of an explosion occurring in a much larger automobile battery. Automakers have invested heavily to develop means to reduce the risk of lithium ion batteries such as replacing the carbon in batteries with titanate, but these innovations in safety often result in decreased performance and power output (Schneider, 2007). These drawbacks of electric cars have been problematic for decades and also play into the mindsets of many consumers. Individuals often consider an electric vehicle to be "a more expensive car, a smaller and less comfortable car, a slower car, a car with a wire (for connection)...a car in need of frequent recharge, a car with limited range, a less reliable car, a less safe car, a golf cart, a low performance car, a city car (a second car for short distances)... [and] a car that does not work during the winter season" (Chéron and Zins, 2007). Clearly, Nissan has many challenges to overcome in both technological difficulties and perception problems if they are to achieve success in the near future in the electric automobile market. As the technology to allow the creation of viable electric vehicles is still in its infancy, it remains to be seen what form future Nissan electric automobiles will take, but it is likely that any entry into the electric automobile market in the near future will largely involve urban communities where travel distances are limited.

AUTOMAKERS OF THE WEST

Although western automakers have taken notice of Toyota's success in the hybrid market, many agree with Nissan that hybrids mark only a step in the journey to a zero emissions energy source. However, many automakers in the West are not as committed to pursuing a specific alternative energy model as their Japanese counterparts. For example, although Toyota invests in a milieu of technologies, they are known for hybrid technology; similarly, Honda is known for fuel cell development and Nissan is pursuing electric vehicles. However, General Motors chairman Rick Wagoner has stated that his company will invest heavily in a variety of green technologies in the future. The most recent development by General Motors has been in the announcement of the release of the Chevrolet Volt. Slated to hit the markets in 2010, this plug-in hybrid will be capable of traveling on battery power for 40 miles before then relying on a photovoltaic engine to recharge the battery. As the future of green automobile technology is unclear, Wagoner has indicated that General Motors will produce vehicles capable of being converted to operate on a variety of sources including fuel cells, traditional engines, or batteries (Hasegawa, 2008).

Ford has also attempted to compete with Japanese automakers by rapidly and aggressively deploying its own hybrid models with licensed Toyota technology, while also looking to the future with the announcement of the Ford Airstream automobile in 2007. This model will utilize a lithium ion battery to power the vehicle for the first 25 miles before then utilizing a hydrogen fuel cell to recharge the battery and power the vehicle. Much like General Motors, however, Ford is not banking on one technology alone; Ford has also invested in the development of automobiles that can operate on both gasoline and ethanol — an energy source promoted by the Bush administration as a clean fuel of the future. Currently in the United States, consumers have the option of purchasing automobiles capable of operating on ethanol, and Ford is continuously working with fuel companies to increase fueling stations throughout the United States (Hasegawa, 2008).

European automakers have taken a different approach, however, in the pursuit of greater research into diesel technology. Although diesel engines have been utilized for decades, they have largely been unpopular in the United States and Japan due to the black smoke and particulate matter that are released as exhaust. Despite the fact that diesel engines are far more efficient than gasoline engines, the visible smoke emitted by diesel automobiles has left many consumers with a negative image of the technology. DaimlerChrysler, specifically, is pursuing diesel technology as a means of entering the green automobile race and establishing itself as a competitor in this lucrative market. This automaker recently partnered with Bosch to develop the next generation diesel engine, which debuted in Tokyo in 2006 and claimed to produce no noise or unattractive emissions that have dissuaded consumers from purchasing diesel in the past. The European market seems more promising than the United States or Japan, however, as diesel engines currently account for 20% of automobile sales across the European Union. Furthermore, DaimlerChrysler engines that utilize diesel power boast up to 30% greater fuel efficiency than the same gasoline models (Hasegawa, 2008).

Despite the growing popularity of diesel, however, not all European automakers are pursuing that avenue of green technology. BMW, for example, is banking its hopes in clean energy on the hydrogen fuel cell. Although hydrogen fuel cell technology offers the promise of zero harmful emissions, the $1 million price tag leaves these vehicles out of the reach of many consumers. However, BMW has developed a hydrogen fuel cell and gasoline hybrid engine that allows the vehicle to operate on either fuel source, thus accounting for the lack of hydrogen refueling infrastructures in many nations. Although BMW appreciates the successes that Toyota and other automakers have had in the hybrid arena, executives in that company do not feel that hybrid technology will ever become a truly long-term market. Rather, as do some other automakers, BMW views hybrids as a stepping-stone to future green technologies. Currently, BMW is devoting significant research to reducing the price of hydrogen fuel cells and to creating more efficient gasoline engines (Hasegawa, 2008).

CONCLUSION

As an author for *The Economist* stated in a recent article, "Whether in Los Angeles, Tokyo or London, the Prius, Toyota's trailblazing petrol-electric hybrid car, has become a common sight... [and] has since achieved cult status among image-conscious Hollywood stars and greener-than-thou politicians. [As of 2007] Toyota said it had passed the milestone of manufacturing more than 1m hybrid vehicles" (Economist, 2007). However, despite this hybrid success, automakers across the globe still do not have a coherent, single vision for the future of green engine technology. General Motors and Ford's attempts at hybrid automobile designs have been met with limited enthusiasm, and Honda has already opted to replace the hybrid Accord with a diesel option. Honda sees hybrid technology as only viable for small, lightweight vehicles and General Motors feels that the market will only grow if advances in technology allow hybrid vehicles to travel greater distances solely on electric power. As a result, General Motors is banking on lithium-ion battery technology to enhance the range of their future hybrids such as the Chevrolet Volt, whereas Toyota executives have opted to continue using the traditional, bulky nickel-metal hydride batteries amidst fears that lithium-ion batteries are dangerous. European automakers seem to be largely banking on diesel technology, but BMW is also investing heavily into hydrogen fuel cell technology (Economist, 2007).

While numerous options and business strategies have been illustrated for prospective designs of the future green automobile engine, a clear frontrunner has yet to emerge. Do Toyota's hybrid vehicles represent the engines of the next century, or is hybrid technology simply a stepping-stone to other technologies as many American and European automakers believe? Will diesel engines gain popularity in Japan and the United States, or will advances in battery technology allow for the emergence of viable electric vehicles? Will hydrogen fuel cells become affordable options for the average consumer? The answers to these questions will ultimately reveal which automaker and technology will represent the engine of the future, but it is safe to say that with the head start and financial resources of Toyota, it is unlikely that they will lose their hold on the green market anytime soon.

QUESTIONS

1) Which different approaches to future technologies can you identify?
2) Which approach is going to be the most successful? Discuss in class.
3) How can a company ensure that it is developing a technology which will succeed in the future?

BIBLIOGRAPHY

Capps, B. (2007). Sustainability a journey, not destination. *Advertising Age*, 78.

Carr-Ruffino, R and Acheson, J. (2007). The hybrid phenomenon. *Futurist* 41.

Cervi, B. (2008). Clean machines. *Engineering and Technology*, 3.

Chéron, E and Zins, M. (1997). Electric vehicle purchasing intentions: The concern over battery charge duration, 31.

The Economist (2007). Beyond the prius. *Economist*, 383.

Frank, A. (2004). Plug-in hybrid vehicles for a sustainable future. *American Scientist*, 95.

Greimel, H. (2008). Japanese carmaker must fix lags and jerks in its hybrid to catch Toyota and Nissan. *Automotive News Europe*, 13.

Hasegawa, Y. (2008). *Clean Car Wars: How Honda and Toyota are Winning the Battle of Eco-Friendly Autos.* Hoboken, NJ: John Wiley and Sons.

Healey, J. Altima hybrid blends power, fuel economy (13 July 2007). *USA Today.*

Kiley, D. Is GM's green tech better than Toyota's? (15 November 2007). *Business Week Online.*

Kranz, R and Sedgwick, D. Nissan: Electric car to get here in 2010 (10 March 2008). *Automotive News.*

Nathanson, S. (2007). Not all hybrids are created equal. *Futurist,* 41.

Rowley, I. (2007). Honda targets Toyota's hybrid dominance (20 December 2007). *Business Week Online.*

Schneider, D. (2007). Who's resuscitating the electric car? *American Scientist,* 95.

Treece, J. (2006). Nissan plans hybrid clean diesels in 2010. *Automotive News.*

Vella, M. (2008). Inside Toyota's hybrid truck (2 January 2008). *Business Week Online.*

Walsh, B. (2007). How business saw the light. *TIME,* 169.

Woodyard, C. Toyota: Extend hybrid tax credit (16 January 2007). *USA Today.*

Index